MW00999526

Democracy Tamed

Democracy Tamed

French Liberalism and the Politics of Suffrage

GIANNA ENGLERT

OXFORD
UNIVERSITY PRESS

OXFORD
UNIVERSITY PRESS

Oxford University Press is a department of the University of Oxford. It furthers
the University's objective of excellence in research, scholarship, and education
by publishing worldwide. Oxford is a registered trade mark of Oxford University
Press in the UK and certain other countries.

Published in the United States of America by Oxford University Press
198 Madison Avenue, New York, NY 10016, United States of America.

© Oxford University Press 2024

Library of Congress Control Number: 2024931148

ISBN 978–0–19–763531–5

DOI: 10.1093/oso/9780197635315.001.0001

Printed by Integrated Books International, United States of America

Contents

Acknowledgments

Writing a book can be a solitary and lonely enterprise. My most uplifting moments while writing this one came when I brought my ideas into conversation with colleagues and friends. For improving both this book and the process of writing it, I am grateful to many people.

This book grew out of my dissertation at Georgetown University. My advisor, Richard Boyd, is a model scholar, mentor, friend, and now coauthor. Richard deserves special mention for reading portions of this book at just about every stage, from dissertation to monograph and the many awkward phases in between. Bruce Douglass pressed me to tackle some of the thorny contemporary implications of my arguments, while Shannon Stimson pressed me in the other direction, urging me to make the historical details as fine-grained as possible. For the extra push from both sides, I thank them. Cheryl Welch has been a wonderful mentor to me since she signed on to be an external committee member six years ago.

I began writing this book in earnest as a Postdoctoral Research Associate at Brown University's Political Theory Project. I finished it (too many years later) in roughly the same location: as a Visiting Scholar at the newly established Center for Philosophy, Politics, and Economics, also at Brown University. Although my affiliation may have changed, many of the faces stayed the same, and my debts of gratitude remain. Rosolino Candela, Daniel D'Amico, Brandon Davis, Dave Estlund, Nick Geiser, Anton Howes, Shany Mor, Julian Müller, Kirun Sankaran, David Skarbek, Emily Skarbek, and John Tomasi offered invaluable feedback on early drafts. Sharon Krause was an insightful reader and interlocutor on the history of liberalism, and Melvin Rogers gave sound publishing advice in the final stages of the project. Aly Laughlin has been everything from a smiling face to a shoulder to cry on, and I cherish our friendship.

Thank you also to my colleagues at Southern Methodist University and in the John G. Tower Center, who hosted a one-day research workshop on the manuscript just before the pandemic. In particular, Joseph Kobylka, Dennis Ippolito, Michael Lusztig, Stefano Recchia, Karisa Cloward, Pamela Corley, Jim Hollifield, Hiroki Takeuchi, and Cal Jillson read my work with care and welcomed a historian of political thought into the department. Special grati-tude is owed to Melissa Emmert and Christine Carberry, who showed me the ropes in Texas.

The following individuals either read some or all of the manuscript, helped to fine tune the arguments within it, or provided me with valuable profes-sional advice when I needed it: Gordon Arlen, Nolan Bennett, Jason Canon, Mauro Caraccioli, Joshua Cherniss, Hank Clark, Kristen Collins, Connor Ewing, Shawn Fraistat, Bryan Garsten, Emre Gerçek, Arthur Ghins, David Golemboski, Christine Dunn Henderson, Jennie Ikuta, Jeremy Jennings, Stuart Jones, Jooeun Kim, Brian Kogelmann, Alan Levine, Jacob Levy, Daryl Li, Alida Liberman, Briana McGinnis, Michael Mosher, Helena Rosenblatt, Stephen Sawyer, and Sarah Wilford. Alan Kahan and Aurelian Craiutu were supportive of this project from start to finish, and a work like this would not have been possible without the strides they made in studying French liber-alism. I owe a special thanks to the very generous Elizabeth Cohen, without whom this book would not have come together in the way that it did. I also wish to thank the Institute for Humane Studies for hosting a virtual work-shop on an early draft of the manuscript. At Oxford University Press, Angela Chnapko edited this book with the perfect balance of enthusiasm and pa-tience, and Alexcee Bechthold expertly guided me through the production process.

I would be neither who I am nor where I am if it were not for the sacrifices and love of my family, both in the present and in past generations. My grandparents have always beamed with pride when I tell them about the work I do. This book is dedicated to the four of them.

Introduction

There are at least two stories we can tell about the relationship between liberalism and democracy. The title of a 1998 exchange in *Foreign Affairs* recounted a version of the first: "Liberalism and Democracy: Can't Have One Without the Other."[1] Or, "wherever one finds liberalism," one of the contributors explained elsewhere, "it is invariably coupled with democracy."[2] The modern-day pairing of liberal states and democratic procedures may give the impression that the two have had a long and happy marriage. And so appealing is the composite of a liberal democracy that Francis Fukuyama once declared it to be "the final form of human government" and "the end of history," a system "arguably free" from "the grave defects, irrationalities . . . and fundamental internal contradictions" that plague its rivals.[3]

Yet in the decades since Fukuyama's 1992 proclamation about the end of history, a second, less sanguine account has displaced the first. A liberal state will not necessarily be subject to popular control through fair and competitive elections. Nor will the choices of the *demos* necessarily produce a government that respects the rights and liberties of citizens. Opinion pieces in *Foreign Affairs* tend to strike a more somber tone today than they did in the light of Fukuyama's triumphalism. Their authors warn of the rise of "illiberal democracies" and "populist autocracies," terms meant to reflect the harsh reality that liberal democracies everywhere seem to be coming apart at the seams.[4]

But for all of the foreboding headlines from the last few years, this skepticism about sustaining a form of government that is both free *and* popular is not new. Despite all appearances, democracy and liberalism did not grow up together in perfect harmony. Nor did they depend on one another for their mutual survival. As this book will show, many of the first self-avowed liberals—those European writers and politicians who adopted the label "liberal" in the decades after the French Revolution—not only distanced themselves from the proponents of universal or near-universal male suffrage, they also fought to halt democracy's political advance altogether. Liberals looked on the essential features of a political democracy, a universal electorate in

Democracy Tamed. Gianna Englert, Oxford University Press. © Oxford University Press 2024.
DOI: 10.1093/oso/9780197635315.003.0001

particular, as imminent threats to the rule of law rather than their natural complements. As liberals defined and delineated the rights of the individual, they also disputed what has since become a self-evident political truth in the Western world: the claim that "the people"—*all* of the people—should control the electoral levers of power. Liberalism and democracy did not begin to uncouple just recently, then.[5] They originated independently, and the representatives for each side were often at odds.

This book is certainly not the first study to recognize the rocky historical relationship between liberals and democrats of various stripes. For historians of liberalism, the basic assertion that advocates for limited government intended to drown out their contemporaries' calls for universal—or anything approaching universal—suffrage will not come as much of a surprise. In his concise but classic exposition of the relationship between liberalism and democracy, Norberto Bobbio admits that "liberal writers regarded the extension of the suffrage as ill-timed or undesirable."[6] Other scholars have been more emphatic. "Liberals defined themselves in opposition to the old regime and to political democracy," Alan Kahan contends, before tracing parliamentary debates over the scope of the franchise in Britain, France, and Germany across the long nineteenth century.[7] In recovering liberalism's "lost history," Helena Rosenblatt highlights its exemplars' entanglements with mass politics. "Since the very beginning," Rosenblatt summarizes, "liberals worried about the 'incapacity' of the masses, whom they thought were irrational, prone to violent behavior, and unaware of their own best interests."[8] One common thesis runs throughout all of these interpretations: many of the key political actors who endeavored to establish free governments across Europe believed that "liberal democracy" was a regime type rife with internal contradictions, a form of government that was unlikely to endure beyond a single generation.

Even so, scholars have tended to treat liberals' documented distaste for the democratic as a mere footnote to the long and dizzying history of the liberal tradition. For although historians from Bobbio to Rosenblatt have acknowledged the liberal antagonism toward electoral equality and even outlined the reasons why it originated, they have said much less about *how* liberals waged their wars against universal suffrage—about the theories that the earliest liberals constructed to repel demands for political democracy and about their proposed alternatives to popular sovereignty.[9] This book uncovers these overlooked alternatives along with the arguments behind them. It reveals that French liberals created a vocabulary all their own to combat the notion that political rights were due in equal measure to all persons and that they aimed to replace the language of "rights" in electoral politics with a more demanding standard. In the nineteenth century, the setting for this book, some of the most influential figures in the French liberal tradition formulated the concept of *capacité politique* (political capacity) in response to "the suffrage question," or the matter of who should receive the right to vote and, just as crucially, who should not. French liberalism crystallized at least partly around debates over the extent of democracy, or so this book will argue. For many of the most vocal and influential self-identified liberals in post-revolutionary France, the extension of the suffrage was not merely "ill-timed," as Bobbio suggests; rather, a universal franchise posed an obvious threat to free governments, an open war on liberal ideals and institutions.

In pursuit of its guiding aim to parse this forgotten liberal language against democracy, this book develops two main themes. First, it explores how, when, and why French liberals mobilized the controversial concept of *capacité politique* to make sense of the democratic age. It begins by uncovering the concept's origins in the liberal political thought of the Bourbon Restoration (1814–30), principally in historical lectures by François Guizot, and concludes with the liberal-leaning essayists of the Second Empire (1852–70) who reimagined the relevance of *capacité* for novel circumstances. But second, this book argues that liberals not only used *capacité* to attack universal suffrage. They also battled for control of the word "democracy" itself, severing the term from both its classical roots in the Athenian *polis* and from its eighteenth-century associations with popular sovereignty. In addition to its analysis of various arguments for (and against) *capacité politique*, this book argues that liberals tried to give new meaning to the Greeks' "*demokratia*," a word which they maintained had no intrinsic connection to popular power or equality or, for that matter, to political institutions or electoral arrangements at all. It was atop their "new democracy"—democracy as a *type of society* rather than a political regime—that liberals surprisingly mounted their assault on the various claims about political equality that held sway in the nineteenth century. Put simply, they turned their democratic society against democratic politics.

The five central chapters of this book illuminate watershed moments and provocative arguments in the liberal struggle to save this, what they called the "new democracy," from falling into the hands of the many. Its analysis begins in the decades following the Revolution of 1789 and concludes with the collapse of Napoleon III's imperial democracy in 1870. The concluding chapter returns us to our present moment and to the enduring challenges of sustaining liberal democracies.

Capacité Politique

Capacité politique was the proper precursor to political rights, or so its advocates argued. They insisted that the individual should exhibit the signs of *capacité* to exercise the right to vote—a right that had to be earned or proven rather than taken as given or "natural." In this way, the right to vote was distinct from those civil rights to a free press or to religious worship, which extended to all persons by nature.[10] By appealing to *capacité* as the only legitimate standard by which to distribute the vote, these "capacitarian" liberals could restrict the suffrage to "the capable," a class sensible enough to see through the shallow rhetoric of a despot or the inciting cries of a mob. The concept of *capacité* emerged in response to universal suffrage, an electoral scheme that most liberals scorned.[11] According to some influential liberal figures, the time for universal suffrage was still far off. Yet for others, it was—and always would be—an unsuitable electoral scheme for a people prone to violence and tyranny, as the French clearly were. The *ancien régime* had been toppled by the Revolution of 1789, and the new society that rose in its place was shaken by the Reign of Terror in 1793–4, only to fall prey to the ambitions of the despotic Napoleon Bonaparte years later. To ensure that France would not repeat the mistakes of its past, a past marked by social unrest and political servitude, liberals sought to empower the possessors of political capacity in their nation, its society recently remade by the Revolution. They began by trying to regulate which citizens could cast the ballot and who would thus lead France into the new century.

To police the boundaries of their capable electorate—however poorly defined those boundaries were, as we will learn in the following chapters—liberals had to get creative. At one time or another, they set taxation, professional, and residency thresholds for the national vote; dreamt up electoral systems that would channel the influence of one part of society to the exclusion of all the rest; and devised imaginative ways to sidestep constitutional mandates for universal male suffrage after the Revolution of 1848. During the Bourbon Restoration and the July Monarchy (1830–48), liberals brandished *capacité* as an unabashedly antidemocratic weapon. Armed with their ideal franchise, many of the influential leaders of the July Monarchy battled both the radical Left and the more moderate political Center to restrict electoral participation—to tame democracy as we have come to know it—for the sake, they claimed, of rescuing their entire nation from either the caprice of the crowd or the heavy hand of a tyrant.[12]

Of course, these nineteenth-century liberals were not the first thinkers to recommend that human societies follow the guidance of a wise or all-knowing ruling class.[13] Writing in the fourth century BCE, Aristotle concluded that politics was a vocation best left to the leisured and ideally to the philosophic few, since the intellectual demands of life in the Athenian assembly would prove too exacting for day laborers, common craftsmen, and slaves.[14] Centuries later, Edmund Burke watched in horror as the French Revolutionaries proposed to empower the lower orders, so much so that he recoiled at the mere suggestion that hairdressers might be entrusted with any degree of political power:

> The occupation of an hair-dresser, or of a working tallow-chandler, cannot be a matter of honour to any person—to say nothing of a number of other more servile employments. Such descriptions of men ought not to suffer oppression from the state; but the state suffers oppression, if such as they, either individually or collectively, are permitted to rule.[15]

Yet other spectators to the Revolution relied upon similar assumptions about political wisdom and rationality to endorse democracy. Across her incisive rejoinders to Burke, Mary Wollstonecraft cited the rationality and virtue displayed by women to vindicate radical proposals for extending the revolutionary Rights of Man.[16] Nicolas de Condorcet reasoned along similar lines in 1790. Since many of his countrymen acknowledged that all "rational and sentient beings" merited the right to vote, anyone who opposed the enfranchisement of women would have to prove that women were not "capable" (Condorcet's term in 1790) of exercising it. At the same time, he warned the Revolutionary generation about setting such a precedent. It was dangerous to send legislators down the slippery slope of disenfranchising "the incapable." They would no doubt have to disqualify just about everyone in the end, leaving only those men "who had completed an education in the law" to cast the ballot.[17]

Post-revolutionary French liberals not only gave a name to such vague notions about political competence or individual rationality that had circulated since ancient times.[18] They also created systematic theories of *capacité politique* and traced the concept's hidden history from ancient Rome to the Revolution, all to justify its essential role in all modern electoral systems. With this approach, they also managed to establish *capacité politique* as the prevailing language for public debate about the makeup of the French franchise. As we will discover across the following chapters, *capacité* became the conceptual axis around which virtually all parliamentary deliberations over the suffrage question revolved, and it survived even the reintroduction of universal suffrage after 1848.[19] Finally, liberals composed electoral laws with an eye toward fashioning the most capable electorate whose members would choose only the most capable representatives, thereby inserting *capacité* all along the electoral hierarchy.

This book follows liberals' lead. It reconstructs their intricate defenses of *capacité politique* while scrutinizing their clever attempts to put those theories into practice in laws to regulate the national vote.[20] Most importantly, its main arguments reveal the degree to which nineteenth-century French liberal thought depended upon its underlying logic of *capacité*. In the eyes of its advocates, a capable franchise was not merely preferable to a universal one. It was the foundation for individual rights and the guarantee for stable constitutions. At times, liberals went so far as depict *capacité* as the sole safeguard for freedom, both for individuals and for entire civilizations. Far from a mere addendum to the long history of political liberalism, *capacité* became the anchor point for liberals' comprehensive vision of a free society.

Despite (or more likely because of) its significance to the liberal project, *capacité* was a contested concept among even its most ardent proponents. François Guizot, who is most famous in French history for upholding the conservative policies that propelled Paris toward revolution in 1848, theorized *capacité* as a transcendent, almost Platonic standard with which to structure the electoral system.[21] Guizot held that the capable were those who acted in accordance with unchanging reason, truth, and justice. His argument would effectively compress the French franchise to disqualify all but an exceptional category of "the reasonable"—a category that, as we will discover, happened to coincide with the nineteenth-century bourgeoisie. While other Restoration liberals shared some of Guizot's reservations about an unrestricted franchise, they had much lower and more attainable expectations for the voting public. The Swiss-French pluralist Benjamin Constant, for one, proposed that voters should exhibit "sound judgment" rather than supreme reason and recommended a *suffrage censitaire* that established a modest (and changeable) property qualification for the vote. Alexis de Tocqueville,

who learned a great deal about democracy from the capacitarian Guizot
of all people, had less confidence in *capacité* and its variants. Guided by
his understanding of American democracy, Tocqueville concluded that
the disadvantages of instituting *capacité* in any form—whether Guizot's
metaphysical ideal for the French electorate or something less taxing—
outweighed the potential benefits. A few lingering questions bedeviled the
theorists of *capacité* throughout the century, from the staunchly capacitarian
Guizot to the reluctant Tocqueville to those post-1848 writers who reopened
the suffrage question after the establishment of universal suffrage. Who were
the capable, after all? By which signs, economic or otherwise, could they be
identified? How could French legislators write their electoral laws to enfranchise the capable segments of their society while disqualifying the incapable
ones? All capacitarian liberals knew how significant these questions were, yet
they could never quite agree on the right answers.

Nor, as this book will argue, did all French liberals across the century invoke *capacité* to undermine political democracy. Because he had observed the
positive consequences that flowed out of universal male suffrage in America,
Tocqueville never fully bought in to the capacitarian logic in France, a point
I will argue in Chapter 3. And although the concept originated as an elitist
rejoinder to populist demands, some of the liberal party's up-and-coming
leaders during the Second Republic (1848–52) attempted to transform their
forerunners' antidemocratic sentiments into firm justifications for universal
suffrage, hoping to embrace political democracy on liberal grounds. These
more progressive liberals after 1848 (the subjects of Chapters 4 and 5) were
among the first thinkers to imagine how liberal democracy might take shape
in France, free from the contradictions and fears that so gripped the minds of
their predecessors.

The Two Democracies

Given this brief overview of the liberal tradition from the Revolution
to the end of the Second Empire, one of the central arguments of this
book is likely to come as a surprise. As we now know, French liberals initially upheld *capacité politique* as their shield against democracy's political onslaught. Yet they also believed that a capable franchise was one of
democracy's firmest bases of support. For while liberals developed *capacité*
to frustrate the ambitions of their egalitarian rivals, they also selectively

borrowed from their opponents' democratic toolkit. Liberals set out to reclaim the word "democracy"—to rescue it from the republicans who stood in the shadow of Jean-Jacques Rousseau and who wished to restore an ancient and, to the liberal mind, archaic form of government in the modern world.

The central assertion of this book, then, is not simply that a small group of elites marching under the banner of modern liberalism detested the very notion of rule by the common people, a historical yarn that other scholars have spun in their own ways.[22] Rather, it tells the more intricate story of how French liberals set out to claim modern democracy as their own—and stranger still, to make their "new democracy" compatible with government by a capable few. As Chapter 2 argues, Guizot and the school of Restoration liberals known as the Doctrinaires believed that the words democracy and aristocracy were in need of updated definitions following the end of the *ancien régime*, definitions that would reflect the complex reality of post-revolutionary society. They theorized democracy primarily as "a social condition" or "a state of society" whose basic elements had nothing to do with universal suffrage or popular sovereignty.

Borrowing from the French Doctrinaires' theoretical framework, Tocqueville (Chapter 3) raised questions about the nature of American democracy that implicated both the novel social democracy identified by his contemporaries and the older political definition of rule by the people. During the Second Empire, the constitutional scholar and self-professed Tocquevillean Édouard Laboulaye (the subject of Chapter 4) would update the term once again. According to Laboulaye, "democracy" had assumed a new meaning since the Revolution of 1848, just as it had after 1789 and at the hands of the Doctrinaire Guizot. For Laboulaye, the once-"incapable" wage-earning classes, those who remained without the vote during the nearly two decades of the July Monarchy, exemplified the post-1848 conception of democracy as "self-government" through their associational activities. Unlike his Doctrinaire predecessors, Laboulaye would exalt the new democracy to uphold universal suffrage, uniting a democratic social state with a government bearing the same name. But he would also take a page out of his predecessors' playbook to do so. Laboulaye turned the notion of democracy as a social state *against* the capacitarian elites who introduced it, thereby nudging his fellow liberals toward the very electoral scheme—universal suffrage—that they had resisted for so long.

Organization and Method

This struggle over the meaning of democracy runs as a continuous story throughout the following chapters. Chapter 1 focuses on a figure who has recently been called the "first French liberal democrat" even though he rarely uttered the word "democracy": Benjamin Constant. Against what has become the prevailing but oversimplified interpretation of Constant as a liberal democrat, this chapter maintains that he spoke the language of political representation rather than political democracy, and that his replies to the suffrage question in the Restoration years were but the means to attain what he envisioned as a "truly representative" end for the legislature. Above everything else, Constant hoped to ensure that society's numerous sectional interests would receive representation in the elected chamber. His plans for electoral reform were crafted to imbue political representation "with real force"—that is, to compose an assembly that would reflect both a pluralistic French society and its (restricted) electorate's capable judgment.

Even so, Constant's essays and speeches about electoral rules and regulations could not help but touch upon those conversations about the value of political democracy in which his successors would engage in earnest after his death in 1830. Constant tried to balance an embryonic version of political capacity with a commitment to social diversity, but he did not quite succeed. His Restoration adversary, the more centrist Doctrinaire Guizot, would seek to resolve some of the contradictions between a capable assembly and a diverse one that lie at the heart of Constant's electoral theory. For Guizot, the theorist par excellence of *capacité politique* and the subject of Chapter 2, rationality—not diversity—was the goal of government, and the most capable men would guide societies toward absolute reason rather than chaotic variety. Chapter 2 disentangles the intertwined lines of argument that comprise Guizot's much-maligned theory of *capacité politique*. It also interprets Guizot as a democratic theorist who attempted to wrest control of the term "democracy" from his republican counterparts who attached it to popular sovereignty and also from his far-Right adversaries who denounced it altogether. An electorate delimited by *capacité* was best suited to what Guizot called the "new democracy," a type of society born in the upheavals of 1789. Guizot's notion of the new democracy suffused his political theory and his plans for French educational reform, and Chapter 2 accordingly sheds light on the complementary electoral and educational components of his particular brand of liberalism, making it one of the few studies to bring Guizot's political and educational endeavors together.

Chapter 3 turns to the most thoughtful observer of the democratic age: Alexis de Tocqueville. But the Tocqueville of Chapter 3 is not exactly the author we have come to know. For he is neither (principally) the celebrated theorist of civil society nor the famed foreign spectator of the American social state. Rather, the Tocqueville presented in these pages is the statesman who rose against Guizot in the heated deliberations over the size and scope of the French franchise—some of which took place on the eve of the 1848 Revolution—and on the very character of a vibrant liberal nation. This chapter reconstructs Tocqueville's overlooked views on the vote in America and France, what I call his reflections on "the other democracy," or democracy understood as an electoral system rather than a particular set of social conditions. It argues that Tocqueville was at least ambivalent on the value of *capacité* in the first volume of *Democracy in America* (1835), only to emerge as a full-fledged critic of the narrow franchise that Guizot's liberal government fought to sustain. If Chapters 1 and 2 showcase two variations on the theme of a capable franchise during the Restoration, the first by the Left-leaning Constant and the second by the centrist Doctrinaire Guizot, Chapter 3 mounts Tocqueville's challenge to each one of them.

Chapter 4 charts one of the many directions traveled by Tocqueville's legacy in nineteenth-century France. It explores Laboulaye's "enlightened democracy," his Tocquevillean alternative to the capacitarian claims articulated by the Doctrinaires, some of which lingered in speeches by the leftover luminaries of the July Monarchy who now squared off against Napoleon III. Laboulaye aimed to shift his contemporaries' focus from delimiting the electorate (a failed and outdated strategy, in his eyes) to enlightening the "soul" of each voter—and he deftly merged Tocqueville's Americanism with Constant's pluralism to do so. He also gave the liberal party an educational purpose to go along with the oppositional role it already played in the parliamentary politics of the period. Only a few years later, Ernest Duvergier de Hauranne, whose work is featured in Chapter 5, would recast the political party as a school for political education, a vehicle for representing society's numerous opinions and perspectives on the national stage, and a beacon of capable citizenship under political democracy. Along with Laboulaye, Duvergier de Hauranne would also carry Tocqueville's democratic torch in the decade following the latter's death in 1859. He would seek to make democracy "profitable to humankind," just as his predecessor advised three decades earlier in the first volume of *Democracy in America*.

While there are a number of ways to partition the arguments and themes within this book, it may be most helpful to approach its organization in this way: Chapters 1–3 feature arguments for and against a capable franchise, with particular emphasis on the period from the Restoration through the collapse of the July Monarchy. Chapters 4 and 5, set in the Second Empire, foreground two *institutional* solutions (education and the party system) to the dilemma of bringing political capacity and political equality together— a dilemma that some of the authors featured in Chapters 1–3 claimed to have resolved by rejecting democratic political commitments wholesale. While this book's central argument sheds light on liberals' reactions to the dawning democratic age, its chapters weave together quite a few accessory threads as well. All of the authors and statesmen in this study searched for solutions to French problems beyond their own borders. Two of the five— Tocqueville and Duvergier de Hauranne—spent a considerable amount of time in America, and the jurist Laboulaye long wished he had. Others, such as Constant, were captivated by the merits of the English constitution. Additionally, the figures featured here stood on either side of what scholars have identified as the liberal divide between rationalism and pluralism;[23] they tried to understand and to redraw the existing class lines separating the old aristocracy from the novel bourgeoisie and both from the emergent industrial classes. They asked not only *who* should vote but *how* and sometimes *where*.[24] The suffrage question, then, went hand-in-hand with what we may call "the voting question"—how to organize elections so as to maximize either political capacity (Guizot and to a lesser degree, Constant), social and sectional diversity (Constant and Duvergier de Hauranne), political morality (Tocqueville in 1840s France), or some other political good altogether.

As this Introduction has already implied, this book does not trace the history of French democratization. Nor does it offer a sweeping word history of *capacité* or its cognates. In general, I have erred on the side of analytical depth over historical breadth to present a number of standout arguments for and against a capacitarian franchise. So while this study does not provide a comprehensive history of the suffrage question, it does gather and reassemble the pieces that made up liberals' protean image of a capable electorate. And it applies that same level of analytical rigor to their depictions of democracy. Methodologically, the central chapters balance textual richness with historical context, while admittedly leaning toward the former. Each chapter gives readers a bird's-eye view of the political world that the key players inhabited and helped to shape, and each includes a concise description of the electoral laws that liberals either backed or opposed. But above all, this book portrays the give-and-take between liberal values and democratic ones, and it disentangles what was characteristically "liberal" from what belonged to democracy as an electoral design.

One final clarifying note is in order. Some of the more contextually minded readers of this book may take issue with my use of the term "liberalism" to describe the perspective adopted by nineteenth-century "liberals," especially those who wrote in the first two decades or so of the nineteenth century. It is true that "liberalism" did not come into use until around 1813, when it appeared in Spain rather than France.[25] Nevertheless, I use liberalism to signify that constellation of first principles and constitutional commitments that were shared by actors who self-identified as "liberal."[26] Still, I do take care to avoid treating liberalism as a fixed set of ideas. In fact, this book depicts how liberals' basic principles clashed with nascent democratic institutions and popular demands, only to be transformed in the *mêlée*. Along the way, its thesis enriches our understanding of the conceptual weapons that liberals wielded to hold their political and intellectual positions, whether they intended to undercut or finally to accept the people's power.

1

"Representation with Real Force"

Benjamin Constant and the Direct Vote

Over the last thirty years, the writings of Benjamin Constant have been revived in academic circles across the French and English-speaking worlds. It is no accident that the latest "revisionist moment" in the study of liberalism followed on the heels of Constant's rediscovery.[1] Along with his intellectual collaborator and romantic partner Germaine de Staël, Constant was the first to apply the label "liberal" to politics. In 1796, he put forth a tempered, open, tolerant—that is, *libéral*—alternative to the extremes of the reactionary Right and the Jacobin Left.[2] Today, Constant is reckoned among those canonical figures who have forced us to reevaluate what liberalism is by reflecting on how it began. Out of liberalism's latest revisionist turn, Constant has emerged not only as one of the first self-professed political liberals, but according to some of his interpreters, also as "the first French theorist of liberal democracy," the first to "hold up . . . popular sovereignty with respect for personal freedoms."[3]

Yet, while no one ought to question Constant's place in the liberal tradition, his stance on the democratic half of liberal democracy is not nearly as clear-cut. Unlike Tocqueville, with whom he is often compared in commentaries on the French tradition, or Guizot, with whom he battled over what an oppositional and later a governing liberal *parti* ought to stand for, Constant never dedicated entire books or essays to the subject of democracy.[4] In those few-and-far-between moments when he identified as a "democrat" (nearly all of them in private correspondence), he intended to distance himself from his reactionary contemporaries who refused to accept the changes wrought by the Revolution.[5] He did offer one definition by way of contrast, at least. As an ancient form of rule in which a small population wields direct decision-making power, democracy was "wholly different" from the representative system that Constant endorsed for modern commercial societies.[6] In their efforts to unveil what one scholar has called Constant's "unwritten theory of democracy," his interpreters have had to distill their conclusions from his

Democracy Tamed. Gianna Englert, Oxford University Press. © Oxford University Press 2024.
DOI: 10.1093/oso/9780197635315.003.0002

comments about related concepts, including popular sovereignty and public assent.[7]

Despite burgeoning interest in Constant as the (first) liberal democrat, most of the Frenchman's original insights about the people's power and the electoral outlets for its expression have gone almost unnoticed.[8] In his signature work of political theory, his *Principles of Politics Applicable to All Governments* (1806), and as one of leading voices of the *Indépendant* Left opposition during the Bourbon Restoration (1814–30), Constant commented at length on the rules for designing elections and for determining who ought to participate in them. At the height of his career, from his own election to the Chamber of Deputies in 1817 until his death in 1830, he wielded electoral reform as a weapon against his illiberal opponents, moving to uproot the restored aristocracy by neutralizing the influence of its wealthy base.[9] So compelling were Constant's Restoration-era pamphlets on elections that they triggered a number of responses—"cries," to cite the sardonic title of one publication—from Ultraroyalists on the far Right.[10] Despite the significance that the thinker himself assigned to electoral rules and procedures at the moment when the term "democracy" resurfaced as a matter for political debate, scholars have generally shied away from tackling Constant's provocative views on the vote.[11]

Granted, the nature of Constant's electoral recommendations may help to explain why. On its face and for its time, his proposal to combine direct elections for representatives with a property qualification for the franchise looks unremarkable—conventional, even, if we zero in on the opinions of other avowed liberals during the Restoration and their preferred suffrage schemes. The Constitutional Charter of 1814 set such a property qualification for the vote; liberals followed suit in the legislation they recommended.[12] Pierre Rosanvallon has deftly demonstrated how the liberal Doctrinaires, who formed the more Centrist opposition of the period and who regularly clashed with Constant and the Left *Indépendants* on a number of issues, championed an electoral scheme in the spirit of the Charter—one that closely resembled Constant's in its design.[13] Given these similarities, other scholars quietly place Constant in the capacitarian camp alongside Guizot and Royer-Collard, who steered their electoral schemes to reach a government based in abstract reason, truth, and justice, evading both the Ultraroyalists' antiquated aristocracy and the republicans' demands for universal suffrage along the way.[14] Most scholars tend to assume that Constant's attitude toward democracy can be understood by scrutinizing the more incendiary Doctrinaires, who proposed the standard of *capacité politique* and railed against the mere suggestion for universal suffrage. Thus, in contrast to those intellectual historians who have recently declared Constant to be the first French liberal democrat, we can trace a second line of interpretation. Insofar as Constant was any kind of theorist of liberal democracy, on this alternate view, it was as one of democracy's elitist detractors.[15]

Against the backdrop of the Doctrinaires' antipathy toward political democracy, it is tempting to see Constant in this long elitist shadow cast by his French contemporaries, some of whom (like Guizot) would later become notorious because they refused to accept a wider franchise, let alone a universal one. Constant *did* favor a censitary suffrage; he *did* draw a distinction between capable voters and incapable others; and he *does* belong within the liberal capacitarian tradition, as this chapter will reveal. Yet Constant built his preferred electoral scheme atop distinctive, radical normative foundations— more radical than either of the two existing interpretive schools have so far been able to capture. While conceding that Constant's external designs for the vote were not especially creative in the context of the Bourbon Restoration, this chapter will argue that the rationale behind them indeed was.

The chapter pursues three aims. First, it reconstructs Constant's singular logic of a representative electoral scheme.[16] Whereas the Doctrinaires devised their electoral plans to rescue democratic society from a political despotism of its own making (a strategy I outline here and explore in greater detail in Chapter 2), Constant saw little reason to shield the government from the *demos*. He chastised his fellow theorists and politicians, from the Revolution's Idéologues to the Restoration's Doctrinaires and Ultraroyalists, for their unfounded fears about popular participation and their proposals to establish indirect elections or elitist colleges that would manage how (and how much of) the popular will could be expressed. When Constant endorsed direct elections for candidates to the assembly, he aspired to reach a different end altogether: to invest representative government with *d'une force véritable* rather than to fortify it against the onslaught of popular power, that is, to ensure that society's numerous sectional interests would be expressed within the elected chamber.[17] It was the prospect of forming a truly representative assembly that motivated Constant to revise electoral rules.

Second, this chapter links Constant's electoral theory to his liberalism in order to cast new light on the latter by way of the former. The ballot, as Constant conceived of it, was a mechanism for translating social diversity into legislative debate. More than this, the direct vote was *the* mechanism for pluralist politics—an assurance that deliberation would take place in the assembly and, as I will argue, that opinions and ideas could circulate freely in a society that respects civil liberties. Constant's pluralist brand of liberalism has been evident to scholars for some time.[18] However, without an appreciation for its *electoral* basis, we have neglected to consider what it would take, in Constant's view, to facilitate political pluralism marked by discussion, disagreement, and negotiation. Many of his contemporaries in the early part of the century, liberal and otherwise, disparaged social difference as a problem to be solved by an enlightened governing class with the final say over the composition of the elected chamber. Constant heard society's discordant opinions, too. But he sought to translate them from society to government via direct elections rather than to quiet them in electoral colleges.

Still, Constant's electoral plan contained a puzzle all its own. Even when he identified as a republican in the decade or so following the Revolution, Constant never argued in favor of universal suffrage.[19] In his quest to shape a diverse and thus a representative legislature, he strangely relied upon what appear to be uniform and unrepresentative means: a "capable" suffrage of proprietors as the sole bearers of the right to vote. In later sections of this chapter, I scrutinize Constant's strategy for managing the tension between inclusive representation and an exclusive franchise.

Finally, as this chapter unearths Constant's disagreements with other theorists on the end of true representation and the electoral means to reach it, it maps some of the political terrain over these issues from the Revolution through the end of the Restoration. It is not an exhaustive overview. Instead, by situating Constant's ideas in their intellectual context, by showing who he was responding to and why, it sets the stage for disputes over the legitimacy of political democracy in which his Doctrinaire counterparts played a leading role. These disputes will then take center stage beginning in Chapter 2.

Before turning to Constant on elections, I open this chapter by drawing attention to the dual dangers that motivated his political thought: despotism and uniformity. Later sections take up his defense of direct popular elections together with his response to the suffrage question, or the matter of who ought to possess the vote at all. The conclusion contrasts Constant's singular stance on representation with some of the debates about the legitimacy and viability of political democracy that would captivate his successors. It points ahead in time to those disagreements over the democratic age that would later unravel other, less pluralist strands of French liberalism.

Popular Sovereignty as Popular Despotism

Constant developed his liberal political theory in reaction to despotism. In his early pamphlets from 1796–7, in which he first defined and defended a "liberal" political stance, we find Constant still reeling from the effects of the Reign of Terror (1793–4) when the Committee of Public Safety under the Jacobin leader Maximilien Robespierre initiated a campaign of state-led violence to expunge France of her enemies.[20] But it was not until he confronted Bonaparte's imperialism that, to quote Helena Rosenblatt, "Constant became Constant."[21] His mature political theory was forged in the crucible of the Consulate (1799–1804) and the First Empire (1804–1814/15) in reaction to a despotic state with faces both domestic and international. Upon the emperor's imminent return from exile in March 1815, Constant deemed Bonaparte more "odious" than either Atilla or Genghis Khan for the skill with which he turned all forces of civilization—conquest and warfare abroad, liberty and equality at home—to satisfy his personal ambitions, and for leading a government so "hateful" that it could not be aptly described in the existing terms of tyranny or despotism.[22] Although he served as *conseiller d'État* during the emperor's subsequent Hundred Days, it was Constant who accused Napoleon of displacing a "regular" monarchy with an "irregular" form of tyranny as yet unseen in modern societies: an "usurpation" that "nothing modifies or softens."[23]

Constant looked on with dismay as Napoleon the usurper "counterfeited" the principle of popular sovereignty by transforming it into another justification for his dictatorship, "invoking the principle only to trample upon it."[24] Alarmed by Napoleon's "corrupting" of the people's power, Constant devoted the opening book of his 1806 *Principles of Politics* to exposing popular sovereignty for what it had become: a guise for usurpation. Such potential for abuse, he suggested, was evident from the earliest philosophical defenses of the concept. When the eighteenth-century philosophers of popular sovereignty, Jean-Jacques Rousseau and Abbé de Mably, crowned the people as a sovereign power, they neglected to set limits on sovereignty itself. However alluring on paper, their philosophies authorized despotism *de facto*.[25] It was no mere coincidence that usurpation emerged in France with the founding of the purportedly "popular governments" of the Consulate and Empire that implemented universal male suffrage and the plebiscite.[26] Napoleon concealed his personal power behind these democratic pretexts, rendering the French people subject precisely by invoking them as sovereign.[27]

In addition to his barely-veiled descriptions of Bonapartism as popular despotism, Constant identified the Terror as another example of dictatorship cloaked in the radical democracy of Rousseau, when the constitution of 1793 received approval in a nationwide referendum.[28] Armed with this mandate from the people, Robespierre declared that a democratically-justified Terror was the order of the day.[29] Nor did France's legislatures escape Constant's critical eye.[30] In the absence of constitutional checks on legislative power, the national assemblies "exercised an unparalleled despotism" after the Revolution, when there was no executive or judicial "counterweight, no suppression, no check on their will."[31] Their usurpation nevertheless bore the stamp of legitimacy; they operated as if "the absolute unlimited sovereignty of the people had been transferred" from the society to the assembly, where it would remain absolute and unlimited.[32] With these, the doctrine's real-world consequences in mind, Constant made no secret of his intention to break the spell of popular sovereignty with which the holders of power, whether individual usurper or despotic assembly, had charmed the French people.[33]

Still, Constant never attacked popular sovereignty because it was *popular*. Nor did he hold ordinary citizens responsible for usurpation. The people's choices were not the wellspring of the new despotism that stirred so much anxiety among his Doctrinaire counterparts, as we will discover in the next chapter. Instead, Constant placed the blame for the rise of abusive governments on "the extent of power," specifically on the constitutions that failed to constrain it, rather than on "those in whom it is vested," in this case the people *en masse*.[34] Given this distinction, scholars are of course right to read the *Principles* as the author's definitive contribution to constitutionalism, a text in the tradition of Montesquieu's *Spirit of the Laws* (1748).[35] In severing political power in the abstract from the human "hands in which it is placed," Constant wrote to re-enliven his nation's interest in constitutionalism after more than a decade of exhausting attempts at constitutional creation.[36] But Constant also aimed to differentiate a fictitious popular government from an actual one, or the "abstract thing" from the "real thing."[37] His message was that the abstract axiom of popular sovereignty can sanction very real political evils. "What no tyrant would dare to do in his own name" could be undertaken without question by the avowed agent of the popular will instead.[38] In the shadow of despots and the feeble institutions through which they proceed unchecked, there was relatively little to fear from the real, direct participation of the people themselves, from their interests genuinely expressed rather than their wills co-opted.

Constant added another accusation to his descriptions of usurpation: as of 1806, the French had yet to hold a popular election at all. This was because popular sovereignty was paradoxically a source of both legitimacy and of anxiety. Although leaders relied upon the *appearance* of popular assent to legitimate their authority and implemented universal suffrage and the plebiscite for this purpose, they feared the real *existence* of a public spirit.[39] "Since the introduction of the concept of representation," the participation of the people had become a source of anxiety for the French, Constant alleged. And they crafted elaborate plans for electoral colleges to quiet the popular voice without muting it entirely. Their fears were unfounded, however: "if, in the history of the ten years which have just passed by, certain facts seem unfavorable to popular election, special causes explain this. First of all, we have never really had a popular election . . . we cannot judge popular election in France because it has simply not existed."[40] The nation's constitutional architects believed that despotism emerged out of the people's unfiltered electoral choices and constructed their electoral schemes upon this baseless assumption. Midway through his *Principles*, Constant, who was always careful to avoid any misunderstandings that might stem from the "vagueness" of words,[41] altered the very terms by which to distinguish one electoral procedure from the other: not direct versus indirect but free "popular *election*" versus an exclusive elitist power of "*appointment*."[42] Constant's choice of words is telling. Anything less than the voters' direct choice could not rightly be considered an expression of popular electoral power.

With this distinction in place, Constant set out to accomplish two objectives at the same time. First, he intended to expose recent invocations of popular sovereignty for the tyrannical pretenses that they really were; second, he sought to dispel the existing belief that the people's choices were responsible for the tyranny of modern governments. Misunderstandings on both fronts, he thought, prompted his countrymen to write ineffectual constitutions with poorly designed electoral schemes, unknowingly creating the conditions for usurpation.

"An Exaggerated Uniformity": Constant Against Indirect Elections

Constant was not the first to find fault with the indirect "vote." Some of the sharpest criticisms of indirect elections came from Jacques Necker, former finance minister on the eve of the Revolution and father of Germaine de Staël.[43] Necker commented on the Constitution of December 1799 (Year VIII of the republican calendar) that created the Consulate and instituted universal male suffrage along with a multi-tiered procedure for electing legislators.[44] Voters at the municipal level chose one-tenth of their number ("those who are most fit to conduct public affairs") to designate a list of "eligibles" from which a subsequent list was drawn, and so on.[45] The constitution left the final selection of officeholders to Bonaparte as First Consul and to the Senate, who appointed legislators to the *Corps législatif* from a finalized national list of 6,000 names.[46] Necker lamented that this complicated process (one that grew too complicated even for Napoleon) rendered the election of representatives "fictional" and the individual vote "insignificant." With time, citizens would come to regard both their individual participation and their legislature with "passive indifference."[47] As the constitution bestowed the title *citoyen* on all adult men, it emptied that title of "the beauty and dignity" it once conferred.[48]

Echoing Necker, Constant found fault with any system that could so detach the voter from the deputy chosen—by someone else, in the end—to represent him.[49] He cited quite a few examples to mount his critiques. The nation had been experimenting with indirect or multi-tiered elections and intricate networks of primary assemblies since the early stages of the Revolution.[50] Years later, Constant regretted that his own contribution to the long line of French constitutions, the 1814 *Acte Additionnel* to Bonaparte's imperial constitution, did not include any major modifications to the 1799 arrangement. In his eyes, the document's electoral measures (or lack thereof) were "unquestionably" its "most imperfect part."[51]

The imperfections of the *Acte* notwithstanding, Constant amplified Necker's complaints about the indirect vote.[52] Since indirect "elections" reduced the casting of the ballot to a ceremony without substance, they also reduced the likelihood that the elected Chamber would be truly representative or, in Constant's revised terms, *popular*. For one, an indirect system incentivizes candidates to seek approval from the wrong places—not from the homes of their constituents but from "the palaces of electoral colleges," inhabited either by a single ruler, government officials, or the wealthiest men of France, depending on the electoral measure in place at the moment and its distribution of electoral choice.[53] To navigate the circuitous channels to public office, candidates will resort to flattery or servility "to win over" the few with final decision-making authority rather than to represent primary voters who were at least twice removed from an election's results.[54]

Constant's pivotal objection to the indirect system hinged on the very meaning of representation. He accused some of France's most outspoken enthusiasts of representative government (and not coincidentally, also of indirect elections) of promoting an erroneous notion of *what* exactly could be represented. Across his writings, Constant targeted a loosely associated cadre of constitutional theorists that included many of his personal friends: Emmanuel-Joseph Sieyès, Pierre Louis Roederer, Pierre Jean-Georges Cabanis, and Nicolas de Condorcet, among others.[55] On the matter of electoral rules, at least, Constant grouped them all together as proponents of "political uniformity." On their shared view, what Constant framed as the prevailing perspective on representative government since the Revolution, the legislative assembly exists to represent a "single general interest," or as he denounced it, to graft a "very exaggerated idea of uniformity" onto institutions that fails to reflect the realities of a diverse country spanning a large territory.[56] To secure this general interest, Sieyès and company subjected politics to the regulating rule of reason, or to borrow from one of Rosanvallon's descriptions, an abstract guideline for accessing truth with no "deliberation or experimentation" required.[57]

To Constant, the Constitution of 1799 reflected the rationalistic aspirations of its architects, Sieyès first among them. In fact, the details of the constitution's final design paled in comparison to the blueprint that Sieyès initially sketched for Napoleon. In that first draft, members of a proposed five state institutions (including a "Great Elector," the seat that Sieyès himself hoped to fill) would be chosen through an indirect process that involved more list-making at every level from department to nation, all of it engineered to blunt the instrument of popular participation.[58] Consistent with the goal to promote the general interest, Sieyès maintained that the concept of representation applied solely at the highest level of political organization: the nation. Over a territory as large as France, it was not only undesirable but impossible to represent local interests, customs, or attachments. To speak of "the people," furthermore, was to refer to a single entity that "exists only at the level of national representation," he held. The choice of legislators must rest with "higher-ranking persons" who alone are able to "represent the nation as a body," since they stand above the popular fray of conflicting opinions and customs.[59] The Idéologue Cabanis, who sat on one of two commissions charged with promulgating the new constitution, likewise insisted that the choice of officeholders should "not flow from below," from the fount of popular direct elections, "but from above, where it will always necessarily be done well." Cabanis gave his approval to systems in which "everything is done for the people and in the name of people, but never by them or from their mindless dictations."[60] To secure this government for the people though never by them, "the nominations to the legislative body can only be adequately made by men who know the object and general aim of all legislation well," those electors who could identify other men of enlightenment and good sense just by, as he put it, casting a single "glance" over a nation's territory.[61]

This penchant for rationality from above had deep roots in French culture and perhaps even deeper ones in human nature.[62] Rosanvallon traces its origins to the Enlightenment ideal of freedom through reason.[63] So entrenched was the French credo of "generality" (or what Constant derided as uniformity), Rosanvallon argues, that it mobilized the French to revere the political imaginary of a nation whole and entire, and to renounce all things local or intermediary—interests, opinions, sentiments, corporations, attachments, associations—as barriers to a unified society.[64] For the Scottish moralist Adam Smith (1723–1790), whose writings Constant studied at the University of Edinburgh, these inclinations were more primordial—the stirrings of the "spirit of system" that drove humankind to systematize the social world, as if the players within it had no more agency than pieces on a chess board.[65] Regardless of its source, the near-aesthetic appreciation for a uniform society went hand-in-hand with a deep distrust of the people. The implication of Sieyès' position was that political elites, as the keepers of the nation's general interest, ought to disseminate those truths to which they alone have access. Electoral decisions emanating "from below" would be partial and therefore imperfect, while those conferred "from above" would further the general interest by shining truth's light on every darkened, provincial corner of the country.[66]

Constant found it ironic that humankind's "spirit of system," a term he no doubt took from Smith, manifested in the midst of a "revolution made in the name of the rights and liberty of men."[67] He acknowledged that the instinct to systematize and centralize would not lead to despotism everywhere and always. And yet this was its result in modern France. In their zeal to efface "parochial" customs and "irrational" ways of life with absolute values, the "so-called patriots" of the Revolution unknowingly undermined local, traditional sites of resistance against the state to give an "immense advantage" to would-be despots.[68] While Cabanis, for his part, could not have predicted the depths to which Napoleonic usurpation would sink when he wrote in support of the Consul in 1799, his commitment to *la représentation nationale* shaped by experts in secondary elections nonetheless fit seamlessly in his pamphlet written in defense of Bonaparte's newly-consolidated power.[69] Constant could thus see very little daylight between the philosophy of uniformity and the politics of despotism.

Popular Elections and Press Freedoms

Writing in 1806, Constant found the same homogenizing ethos contained in all French constitutions since the Revolution, where it lent support to a mistaken view of national representation and a flawed formula for elections. From 1814 onward, he found it restated in the agendas of his Restoration adversaries, both the reactionary Ultras and the just left-of-center liberal Doctrinaires, who anchored their respective policies about civil and political rights on a similarly uniform ideal. Ultraroyalists such as Louis de Bonald and Joseph de Maistre esteemed the *ancien régime* as a hierarchical golden age that stood outside of history, and aimed to restore its absolute monarch allied with the Catholic Church with the support of the *grands propriétaires*. Their plan also involved retooling the nation's electoral machinery, and this culminated in the 1820 Law of the Double Vote.[70] The law added 172 extra seats to the Chamber and gave the choice of candidates for them exclusively to the wealthiest quarter of the electorate, who literally had a double vote: the first to fill the original Chamber seats in the district colleges and the second for the newly-added seats in the departmental colleges. Those wealthy electors, who also happened to comprise the demographic most sympathetic to the royalist Right, held the largest share of influence over the composition of the elected chamber.[71]

With the Double Vote, the Ultras overturned the liberal-backed (and Constant-supported) Lainé Law of 1817 that gave the direct vote for deputies to 90,000 men, including small proprietors and members of the middle-class occupations who met its property qualification.[72] In their attacks on the 1817 law, the Ultras accused the Chamber of having grown "factional" by dint of the mechanism through which its deputies were elected—that is, *directly* by voters in the departmental colleges rather than by second-level electors who could speak for the whole nation at once.[73] Pushing the charge further, the Ultras restated some of the ideas about national unity that circulated during the Revolutionary debates. They associated indirect elections alone with a *representative* assembly, by which they meant one that reflected the common good of the whole nation over the dissimilar sentiments of its parts.[74]

For his part, Constant accused the Ultras of "conspiring" to "suffocate public opinion" in elections and in the press at the same time.[75] He had good reason for his suspicions. Broadly speaking, the Restoration years were characterized by censorship punctuated by moments of liberalization[76] One "liberal" moment followed immediately on the heels of the restoration of Louis XVIII in 1814; soon thereafter, the Bourbon monarchy imposed legal measures subjecting all publications under twenty pages long to government oversight, a law framed to target the pamphlets and journals that surfaced after Bonaparte as lively outlets for public dialogue. Following another short-lived experiment with less-stringent restrictions a few years later, the 1820 assassination of the Duc de Berry led to the most severe crackdown on press freedoms. The Ultras then fueled fear and distrust to justify suppressing the written word.

The issues surrounding free expression during the Restoration made strange if temporary and unacknowledged bedfellows of politicians at the reactionary extreme and the liberal Center.[77] Before he emerged as the most outspoken of the Doctrinaires, the young liberal Guizot was always hesitant about testing the social waters with a freer press.[78] On the one hand, he saw the value of a free press as a key instrument of representative government, an open line of communication between society and those who occupy the seats of power.[79] On the other, he feared that truth and reason would be drowned out in the unregulated, cacophonous expression of ideas across newspapers and journals.[80] He found a middle way, he thought, when he advocated for the *cautionnement*, a monetary deposit paid by newspaper publishers to the state in order to secure the "privilege"—not a civil *right*, we will note—to publish, and a sure sign of a journalist's *capacity* (a term we will see again) to promulgate the truth.[81] In exalting absolute reason over ever-changing opinions, Guizot breathed new life into the Revolutionary ideal of uniformity by using it to condemn universal suffrage, which he warned was too unreasonable and unruly to yield capable government. His idiosyncratic belief in the *sovereignty* of reason (which we will explore in Chapter 2) manifested in his proposals to narrow the exercise of both press freedoms and political rights. He hoped to control the privilege of publishing and to limit the franchise to the politically capable few, or, as will discuss it in the next chapter, the new, natural, and rational aristocracy for post-revolutionary society.[82]

Constant contested the agendas of both parties, Doctrinaire and Ultra, under which the restrictions on civil rights and political rights, on press freedom and electoral power, overlapped.[83] He spoke out vehemently and often against the Double Vote and the censorship of the press, and delivered impassioned refutations of Guizot on the *cautionnement*.[84] One conviction underlay all of his critiques: that "there never has been, on important and complex questions, unanimity without servitude."[85] Or as he stated in a different context, "variety is what constitutes organization; uniformity is mere mechanism. Variety is life, uniformity death."[86] Against Guizot's politics of absolute reason, Constant emphasized that difference and discord were the social background conditions for political debate. While Guizot encouraged the nation to vest power over the printed word and control over government in the capable few, Constant championed the proliferation of ideas and interests in the press and in the legislature, regardless of the source of those ideas.[87] Conflict and contestation were empirical facts, he insisted. They were also valuable features of political life, not problems to be solved by a priori reasoning. And for Constant, the value of diversity could be felt well beyond the political. It is the basis for a human life well-lived, that which makes our self-development and self-knowledge possible.[88]

When compared with the Doctrinaires' outlook on the press, Constant emerges as the liberal champion of civil liberties. This is how he has come to be known to scholars.[89] But specifically for him, civil liberties sat atop the foundation set by popular elections, a point that has received little attention from scholars, even those who set Constant's pluralism against Guizot's rationalism. He stressed just how *fragile* the civil freedom of the press was in those countries where citizens were denied the direct vote. "It is through popular election that press freedom, under very easily offended ministers, has survived every crisis," he declared, since press freedom "is never other than precarious where political rights do not exist."[90] If that freedom comes under threat from the legislature, a "people who do not have the right of election can change nothing about the composition of assemblies that speak in their name." If those threats originate with the executive, the people again have no recourse: "when assemblies that call themselves 'representative' are not selected by the people" but by an electoral college, "they are helpless before the executive power. If they put up some resistance to it, it demands to know by what right. How can you be the representatives of the people? Did they appoint you?"[91] Whether despotism takes on a legislative or executive hue, a citizenry without direct representation—even under a well-designed constitution that constrains the rulers, he suggested—remains powerless to resist it. A nation denied the chance at real popular election lacks any standing to resist usurpation based in abstract "popular" power. Nor can citizens hope to safeguard their civil liberties, a free press among them, without exercising some binding accountability over their representatives through direct election.

Thus, even well before he carried the liberal mantle of a free press against the Doctrinaires and denounced the aristocracy of the Ultras, Constant worried about what would be lost in constructing the legislature around a national interest that was untouchable by the people and defined by a network of elitist electors. Out of their "mania for uniformity" and complementary fear of the people as a power, Constant's contemporaries sacrificed what he regarded as the two great advantages of a representative government.[92] The first was political: its ability to translate society's interests into the elected assembly. The second was social: to forge links between all social classes by giving candidates an incentive, albeit an incentive out of self-interest, to consider the welfare of the lower classes.

Diversity through the Direct Vote

Put otherwise, Constant was more than willing to trade the futile pursuit of abstract enlightenment for the real representation of society's varied and variable interests. Still, he never denied the existence of a "general interest" altogether. *Contra* Sieyès or Guizot, he insisted that it was not the product of the a priori reasoning of an enlightened few.[93] As scholars such as Bryan Garsten and Jacob Levy have shown in different ways, Constant believed that the general was to be found in and only in the interactions between particulars.[94] "What is the general interest if not the negotiations which operate between particular interests?" Constant asked. What is general representation, furthermore, "if not the representation of all of the partial interests that must negotiate over the objects common to them all?"[95] When Constant discussed "partial interests," he used the term in a capacious sense to encompass those held by individuals, as well as those interests most relevant to particular sections of the country.[96] Individuals and local communities are the building blocks of the nation, the organs of the body politic, and their interests are the only objects of representation.[97] Elsewhere, he spoke of those interests as the natural outgrowths of longstanding institutions, of organic customs and practices so deeply rooted that they could never be effaced by a nation's written constitution—no matter how much his rationalist contemporaries had hoped.[98]

Whereas Sieyès asserted that local representation was impossible to sustain across a large territory, Constant invoked "nature" as his standard to assert otherwise.[99] It was "natural" and in fact desirable that deputies across a country as large in territory as France should "bring the individual interests and local preferences of their constituents inside the assembly."[100] Direct elections infuse national politics with much-needed local knowledge in the person of each deputy, who serves unapologetically as the "biased instrument" of "that section of the country whose mandatory he is."[101] They incentivize deputies literally *to re-present* the interests of their constituents, thwarting the evils of corruption that plague indirect systems where candidates appeal to the already-powerful few. Seen from Constant's vantage, what the Ultras denounced as the deputies' "factionalism"—their partiality for the wishes of their respective departments—was suggestive of a healthy representative body, operating just as nature intended.[102] In addition, Constant emphasized that his schema for representation had social repercussions beyond the electoral sphere. Since legislators would be chosen directly, they would be forced to weigh the opinions of all classes in their departments rather than those of high-ranking electors alone. Constant was confident that a truly representative system, one in which the vote remains unmediated, would also "establish frequent relations between the diverse classes of society. Sectional election requires on the part of the powerful classes sustained consideration for the lower classes. It requires wealth to conceal its arrogance, power to moderate its action by placing in the people's votes a reward for justice and kindness and a punishment for oppression."[103]

Direct elections also enhance the inner workings of the assembly. As William Selinger shows in his work on parliamentarism, Constant celebrated a legislative assembly as *the* defining feature of a representative regime and valued its processes of deliberation.[104] For Constant, two factors distinguish deliberation from mere talk. First, deliberation requires diversity. Without an array of prejudices, preferences, ideas, habits, or interests, it is unclear what exactly will be up for discussion. Second, deliberation entails compromise among competing interests. It was in the negotiations among differing ways of life that Constant discovered a "general interest" very different from the abstract, disembodied truth that Sieyès envisioned. Constant identified the general interest as a much thinner *modus vivendi*, as "nothing other than individual interests rendered incapable of harming each other." Deputies find commonality in disagreement: "forced to debate together, they notice respective sacrifices that are indispensable." Alongside his modest hopes that violent interests could be disarmed and some common ground could be discovered, Constant arrived at a far-reaching conclusion about the electoral process: "the principle of unity in the electoral body," the principle behind indirect elections, is "completely erroneous."[105]

With this conclusion, Constant turned the arguments of figures such as Cabanis and Sieyès on their heads. They contended that local interests and habits ought not and could never be represented in the national legislature and created their electoral plans accordingly. Absent such variety, however, Constant held that there was nothing to represent—and little about which to deliberate. In his conclusions on elections, we find Constant's liberal pluralism wedded to his novel view of representation: "in sum, *only* sectional election by the people can invest national representation with real force and give it deep roots in public opinion."[106] Only popular election can guarantee a pluralistic assembly with real representative force, a balance of sectional and individual interests as they exist.[107]

However resolute Constant remained in favor of true representation, the second pillar of his electoral theory—a property qualification for the vote—stands uneasily alongside his defense of direct elections. Can the legislature truly represent a range of society's sectional and individual interests if most of those interests will never actually be expressed in elections? How is real representation possible with a franchise of the (relative) few?

In order to square the circle regarding Constant's electoral commitments, it is worth clarifying two points at the outset. First, Constant himself anticipated a similar objection. He acknowledged that his two electoral proposals, one for electoral design (how the vote ought to happen) and one for the franchise (who would vote at all), might operate at cross purposes. "Perhaps it will be objected that in granting political rights only to property owners, I am lessening the advantage of the representative system," he wrote.[108] Strikingly, however, he also doubled down on his earlier claims about the inclusivity of his proposed system. Under a direct system, *all* segments of society, including those that may be disqualified from the vote, would nonetheless find their interests reflected in the legislature through a franchise limited to the propertied. Second, although Constant inherited the Physiocrats' definition of property as land and continued to invoke that same definition during the Directory and the Empire, he later arrived at a more dynamic meaning of the term. Property came to include industrial property and as a result, opened the electorate to new persons and occupations, thereby encouraging a broader suffrage over time. The following section takes up these two points, the first on the political merits of proprietorship, the second on an evolving electorate.

A Propertied and Evolving Electorate

All political societies make distinctions among those within their borders. With this, one of his "principles of politics," Constant opened a sprawling inquiry into the relationship between property and political rights in *Principles* Book X. Even "the most absolute democracy," if one ever came into being, would prove the rule rather than the exception, he claimed. It would grant certain rights to adults but deny the same to children and foreigners.[109] Of course, not all distinctions are legitimate. The fixed binaries of the ancient world (slaves and freemen) and the feudal age (nobles and lowborn) reveal the arbitrariness with which nations may discriminate among their inhabitants. In place of these arbitrary, outdated divisions, Constant looked on property as the rightful standard for organizing modern societies into two classes of owners and non-owners and therefore into citizens and non-citizens. In choosing *"citoyens"* over *"électeurs"* to designate the holders of the vote, Constant (ever careful with his words) attempted to redraw the electoral dividing line to complement his preferred designs for direct elections. The relevant partition, then, was not between second-level electoral colleges and primary voters, but between citizens with the vote and inhabitants without.[110]

As he replaced the existing distinction between citizen and elector with his own, Constant also revived an earlier way of thinking about citizenship. Though written during the Empire and in response to its constitution(s) of universal suffrage, the *Principles* echoes the Revolution's lapsed language of passive and active citizenship. It was Sieyès, the eventual architect of the indirect system, who once turned his attention to the voters themselves and proposed to distinguish between passive and active citizens just days after the fall of the Bastille. He began with the premise that political rights are predicated on a more fundamental distinction between society's active, propertied "stakeholders" and its passive, non-propertied residents. As such, the political or "active" rights "by which society is formed" belong only to "those who contribute to the public establishment."[111] But who were society's contributors? Sieyès offered different answers to this question at different times, and his particular proposals for classifying citizens never gained much traction.[112] Nonetheless, his key intuition relating social contributions to citizenship rights resonated in the National Assembly. The Assembly bestowed the title of active citizen on adults who could pay a direct tax of three days' wages, designating all those who fell below the new *cens* as "passive citizens." Although the language of active and passive citizenship disappeared from the constitution once fiscal requirements for the vote were abolished, variations on Sieyès' distinction resurfaced in debates over the franchise and its extent before 1830, often from liberals—Constant among them.[113]

As Sieyès had done, Constant isolated political from civil rights. He recast the distinction in his own terms, carefully distinguishing "powers" from "protections" or electoral "weapons" from civil "shields."[114] Civil protections are owed to everyone and anyone, including the foreigner who crosses the country's border. But because they bestow power in the form of the vote, political rights occupy a different status than civil rights. For Constant writing during the Empire, as for Sieyès in the early stages of the Revolution, the individual entrusted with such power had to be much more than a "passive" inhabitant of a place. To merit Constant's title "citizen" (or Sieyès' active citizen), one had to exhibit "a certain degree of informed outlook and common interests with other members," provable by taxes paid on landed property.[115] The individual's private "enlightenment" could be joined to a common "interest"—though not an abstract one—that he shares with other members of society. This combination could be cultivated while at leisure, Constant stressed, and leisure belongs to those who possess land. In this way, taxes on property (the *cens*) serve as an outward sign of the individual's fitness to exercise the power of the vote.

Ultimately, Constant's description of the modern citizen owes just as much to Aristotle's ancient arguments as it does to Sieyès' distinction. In his book on the best regime in *The Politics*, Aristotle portrayed citizenship as a vocation best left to the leisured few who could undertake the responsibilities of ruling and being ruled in turn.[116] Just as Aristotle disqualified slaves and vulgar laborers from the demanding civic life of the *polis*, Constant agreed that poverty holds individuals in "endless dependence," whether on labor itself, the wage, or the proprietor, leaving them with little personal freedom to invest in public affairs and rendering them unfit for the franchise.[117] He seconded Aristotle's critique of ancient Athens, a *polis* that vacillated between the extremes of oligarchy and democracy without ever finding its mean in a middle-class polity.[118] In his own time and against the status quo of universal suffrage joined to the indirect vote, Constant recovered an "abandoned" qualification for the franchise (though a property qualification would reappear in the Charter years later).[119] "Only property can render men capable of exercising political rights. Only owners can be citizens," he declared, blending Revolutionary and classical arguments in his support for modern reform.[120] Any man who "has the necessary income to exist independently of another party's will" fulfilled Constant's criterion for proprietorship.[121] A lower standard would never suffice to ensure that only enlightened, socially invested individuals held the power of the vote. A higher one, Constant warned, would tend toward oligarchy.[122]

Even granting such a low floor for proprietorship, it bears asking why Constant insisted on a limited, capacitarian franchise at all. For one answer, we have to remember that the right to vote was construed as a "power" that, like all other powers, had to be constrained and controlled, lest it become arbitrary. In this case, any "controlling" of electoral power meant limiting precisely who could wield it. As a second response, we also have to recall that Constant's plan pivoted around rewriting electoral *rules*—*how* the deputies were selected. If France adopted direct elections, meeting Constant's first criterion for representation through "popular election," then it would have to impose some restrictions on the makeup of its electorate. This point is worth restating. While Constant saw no benefit in stopping up the electoral channels connecting the people to their representatives, he did see the wisdom in delineating who "the people" were before an election ever took place.[123] This move to delimit the franchise may initially be surprising, given that Constant gave such a rousing defense of popular elections after the Revolution and would continue to do so through the end of the Restoration. Furthermore, we cannot ignore the reality that, just like those theorists whose proposals he denounced as either oligarchic or illusory, Constant built a mechanism for electoral filtering into the framework of his own plan. On this point, how different, if at all, was Constant from the uniformists he claimed to stand against?

One key difference is that Constant's mechanism operated by delimiting the suffrage—by restricting who could exercise the "power" of political rights at all—rather than relying on the electors' appointment power *ex post* to mold an election's results. Under his plan for direct election by a curated, capable "citizenry," he was able to retain those salutary popular elements of the electoral system—its ability to channel particular interests, to represent diversity, and to tie government authority to society—while also controlling *who* participated electorally. On this matter, Constant was unbending: the suffrage should remain only with those individuals who can make proper use of it.[124] Even when he anticipated the arrival of a broader suffrage for France in the late 1820s, as we will soon learn, he remained steadfast in the view that individuals had to rise to meet the bar for capable citizenship.

Constant's proposal for a limited, propertied suffrage would have both inclusionary and exclusionary implications for the composition of the electorate. On the inclusionary side, it would enable legislators to stretch the boundaries of the electorate as far as they could reasonably reach, that is, to bestow the right to vote on all persons who qualified as propertied and independent, not solely the grand proprietors or the Ultras' wealthiest few. It also meant that the politically excluded category of non-voting inhabitants, what Sieyès called the "passive citizenry," had to be just as clearly delineated. Although the non-propertied often display the *moral* virtue of "heroism," Constant was adamant that they lack *political* judgement, or more immediately, the time and energy to stand vigilant against usurpation. "The patriotism which gives one the courage to die for one's country"—the self-sacrifice undertaken by the lower classes—"is one thing, while that which makes one capable of understanding one's interests"—the political judgement of the citizen—"is quite another."[125] In the same text in which he was clear to condemn the extent of power rather than the hands in which it rests, Constant, too, aimed to control who would wield the power of the suffrage in the first place.

And although he began by reflecting on the unique virtues of the leisured class in the *Principles*, Constant's analysis soon diverged from the Aristotelian ideal of a detached, enlightened aristocrat. In the end, it was not the proprietor's *enlightenment*, the product of his leisure, but his personal-cum-political *interests*, the consequences of owning property, that Constant came to regard as the surest safeguards for liberty. "Always bothered by power," the proprietor will resist any potential encroachments into what is his own, and such a distrustful disposition toward the powerful makes him well-suited to resist arbitrariness and despotism.[126]

For Constant, a franchise of proprietors could also function as a practical counterweight to prevailing ideas about political uniformity. The Revolution revealed the ease with which France's intellectuals, its "scholars, writers, mathematicians, and chemists"—including Cabanis, a scientist and physician[127]—"lent themselves to the most exaggerated opinions" and erected institutions in line with their theoretical science of man.[128] But the proprietor's influence balances the social scales. It offsets the intellectuals' detached "disdaining of facts and scorning of the real sensory world" with a grounded feeling of community.[129] Consider Constant's contrast between the "chimeras" of intellectuals and the actual complexities of social relations:

> Every science ... gives to the mind of him who cultivates it an exclusive slant, which becomes dangerous in matters political, unless it is counterbalanced. Now, the counterweight can be found only in landed property. This alone establishes uniform ties between men. It puts them on guard against the imprudent sacrifice of the happiness and peace of others by enveloping within this sacrifice their own well-being. . . . It makes them descend from lofty, chimerical theories and inapplicable exaggerations by establishing between them and other members of society numerous complicated relations and common interests. Let it not be thought that this precaution is only useful for maintaining order. It is no less so for maintaining liberty.[130]

However elegant, Constant's descriptions of a proprietor class and its signature virtues warrant more careful scrutiny. It is not always clear, for one thing, where that class begins and ends. In some instances, the propertied class is presented as a homogenous stratum of society. Its members share a "love of order, conservation, and justice" for which they readily earn the public confidence.[131] At other points across Constant's writings, its members cross porous boundaries between social classes in the commercial age when "the interests of proprietors are not separate from the interests of the industrial or wage earning classes," or from those of the "artisans of small towns and day-laborers of hamlets" with whom they share "common cause."[132]

Constant thus never gave precise shape to the propertied middle class. And in this, he was certainly not alone. Similar ambiguities can be found in the writings of other liberals of every stripe, as we will discover in later chapters of this book. Guizot, for one, tried to own his imprecision; he claimed that any remaining ambiguities on his part were deliberate, since they reflected the fluidity of social classes in the mobile age of democracy. Likewise, there is little reason to assume that Constant ever intended to circumscribe a middle class with anything approaching sociological precision. In Constant's case, in fact, such a hazy conception of the "propertied" gave his theory at least one advantage over those of his contemporaries: it functioned as a defense against the charges of unrepresentativeness and exclusivity that he leveled at other theorists of representation. On Constant's account, inhabitants without the vote will nonetheless have their interests expressed in the legislature, transported there by the direct vote of individual proprietors who share their interests despite the distinctions of class or inequalities in wealth. Whichever other factors divide individuals, Constant was confident that direct, sectional election for the deputies would override them. He was also quick to advise that such an "everyday device for happiness and harmony" in social relationships "ought not be easily renounced" as a mere electoral calculation on the part of the powerful. What begins out of the self-interest of the few may become a habitual virtue.[133]

Another feature of private property—its mutability—provides another point in favor of the thesis that a propertied franchise could be a representative one. "Since the birth of commerce," Constant wrote, "proprietors have no longer formed a distinct class, separated from the rest of men by lasting prerogatives. The membership of this class renews itself constantly. Some people leave, others enter it."[134] Constant denounced English entail and the Napoleonic inheritance laws for obstructing the natural and free circulation of property. In their place, he proposed a more laissez-faire, *laissez-passer* system that might encourage private property to change hands, yielding both an evolving landowning class and an evolving and more expansive electorate.[135]

Constant's appreciation for the natural mutability of property led him to modify the very meaning of the term. Though he once defined it as land or territory alone, by 1822 he celebrated the inherent mobility of industrial "property" that elevated a class of the "newly-wealthy," a social category that was inconceivable in the days of the Old Regime.[136] With this wider notion of "property," Constant's citizenry would evolve in turn. In 1829, the year before his death, Constant suggested that history was moving in the direction of near-universal suffrage. He envisioned an economic future free from the aristocrats' "monopoly privilege" and with it, a political future in which virtually all Frenchmen, by then proprietors, could be called upon to exercise the franchise. He was consistent in his assertion from 1806 that citizens were made rather than born. Now, he anticipated that equalizing conditions, economic and social, would help to make a growing number of them.[137] And he trusted, as he always had, that such an active citizenry would function as one of the surest safeguards against usurpation.

Conclusion

Against those Revolutionary "rationalists" who saw representation embodied in the whole nation and in the elite electors who could supposedly speak for the national interest, Constant defended the value of local communities and partial interests and even of half-truths and fragmentary opinions. Unlike Sieyès or Guizot, who each in his own way refused to allow anything resembling the unregulated power of the people to determine legislative elections, Constant did not craft his electoral plan out of a deep-seated fear about what universal suffrage could produce. Given his insistence on a limited suffrage, that thesis—the central argument of this chapter—may have initially seemed puzzling. I have shown that Constant did, after all, differentiate the non-proprietors' admirable moral virtue from the proprietors' obligatory political judgment, and that he was clear to classify electoral rights as contingently granted powers rather than universally bestowed civil protections, thereby limiting who could hold them. I have shown, furthermore, that Constant belonged broadly in the capacitarian tradition of liberalism. And yet, Constant did not create his liberal political theory either for or against political democracy as such. Instead, he formulated the foregoing arguments about the vote in light of his overriding aim to see true representation realized, not political democracy either thwarted or embraced. And as I have argued, Constant's stance on representation and his call for direct elections to achieve it were inseparable from his plea for press freedom in times of censorship—and thus from his vision of a *liberal* society that could defend civil freedoms against state power. For him, a liberal social order that preserved such freedoms and a pluralistic, representative political assembly originated from the same source: the direct expression of the people's voice.

Insofar as his plan involved reforming electoral rules, Constant's theory of representation cannot help but touch on at least some of the issues surrounding political democracy as well, even if this is not what the thinker himself intended. In reaction to France's short-lived constitutions and their complicated electoral arrangements, he distanced himself from those theorists who dismissed popular choice outright as either too partial or insufficiently enlightened to dictate the outcome of national elections. His greatest, though still indirect contribution to debates over democracy in this period grew out of his reflections on despotism. He chastised his contemporaries for tracing despotism to the wrong source. In his eyes, it was not the upshot of the people's unfiltered political decisions, but of the French

attachment to philosophical uniformity and to the ineffective institutions
that the doctrine inspired. In fact, a public spirit energized by what Constant
called the "popular election" of representatives may work to counter usurpation, even when constitutional guarantees proved too weak.

After his death in 1830, Constant's pluralist liberalism and his quest for
"real" representation were soon eclipsed in France (as Constant's personal
and professional reputations also would be) by Guizot's Doctrinaire liberalism that put the risks associated with political democracy front and
center.[138] While Guizot likewise recommended a representative government, he did so to complement what he called a "democratic" form of society,
and preferred a *rational* legislative body filtered through a rational electorate
over what Constant would have ever recognized as a *representative* one. The
next chapter examines Guizot's complex arguments for a capable government led by a capable aristocracy and chosen by a capable electorate. On
the surface, as we learned in the opening pages of this chapter, Guizot's electoral plan appears to align with Constant's. And yet the former's aspiration
to see France's democratic society ruled by a capable aristocracy drove his
arguments in divergent and politically antidemocratic directions.

2

François Guizot and Democracy's
"Capable" Aristocracy

While Benjamin Constant said very little about democracy directly, his fellow liberal (and political rival) François Guizot never shied away from expressing his opinions about a democratic France.[1] In his roles as minister of foreign affairs and later prime minister during the July Monarchy (1830–48), Guizot defended electoral laws that went unchanged for nearly two decades and enfranchised approximately 240,000 men at the most. When confronted with demands for electoral reform within the Chamber, the Guizot-led *parti de la résistance* countered measures to broaden the franchise in 1842 and again in 1847. "There will never be a day for universal suffrage!" Guizot declared to the deputies then. Even democracy's leftist "partisans," he railed, knew how absurd their vaunted principle of universal suffrage truly was.[2]

Less than a year after Guizot uttered these words, insurrectionists took to the streets of Paris, where they alternated cries of "*à bas Guizot!*" and "*Vive la Réforme!*"[3] *Capacité politique*, the standard with which Guizot justified his liberalism of resistance, had grown synonymous with exclusive, classist politics. Ever since, it has been dismissed as little more than a failed strategy to forestall the emerging democratic age, its liberal defenders—Guizot first among them—paralyzed by their fear of the mass vote.[4]

But beneath Guizot's thundering verdicts against universal suffrage lay decades of reflections on equality. This chapter will argue that we cannot understand his pleas for *capacité* or his animus toward democracy apart from them. More controversially, it positions Guizot, the sworn enemy of universal suffrage, as one of the nineteenth century's most sophisticated theorists of democracy, if also its most complicated.[5] As the Parisian revolutionaries knew all too well, Guizot did condemn democracy in one sense: as a government founded on the "sovereignty of number" (his disparaging term for the sovereignty of the people), which manifested in an electoral scheme with universal male suffrage.[6] At the same time, he welcomed the equalized society that rose alongside the Third Estate—and in a striking move, claimed

Democracy Tamed. Gianna Englert, Oxford University Press. © Oxford University Press 2024.
DOI: 10.1093/oso/9780197635315.003.0003

it as "democracy." His calls to insert *capacité* into the electoral process went hand-in-hand with these ambitious attempts to redefine "democracy" while also containing its spread. Precisely because post-revolutionary France was "democratic," by which Guizot meant that it was a leveled but also a disorderly type of society, he maintained that its political institutions, its franchise, even its educational system, should not be. As a single standard to delimit the electorate and to judge the elected, *capacité* would temper the democratic desire to see equality imposed everywhere. And as the voice of absolute truth and reason, Guizot's capable governing class—what he called democracy's new aristocracy—would piece together the fragmented society left in the Revolution's wake.

Guizot was certainly not alone in his resolve to enfranchise "the capable." Whereas Constant and other Restoration liberals equated electoral capacity with some demonstrable though inexact degree of judgment, moral intuition, or intellectual competency, Guizot took their capacitarian inclinations further. He wished to hold potential voters to a fixed, metaphysical standard of truth, reason, and justice. The differences between Guizot's strict version of *capacité* and liberals' more amorphous conceptions of the capable have been elided in recent histories of liberalism.[7] From scholars' existing interpretations, we may be left with two related impressions: first, that liberals posed impoverished objections to universal suffrage and second, that they clung to an unforgiving elitism propped up by a fragile theoretical framework, if any theory at all. And yet many of the reform-minded liberals, represented in this book by Alexis de Tocqueville in Chapter 3, treated capacitarian justifications as powerful arguments that warranted thoughtful refutations. As for Guizot, his *capacité politique* was the instrument for managing democracy by means of right reason. By attaching to *capacité* to abstract reason, Guizot attempted to resolve the problems with other, less precise allusions to a capable suffrage.

The concept did a lot of heavy lifting for the *résistance* liberals. It fused aristocratic and democratic elements. It joined equality to merit. In a single breath, liberals invoked *capacité* to authorize civil equality *and* political hierarchy, to enfranchise entire classes *and* to scorn universal suffrage. It also seemed to be a concept rife with contradictions, as some scholars have noted.[8] While objective and unchanging, *capacité* in the individual was revealed by variable, inconstant signs. By reinterpreting *capacité* as a reaction to democracy, this chapter provides what is still missing from the literature: a careful reconstruction of the concept that tries to make sense of those apparent contradictions—or at least demonstrates how Guizot, the foremost theorist of *capacité*, set out to resolve them.[9] It begins by comparing Guizot's criticisms of the old aristocracy with his judgments of the new democracy, which ranged from laudatory to ambivalent. The central sections of the chapter delve into *capacité* in detail. There, I focus on *capacité* as a fixed standard that was revealed by flexible signs. Since Guizot's evaluations of democracy spilled out from the pages of his essays into the domains of parliamentary politics and public education, I tie his arguments for *capacité* to his lifelong passion for educational reform, two threads that have been seldom woven together by scholars. Looking ahead, Chapters 4 and 5 tell the next part of the story about liberals' reactions to democracy that begins here with Guizot. Writing in the 1860s, the constitutional scholar and avowed liberal Édouard Laboulaye would draw on the logic of variable *capacité* to embrace universal suffrage without reservation—an electoral scheme that Guizot himself was always unwilling to accept.

A few additional notes about the contributions of this chapter are in order. By reimagining Guizot as a democratic theorist, my argument complicates the prevailing understanding of his ideological trajectory. It blurs the circa-1840 dividing line drawn by scholars to separate the two Guizots: the first, a liberal open to a wider suffrage during the Restoration and in the first decade or so of the July Monarchy; the second, a conservative, unswerving in his commitment to preserve the middle-class monopoly on political power—and willing to dismantle his own theoretical framework to do so.[10] However, most of Guizot's evaluations of democracy straddled scholars' rough 1840 divide, and his principles remained intact despite regime change. Indeed, the books documenting Guizot's political missteps during the July Monarchy, when he purportedly drifted from his "liberal" moorings, have already been written.[11] What we still lack, and what this chapter provides, is a thorough study of what was a remarkably consistent theory of political capacity and of the concept's role in a modern democracy.

The Old Aristocracy

During the Restoration, Guizot offered two courses at the Sorbonne—one on the history of civilization, the second on the history of representation in Europe. A professor of modern history since 1812, his turn to *those* subjects at *that* moment had a broader political purpose: to consolidate the liberties enshrined in the Charter of 1814 and the institutions to protect them. The written Charter established a constitutional monarchy and a two-chambered parliament, and it guaranteed freedom of the press and of religion and the right to trial by jury.[12] Guizot and his fellow Doctrinaires, a group that included Pierre-Paul Royer-Collard, Prosper de Barante, Hercule de Serre, Victor de Broglie, and Charles de Rémusat, regarded the Charter as the legitimate French constitution and emerged as the Center-Left opposition to an Ultraroyalist majority that held otherwise.[13] Too young to stand for election to the Chamber during the ministry of the Ultra Joseph de Villèle (1821–7), Guizot joined his party as an oppositional voice from the lecture hall and as a prolific writer for the Doctrinaire cause. His 1820–22 lectures on representative government contained thinly veiled criticisms of the Ultras' agenda.[14] Six years later, following Villèle's resignation and the end of his ministry's ban on university lectures, Guizot resumed his teaching. He was greeted by an enthusiastic young audience that included Alexis de Tocqueville and Gustave de Beaumont, who would soon set out for America with Guizot's lessons still fresh in their minds.[15]

By appealing to historical "facts" rather than present-day opinions, Guizot shrewdly accused the Ultras of imposing an antiquated form of government onto a modern society. He reconstructed the etymology of "aristocracy" to mount his critiques. Although the word originally signified "the rule of the strong" and later "the rule of the morally and intellectually superior," its definition had since drifted far from its origins. It had come to designate "a government in which the sovereign power is concentrated in a particular class of citizens, who are hereditarily invested with it by the sole right of their birth." The Ultras failed to understand that an aristocracy, like all forms of government, had social preconditions. In order to have concentrated sovereignty in the noble class, aristocracy needed a specific type of society as its basis. The nobles "must necessarily establish a great inequality in fact, as well as opinion, between [themselves] and the rest of the citizens" to erect their government upon a divided and stationary society in which "the sovereign class does not descend and others do not rise."[16] Aristocracy also derives some of its legitimacy from public opinion. The people have to believe in inequality as a "fact" in order to sustain a government of the privileged few.

In Guizot's revised definition of aristocracy, we can also find the Doctrinaires' shared approach to politics.[17] The social state (*l'état social*) or social condition (*la condition sociale*) is logically prior to the political order, such that the structure of a society determines its appropriate form of government.[18] Any legislator or self-styled reformer must study the "facts" of the social world, in particular the relations between social classes, whether equal or unequal in material wealth, in social status, or before the law. "Prior to becoming a cause," Guizot summarized, "political institutions are an effect; a society produces them before being modified by them. Instead of looking to the system or forms of government in order to understand the state of a people, it is the state of people that must be examined first."[19] With this single claim, he rejected both the ancients' search for the best regime and the moderns' social contract. Against the ancients, Guizot advised the legislator to act as an astute social observer rather than a moral philosopher in pursuit of the ideal. The moderns committed other errors. They failed to recognize the social as the foundation of the political, and as John Locke had done, also entertained the "absurd hypothesis" that governments could be cherry-picked by the majority rather than determined by the social state.[20] Guizot pressed the constitutional architects of his day to correct ancient and modern mistakes—to discover the most fitting regime tailored to society.

France's Ultras were similarly guilty of ignoring the causal connections between social conditions and political institutions. Their static aristocracy was poorly-suited to the dynamism of a post-revolutionary society in which "all classes are perpetually invited and urged to elevate and perfect themselves," a departure from the days of the *ancien régime* when individuals could neither "rise nor descend."[21] Following a centuries-long process that involved the collapse of feudalism, the rise of a commercial economy, and finally the victory of the Third Estate over the nobility in 1789, the inequality underlying aristocratic rule had been overtaken by an egalitarian social condition.[22] Guizot and the Doctrinaires called it *l'état social démocratique*—"democratic" as opposed to aristocratic and a "social state" as opposed to a political regime.[23] They gave a novel, modern meaning to an ancient term. The Doctrinaires retained the element of "equality" at the heart of democracy, but removed it from government altogether, placing it within society instead.

Still, democracy's equality should not be confused with either political or material equality. What Guizot exalted as "equality under the hand of God" was more leveling than elevating; it undermined the prestige of great families and eliminated the old order of fixed ranks. *Grandeur* waned. Equality rose to take its place. The edifice of the Old Regime crumbled under democracy's weight. France after the Revolution had "fewer great lords," though it had "more men, and they stand together," members of one society "without ineffable inequalities, without the privileges" that once sustained aristocratic rule.[24] Democratic individuals share the "same laws and same opportunities, common ideas, feelings, interests," and sympathies as well. Each "recognizes himself in the fate of his neighbor."[25] For the Doctrinaires collectively, the Charter was the legal culmination of democracy's social transformations and the guarantee of its novel form of equality. To cap off the Doctrinaires' efforts at reclaiming and redefining the term, Royer-Collard celebrated "*the true meaning of democracy*" not in popular political participation, but in "the equality of [civil] rights . . . recognized, consecrated, guaranteed by the Charter" and made "universal in society," granted to all regardless of title or lack thereof.[26]

This democratic social condition was novel, and its existence unmistakable. "Everyone agrees," Guizot wrote with confidence in 1837, "that today's society is democratic."[27] Everyone, he more subtly suggested, had by then bought into the Doctrinaires' thesis about what France had become. Democracy's fait accompli rendered aristocracy an unreasonable, unsuitable regime type. Aristocracy was now a social impossibility, an institutional blueprint unfit for the social, economic, and moral condition of a democratized people—or to quote one of Guizot's most striking formulations, a legal order "repelled" and "refused" by the new democracy itself. "Not only does public opinion in France repel this legal and fixed classification of society, but the social state itself refuses it."[28] In his rejoinder to the Ultras before the Chamber in 1822, Royer-Collard uttered a similar conclusion about the "refused" (as opposed to restored) aristocracy in an equally resonant way: "this is not where the torrent of democracy has carried us."[29]

The New Democracy

Nor had democracy's torrent swept France headlong toward *political* democracy. Guizot condemned political democracy by restating many of the arguments he first marshaled against the aristocratic renaissance. Both regimes erroneously attach rights to "birth alone."[30] Under aristocracy, the right to rule belongs to the sovereign privileged caste. Democracy, by contrast, universalizes that right; all are born sovereign by virtue of being born human. Whereas aristocracy mirrors the inequalities of its exclusive society, democracy "violently introduces equality" into the political world, where Guizot insisted that none should exist. Yet the two regime types seem to spring from the same roots. Political democracy is no more than "aristocratic despotism" with an unfamiliar face, the "privilege" once reserved for men of noble birth now bestowed in error upon all men as the "right" to govern.[31]

At first glance, Guizot's trenchant resistance to political democracy seems to be at odds with his stance on the novel "fact" of equality. Although aristocracy was an antiquated form of government for the egalitarian *l'état social*, how could the same argument be made for rejecting political democracy? Universal suffrage may actually *complement* post-revolutionary France, a society marked, in Guizot's own words, by equalized conditions. Democracy's driving fact of equality in the social sphere would translate into the political one. Politics would reflect society. Equality would prevail in each.

Despite the apparent congruence between a democratic society and a democratic regime, Guizot refused to recognize democracy in its original, political sense—the rule of a sovereign people—as a viable regime type in the modern world. Although he regarded democracy as a *social* fact, its equality never to be undone by the Ultras who intended to see a lost social world restored, we will remember that Guizot himself announced to the deputies in 1847 that the day for universal suffrage—for radical *political* equality—would never dawn.[32] Consistent with what I have characterized as the "two Guizots" thesis, scholars have read this 1847 statement either as the last gasp of a defeated politician with few allies or as Guizot's complete repudiation of liberalism.[33] Yet Guizot denounced political democracy well before he felt the first tremors of revolution. What is more, he relied on the Doctrinaires' established *liberal* arguments to do so, citing the particulars of the reclaimed democracy, a democratic society, to represent political democracy as a threat akin to despotism.

Guizot employed this strategy for segregating the two democracies in his 1837 essay, *De la démocratie dans les sociétés modernes*, which opened with a puzzle. With the fall of the Bourbons, virtually all of France's people and its parties came around to the belief that democratic society was there to stay, though they continued to clash over its corresponding form of government. Two publications from earlier that year showcased the French divide over democracy. The first, the Doctrinaire Édouard Alletz's *De la Démocratie nouvelle* endorsed a representative monarchy with a middle-class franchise as the only suitable regime for the "new democracy," a term that Guizot appropriated to differentiate the social state of his day from the destructive institutional schemes of the past.[34] In the second, titled *Essai sur l'Organisation démocratique de la France*, Auguste Billiard pushed for perfect symmetry between society and government.[35] He favored a republic with eventual universal suffrage in reaction to democracy's equalized conditions.[36]

A phenomenon as "uncertain" as democracy was sure to provoke deep disagreements over France's political future, Guizot agreed. "Victorious," "vast," and "still growing," the democratic social state had arrived only yesterday for modern peoples, who could neither foresee its "distant consequences" nor yet grasp its "true nature." Despite so much uncertainty, Guizot himself remained quite sure of at least one thing: writers such as Billiard were too quick to endorse *political* democracy as the inevitable outcome of what remained an unfinished process. By dissolving all of the distinctions between the social and the political, Billiard and the partisans of universal suffrage mistook democracy to be "the government of society itself."[37]

Worse still, Billiard and his fellow republicans failed to heed the lessons of history. The historian Guizot reminded his readers that the word democracy long served as a "war cry," the rallying call of the lower ranks to topple society's elites. Hence the Doctrinaires' desire to recapture it.[38] Even so, those who once fought their battles in its name did not always recognize their enemies. It was invoked "sometimes in the name of the most sacred rights, sometimes in the name of the most senseless passions; sometimes against the most iniquitous usurpations, sometimes against the most legitimate superiorities."[39] Guizot's choice of words here—sacred *and* senseless, legitimate *and* usurpative—reveals his wider ambivalence toward democracy as a social form, which he accepted as an unassailable social fact though with obvious trepidation. Although providential and irreversible, its ultimate consequences were still too far off to imagine or to judge. And given all of the uncertainty about what it might become, the French should resist the temptation to govern their new democratic society with institutions of the same name.

If democratic society was still shrouded in mystery, political democracy had already been seen and tried in the ancient world, only to be renounced by its greatest philosophers. Plato and Aristotle disparaged it as the "absurd and disordered empire of the poor over the rich, of the ignorant over the wise, of the multitude over the elite." It was no surprise to Guizot that democracy's disruptive and indeed denaturing doctrine of popular sovereignty had fallen out of favor for entire centuries before its revival in Rousseau's "perplexing" philosophy.[40] If the Doctrinaires' new France hoped to sustain the freedoms granted in the Charter, democracy's political and social forms had to remain analytically distinct. Indeed, Guizot sought to displace the second entirely, to take back "democracy" from the lower ranks of antiquity and to imbue it with a modern meaning so as to weaponize it against universal suffrage as he had once weaponized it against the Ultras. "What was once democracy," Guizot declared at his essay's end, "would now be anarchy."[41]

Political democracy, the new anarchy, was as inappropriate for the new society as the Ultras' politics of privilege. Guizot concluded as much at least as early as 1821, when he remarked that the French were so intent on exorcising the specter of the old aristocracy (as was he) that they embraced the "confused but powerful dogma" that equality should prevail at all times and in all things, politics included.[42] As he denounced the Ultras' counter-revolution, he cautioned that the opposite extreme of a universal or even an insufficiently-restricted suffrage, unmoored from the standard of polit-ical capacity, jeopardized the liberties enshrined in the Charter. This was, in part, because the intrusion of irrational, impassioned, incapable instincts into government via universal suffrage—that is, via unfounded claims to *po-litical* equality—left a nation susceptible to short-term violence and lasting tyranny. Guizot's evident unease about popular rule arose out of concrete experiences with state-led violence sanctioned by appeals to a "sovereign" people. His Girondist father was guillotined during the Terror of 1793–4.[43] Much like Constant in reaction to Bonaparte, Guizot resolved to expose the doctrine of popular sovereignty for what it truly was: a sad sign of national resignation, of a country's willingness "to live in the ways of tyranny."[44]

Both Constant and Guizot could thus trace a straight line from the principle of popular sovereignty to their experiences under despotism. For his part, Constant never challenged the claim that the people (as opposed to their elite agents in electoral colleges) ought to choose for themselves in elections, as the previous chapter revealed. He was adamant that an active public served as a permanent restraint on power, and to this end, took pains to distinguish the legitimate exercise of popular power from the despot's empty claims to bear it. Guizot set his sights on popular sovereignty itself. Breaking with Constant, he took issue with the mere suggestion that "the people," whether it was un-derstood as a unified body or an amalgamation of individual wills, could be sovereign at all. It was Bonaparte who in fact "personified the sovereignty of the people, and constantly expressed himself to that effect," Guizot alleged.[45] Bonaparte made use of four plebiscites (what were then called constitutional votes) to legitimate his rule.[46] To Guizot's eyes, the plebiscites exposed just how absurd the notion of popular sovereignty was. Napoleon called upon the people to authorize the government, this much was true. But he did so in order to "absorb" each of them, transforming the so-called sovereignty of all wills into the absolute rule of one. Under popular sovereignty, "those individual wills which have created the executive and legislative power are, so to speak, absorbed into it; they have abdicated in favor of the power that represents them. This is obviously pure and unmixed despotism."[47] Whereas Constant attributed Napoleon's usurpation to the emperor's abuse of popular sovereignty, Guizot suspected that the problem was in the doctrine itself, regardless of what kind of man may appeal to it.

Following another one of his liberal predecessors, Madame de Staël, Guizot denounced the "corrupt, debased" Napoleon for having reduced society to a loose aggregation of atomized individuals who were joined exclusively in their common dependence on the emperor.[48] Yet for Guizot, the fault was not entirely Napoleon's. During the reign of Louis XIV, the destruction of the diverse, communal societies and associations transformed subjects into "mere spectators" when it came to the administration of their local affairs, which had been concentrated in the monarch.[49] Guizot believed that the Revolution hastened what Louis XIV initiated. It abolished the privileges of noble families that united subjects from above, thereby assigning significance to the individual over a class of nobles. At the same time, it eliminated intermediate bodies along with the few sites of local liberty that remained.[50] As the individual's will gained strength, as he grew more like his fellows in rights and standing, his social existence narrowed. Bonaparte's despotism marked the culmination of these centralizing and alienating processes. After the emperor's Hundred Days in 1815, Guizot looked on a nation of "wearied spectators . . . blindly and completely divided in their apathy" lacking in "moral unity, common thought or passion, their common misfortunes notwithstanding."[51] Years later, Royer-Collard regretted that France had become *la société en poussière*, an atomized and administered people clutched firmly in "the hand of irresponsible civil servants, themselves centralized by the power of which they are agents."[52]

As he weighed the options for France's political future, its suffrage scheme included, Guizot sought a cure for the Revolutionary-Napoleonic pathologies of political dependency and social isolation. For all of his cautionary messages about democratic uncertainty, he was convinced that the cure would never come from political democracy. Guizot recommended a form of representative government that would complement his changed society, for better or worse. But he had a very specific sense of what it meant to complement democracy. The ideal representative government would neither reproduce democratic equality, as with Billiard's republic, nor "personify" popular sovereignty in another tyrant. Remarkably, it would reintroduce *in-equality* into politics, compensating for exactly what the social state lacked while nevertheless respecting an equalized France. An electoral system and thus an assembly tuned to the harmonizing principle of *capacité*, while unequal and hierarchical, best suited the society of equals.

Capacité Politique

Guizot's critical stance toward political democracy highlights his belief in the sovereignty of reason, an idiosyncratic theory of sovereignty that has been masterfully recovered by scholars such as Rosanvallon and Craiutu.[53] The brief discussion of sovereign reason in this section is intended to supplement their interpretations. Most importantly, it frames the theory of *capacité*, which has received less careful analytical attention and in which reason features as central.

Claiming to speak as "the voice of humanity," Guizot wrote that "the right of sovereignty vested in men is an iniquitous lie."[54] It supposes "that [humanity's] ideas and inclinations are in all cases correspondent to the dictates of justice and of reason—a supposition which the radical imperfection of our nature will not allow us for a moment to admit." Sovereignty instead rests in the metaphysical law of reason, justice, and truth, a law to which all human beings must submit though none have had a hand in creating.[55] No one can grasp reason completely. Nevertheless, all "can be brought more and more to conform to it in their conduct." This is where government comes in: "all the combinations of the political machine must tend . . . to extract from society all that it possesses of reason, justice, and truth."[56]

Of all possible regimes, only representative government can perform this reason-extracting role. Through elections, legislative deliberation, open judicial proceedings, and the press, it invites "those who exercise power and those who possess rights to enter upon a common search for reason and justice," a search that political democracy, based as it was in a naïve optimism about humanity's potential to reason, could never undertake. In elections, voters "confer a mission" upon their chosen candidates, charging them with bringing society closer to the rule of reason. Representatives deliberate under the watchful eye of a capable electorate that checks their "good faith and intelligence."[57] As we learned in Chapter 1, Guizot proposed to control *who* could publish with the *cautionnement*. At the same time, he looked on the press as a vital organ of representative government that "develops and manifests" public reason, enabling citizens to scrutinize the decisions of their representatives.[58] Therefore, it was imperative that newspapers and pamphlets disseminate public reason rather than private opinions.

Guizot's system relied on a peculiar logic of representation. It did not aspire to reach the Madisonian end of "refin[ing] and enlarg[ing] the public views," views that Guizot assumed were likely to be the products of passion over public reason.[59] Nor would his system represent sectional interests, as Constant had hoped, and which Guizot feared would propagate error and encourage disorder. It was engineered to meet a single goal: to empower the capable, or those who rule with the law of reason. In placing reason first, Guizot was unapologetic about *what* (rather than who) was to be represented. "What we call representation," he admitted, "is nothing other than a means to arrive at this result," to "erect a barrier at once to tyranny and confusion and to bring the multitude to unity."[60]

Unlike either aristocracy or democracy, representative government demands that its participants prove *capable* of holding power. It alone arranges *capacité*, rights, and power in their logical order. *Capacité* precedes and confers the *right* to exercise political *power*, whether as voter or as representative. If institutions must conform to reason, truth, and justice, then the individuals who lead them—who exercise power with the vote and wield legislative power in the assembly—must prove capable of guiding society toward those fixed ends.

What makes certain individuals *capable* of taking part in the reason-finding mission of representative government, and what renders others incapable? Guizot's Italian contemporary Giuseppe Mazzini, to name but one of his many contemporaneous critics, could find little value in a concept that even its greatest proponent could not explain to anyone's satisfaction. "What is *capacité*?" Mazzini asked in a review of Guizot's 1837 essay. "Is it intelligence? Is it morality? Who is to measure it? What is to be the standard? . . . Can we just take the tax collector's list as a correct valuation of human faculties and translate intellect into money?"[61] While Guizot was chastised for upholding an ideal so vague—so cryptic, in Mazzini's view, that it required a divine interpreter to determine who should vote—he did devote some of his historical lectures to unraveling its mysteries. There, he categorized the internal, consistent qualities of individuals that make them capable of holding power: reason, independence, and an awareness of the social interest. The remaining parts of this section guide the reader through Guizot's logic.

Reason

Guizot repeated the same definition of *capacité* throughout his writings: it "is nothing else than the faculty of acting according to reason."[62] Behind such a straightforward statement rests a rather rich account of reason itself. The individual who obeys reason does not follow his own lights. Instead, he "submits" to an external law, which also "dwell[s] in every human spirit."[63] It is by acting with reason, that is, by regulating his will according to that law which *ought to* govern him and his society (we will note, whether he wants it to or not), that the individual proves capable of holding political power. During an election, the "reason scattered across a society" is "collect[ed] and concentrate[d] and appl[ied] to government."[64] Guizot's choice of words is revealing. It is neither wills (Rousseau) nor interests (Constant) nor reasonable representatives (Madison) that are looked for, found, and empowered— but *Reason* itself. By framing *capacité* as an absolute standard, Guizot set the bar for a capable franchise higher than his fellow liberals ever had. He equated *capacité* not merely with sound judgment or with competence, but with the ability to separate objective truth from falsehood.

Guizot's reliance on transcendent reason has familiar antecedents in the history of political thought.[65] For Thomas Aquinas, reason grants humanity access to the natural law derived from the divine. The Protestant Guizot, too, presented reason as a divine and natural law, though without referring to Aquinas' hierarchy as an influence. Reason has a moral component as well; it is a shorthand for "reason, truth, and justice," which act in concert as the "true law of government" and the "true source of right."[66] However, Guizot's definition of *capacité* as the "faculty of acting according to reason" is more clearly seen through the lens of Aristotelian virtue than Thomistic law, even if it is not identical to virtue. The capable use their knowledge (what Aristotle called *theoria*) of reason's rule "in order to apply it to the practical requirements of governing."[67] They combine *theoria* with *phronesis* or practical wisdom, uniting intellect to action to bring universal reason to bear on particular circumstances. Representatives must know what reason requires. But they also must "render" reason into human laws that will circumscribe the actions of capable and incapable alike.[68] This point about metaphysical reason distilled into political practice has been overlooked by most scholars of French liberalism, who more often than not portray *capacité* as a purely intellectual faculty, akin to philosophic wisdom.[69] In that same 1837 tract on modern democracy in which he rejected universal suffrage, Guizot refined the concept further to highlight its active, practical dimension: "it is not just intellectual development or the possession of any particular faculty . . . it is in fact a certain aggregate of faculties, knowledge, and *methods of action* . . . which decide on his course of conduct and the use he will make of such power."[70] By the mid-1830s he arrived at the conclusion that the purpose of the capable—the *politically* capable, we should keep in mind—is to apply objective truth to the act of lawmaking.

Independence and the social interest

The remaining two elements of political capacity—independence and an awareness of the social interest—emanate from reason. Although subject to reason's dictates, the capable individual is not beholden to "foreign will or judgment" of any other person.[71] Reason, after all, is sovereign; human beings never will be. The Doctrinaires searched for the individual's inner capacity in the outward sign of property measured by the *cens*—an imperfect sign that, we will learn later in this chapter, Guizot did not always find satisfactory. On a basic level, however, he shared Constant's perspective on private property. It signals that the proprietor is not reliant upon anyone else for his livelihood, and therefore that his intellect, as far as possible, can be captured by reason and not the fallible minds of other men.

Hoping to free individuals from unreasonable influences, Guizot proposed to reform elections during the 1820s following the passage of the Double Vote. Realistically, he knew that not all influences could or should be minimized in the electoral process. Some are beneficial, even if most are pernicious. His argument rested on two premises. First, voters are neither isolated nor disinterested spectators, so it is impossible to emancipate them completely from all opinions. Second, even if reason is the proper end of human action, it should never be imposed. "The soundness of elections" actually "arises from the *conflict* between influences and ideas."[72] In sifting out true ideas from false, the capable individual will be *persuaded* about where the truth lies, making his obedience to reason "voluntary, an act of judgment and of will," never compelled, and his society progressive, not despotic.[73]

We may be surprised to hear that the rationalist Guizot encouraged any pluralism at all in the electoral process, even if he did expect plurality to converge on a single point. But his was pluralism with an important caveat. Not all opinions are worthy of thought and discussion. "The law must allow [opinions] to reach the elector, and grant them all natural means of acting upon his judgment; but it ought not deliver them up to him defenseless."[74] Guizot wished to shelter "well-tried and freely-accepted influences," allowing those views alone to compete for the voter's attention. Hence his desire to regulate the printed word by vetting the rationality of publishers.[75] Above all, he sought to preserve "natural influences," or those that operate on the minds of voters before an election ever takes place and endure long after the votes have been counted. He instructed that elections should take place where voters live and conduct their ordinary business, in that "habitual sphere in which their lives are passed, their activity displayed, and their thoughts exchanged" rather than in a centralized department.[76] He thus endeavored to abolish electoral colleges and intermediate assemblies, those unnatural institutions that would otherwise never affect the voter in his daily life.

During the Restoration, Guizot grew acutely aware of the need to shield voters from such reason-obscuring practices. One scholar styled the typical election in this period as *une affaire de salon*—more intimate than public, since it was conducted by a small number of electors (approximately 90,000 out of 32 million in 1828), most of whom came from the upper echelons of society.[77] Members of the clergy sometimes worked as electoral agents to sway their parishioners who had the vote, bringing divine authority to bear on the choice of a representative. Overall, elections in this period lacked the publicity vital to representative government. Whatever transparency there was threatened the elector's independence; votes were not secret, and electors handed their unfolded ballots to officials of the college.

Guizot directed all of his reform efforts in this period to enable voters to "act *freely* and *reasonably* in the *social interest*."[78] Even so, the term "social interest" rarely appears across his 1820–22 lectures. As we know from Chapter 1, the idea of a general or national interest had become common currency among certain advocates of representative government since the Revolution. Guizot, for his part, never referred to his famed predecessors, either to Sieyès or Roederer or others like them, or to their allusions to an overarching interest in these lectures.[79] Nor did he align his theory of *capacité* with their calls for elitist intermediary assemblies. When Guizot did use the term "social interest," it was to reinforce *his* notion of sovereign reason and the original model of representation that followed.[80] His legislature would not represent anything like a popular consensus or majority will, each of which he decried as outcomes of that "iniquitous lie" of popular sovereignty. To a point, he took this perspective against popular choice alongside Sieyès and the Idéologues, those whom Constant disparaged as the uniformist "patriots" of 1789. In the end, Guizot's "social interest" was coterminous with *reason*—no less and no more. His system was designed to ensure that the powerful—the capable—would accept and reflect reason, society's sole *true* interest.

A New Aristocracy

But not all capacities are created equal. Representative government, in fact, hinges on recognizing inequality. Guizot chastised republicans and Ultras alike for refusing to admit some basic if uncomfortable truths about humanity. It is a *fact*, he asserted, that some are more capable than others, and that political inequalities rooted in *natural* and unequal capacities are both legitimate and necessary. Of course, the Ultras structured their policies around inequality as well. Yet they failed Guizot's test of legitimacy. Their aristocracy conferred power on the noble, not necessarily the capable. Political democracy failed, too, though from the opposite direction. Entranced by newfound equality, its proponents "paid no regard to the legitimate inequality" that should prevail in politics.[81] Only representative government makes use of the legitimate inequalities that distinguish one person from another. It summons superior men to the assembly, unites capable voters in elections, and allows the rest of society to follow reason by following human laws.[82]

Guizot identified a hierarchy of *capacité* with representatives at the top and the enfranchised just below. The latter determine which among the former can best steer society toward reason, justice, and truth, without doing any of the actual steering for himself. The voter's *capacité* consists in *recognizing superiority* where and in whom it exists. Trusted to "choose wisely," he searches for "men capable of thoroughly comprehending the interests upon which they will have to administrate."[83] While no individual is sovereign, some prove more capable of governing according to reason than most. These superior few, those who serve as reason's representatives, possess the superior *capacité* "to enforce reason's recognition and observance by citizens in general."[84]

With his claims about superiority, Guizot intended to uplift a new aristocracy.[85] He envisioned a political role for *an* aristocracy after the *ancien régime*. This point alone is worth emphasizing. Still, it was neither the same role nor the same aristocracy that the Ultras aspired to resurrect. Unlike the landed elites of earlier centuries, Guizot's new aristocratic class did not possess the *privilege* to govern. Instead, it earned the *right* to rule because of the "beautiful, legitimate superiorities" displayed by its members.[86] Authorized by "*nature's* inequality," the new aristocracy leads the political world just as superiors guide the natural one—just as "the timid follow the brave, the incompetent obey the competent." Guizot took it on faith that "every superior," whether in nature or in society, "has a certain sphere of attraction in which it acts and gathers around itself real inferiors."[87]

Guizot's capable aristocracy was the order of nature mirrored in politics, an image akin to Edmund Burke's natural aristocracy eminent in virtue. Rooted at once in nature and in history, it was a modern alternative to the denaturing doctrine of popular sovereignty. Guizot's aristocracy was also, counterintuitively, a democratic institution. By placing his aristocracy atop a democratic foundation, Guizot departed from Burke. A new aristocracy conforms to nature, as Burke argued. And yet it derives some of its *aristocratic* legitimacy from the *democratic* process of elections, in which a capable electorate not only discerns but "feels and freely accepts" the superiority of the few. "Election is a trial imposed on those who aspire to power," Guizot wrote, a test through which a new aristocracy proves its right to govern.[88]

Just as he joined the Doctrinaires to modernize the word "democracy," Guizot redefined aristocracy as well. But in this instance, he hoped to redeem what was lost. As he identified his new governing class as a modern *aristoi*, Guizot revived one of the original definitions of aristocracy as rule by the "best," both intellectually and morally, a definition that had been lost to time. According to Lucien Jaume, who traces the theme of a new aristocracy across nineteenth-century France, Guizot envisioned the governing relationship between aristocracy and society as one of prestige, the rule of true, natural superiority.[89] Out of an even deeper dive into Guizot's writings and speeches, we can further sharpen the characteristics of his novel *aristoi*. While superior in rationality, a new aristocracy would not act with the lofty honor of the highborn or exhibit the *grandeur* of a bygone age. Nor did it have to. It had only to possess the political capacity—a modest, political "excellence" relative to the traditional aristocratic virtues, if a demanding one nevertheless—to answer reason's call.[90]

As he rejected political democracy and popular sovereignty and uplifted a new aristocracy in their place, Guizot spurned the republican legacy of the Revolution. But it is more illuminating to delve into his disputes with the reactionaries on the far Right, with whom he shared an obvious distrust of popular sovereignty but disagreed about the nature of a true aristocracy. It is in the space separating Guizot from the Ultras that we find the Doctrinaires' original contribution to the Restoration's "Great Debate" between aristocracy and democracy.

The Ultra Joseph de Maistre deemed the idea of an aristocracy of talent— and by extension, of *capacité*—as "unprofitable" and likewise belittled an elective aristocracy as "democracy masquerading under another name."[91] The only legitimate aristocracy, Maistre asserted, unites noble birth with wealth. By contrast, Guizot's vision of aristocracy was motivated by a suspicion of power that partisans of the far Right such as Maistre did not share. Guizot lauded the elective principle as a bulwark against absolutism and arbitrariness, a "precaution" against legislative despotism that forces members of the new aristocracy to continue to demonstrate their *capacité* to rule before the people.[92] Under a democratic social condition, power should be forced to prove its legitimacy. This was a necessary consequence of the Revolution. "The government that in earlier times had its separate, higher, greater, but nevertheless special and restrained sphere has itself become more general, more direct and universally associated with the interests and lives of all citizens."[93] If, as Guizot put it, society "rebuffed" the aristocracy of the past, it also revealed the necessity of a new aristocracy, beholden to democratic society even as it stood above it.

The voter's relatively inferior *capacité* was no less essential to the existence of representative government than the representatives themselves. Present from election to parliamentary deliberation, *capacité* ensures that reason will rule. No less important is the tie that binds capable electors in society to their representatives in the assembly. Every superior, on balance, needs inferiors, and the political world that Guizot set out to construct was no different.

A similar argument informed Guizot's critique of indirect elections. Like Constant and Necker before him, he maintained that the outcomes of indirect elections felt too "distant and uncertain" for the initial voter, who "gives his suffrage coldly and blindly to subsequent electors, whom his thoughts never follow into a future in which he interferes so little."[94] Necker worried that an indirect system would demean the vote itself; Constant accused its advocates of privileging the few instead of representing the many. Guizot attacked that same system from another angle. Indirect elections displace *capacité* from politics by severing the connections between inferior voters and superior representatives, he contended.[95] Without any direct tie between capable voter and candidate, the former will not judge the *capacité* of the latter. Nor will the voter care to scrutinize the decisions of the chosen deputy—though not *his* chosen deputy—within the assembly. Indirect elections thus extinguish the usefulness of the voter's *capacité* the minute that votes have been counted. They break the obligatory cycle of *capacité*, publicity, and legitimation at the heart of a representative government. Of course, representative institutions could not reach toward reason without a capable aristocracy at the helm. Guizot was insistent, however, that it would be an aristocracy summoned to power by the choices of the capable, if limited, portion of society.

By tracing *capacité* as a single thread running from voter to deputy and from election to assembly, Guizot endeavored to rewrite the terms of debate over popular government in this period. As Bernard Manin writes, most of the legislative back-and-forth "did not center on who could vote . . . but on who could be voted for."[96] Indeed, at least one deputy of the Third Estate admitted that he had acquiesced on universal suffrage *only* because elections were decided by second-degree electors, and here we can think of Cabanis' vision of a government for the people but never by them.[97] Guizot, by contrast, gave his attention to the voter and to the "voted for." In a system of direct elections, the quality of the individual voter matters. Constant reasoned along similar lines as early as 1806. We should not be shocked by now to hear that Guizot reframed the issue in his own way: the *capacité* that unites voters to representatives, rather than the filtering function performed by intermediary colleges, leads to rational government. He wrote of voters simply as *électeurs*, erasing existing distinctions between primary and second-order electoral institutions. When Guizot endorsed direct elections, then, he never intended to follow in the pluralist footsteps of Constant. On the contrary—he believed that direct elections would reinforce the chain of *capacité* that links a society to its government and binds both to uniform reason.

Variable *Capacité*

Yet for all of Guizot's language about "discovering" and "collecting" *capacité*, the process proves to be more of an art than a science.[98] "Concealed" and

"constantly variable," *capacité* is distributed unevenly across society—
"scattered," to borrow Guizot's favorite description. Its distribution varies
with social change; it is "subordinate to a host of other circumstances, to the
number of citizens, [and] to their social situation," such that the search for
the capable will yield different outcomes for different times and places.[99]
Mazzini, for one, cited the concept's variability as evidence for just how indeterminate and useless it was. But Guizot tried to spin the concept's inde-
terminacy into its greatest advantage. An electoral system designed around
capacité, a variable standard though one anchored to invariable reason,
would best keep pace with democracy's more mobile social order.

Using England as his example (pre-Reform England, we will note, given
the timing of his lectures), Guizot reminded his lecture audience that political rights once rested with freeholders (landowners), the clergy, and
burgesses of major towns prior to the seventeenth century, all of whom
participated in elections in the counties and boroughs.[100] Changes in patterns
of landholding then expanded the capable from freeholders (landowners)
to copyholders, whose tenure of "free, secure, fully hereditary" land served
as a sufficient *external* sign of *internal capacité*. Commerce allowed the
merchants to acquire wealth; in turn, it "develop[ed] the mind" of the once-
poor and once-incapable.[101]

Guizot once again drew from the past to instruct France in the present. He
endeavored to expose the harms that could plague any nation that neglects
to enfranchise *capacité* wherever it happens to appear. Over centuries, the
English did not adjust the land-tax requirements for the local vote. Nor did
they modify their system that "attributed electoral rights by name and *forever*" to most of the inhabitants of particular towns which had declined in
importance over the centuries. Guizot concluded with a rather bold claim: if
the nation had been willing to amend its laws to reflect *capacité*, it could have
avoided "rotten boroughs" altogether.[102]

Even if we grant the point about variable *capacité* and its potential democratic advantages, its discovery poses another challenge: *capacité* is an *internal* characteristic that is perceived only by its *external* signs—and not very
clear ones. "The *capacité* of acting freely and reasonably for the promotion of
social interests," Guizot conceded, "is revealed by no more distinct signs than
any other internal disposition." Nor are such signs, when they are observable,
always the same. "The external characteristics which reveal it, possess, by the
very nature of things, nothing universal or permanent."[103] Those imperma-
nent signs depend on independent variables as intricate and inexact as the

relations between classes, the concentration and circulation of land, the division of labor, the distribution of education, the size of the population, and the extent of civil liberties.[104] Changes in just one variable would alter where and in whom *capacité* might later manifest *and* how it would be revealed. In light of so much mutability, Guizot advised legislators to reject *any* fixed criterion for the vote. Electoral standards should remain ever open to "legal suspicion," or reevaluated at least with each generation.[105] Thus, to echo his own contentious point, there will *never* be a day for universal suffrage. Once it grants the vote to everyone, a nation no longer holds onto any "suspicion" about where *capacité* resides and, by extension, who merits the right to rule.

As retold by Guizot, England's electoral history showcased its failure to redistribute electoral rights to match expanding *capacité*. By contrast, the French electoral law of 1817 (*la loi Lainé*) demonstrated how the law could reflect society. To vote, a man had to be at least thirty years old and pay 300 francs in direct taxes. To be eligible for direct election as a deputy, a man had to be at least forty years old and pay a direct tax of 1,000 francs. Roughly 90,000 men qualified as electors out of a population of 29 million; approximately 16,000 met the requirements for election as a deputy.[106] The law replaced indirect with direct elections and was less restrictive on age and property requirements than the Ultras preferred. Those wealthy landowners who leaned toward royalism certainly met the fiscal requirements, but so did tradesmen, clerks, lawyers, university professors, and civil servants who could pay the direct tax, crowding out the electoral influence of the rural proprietors who trended conservative in their politics.[107] The law's effects were short-lived, however. Three years later, the Ultras' Double Vote that so stirred Constant became law.[108]

Nonetheless, the 1817 law had an enduring legacy in French electoral politics through 1848. Although demands for universal suffrage saturated the rhetoric of the Revolution, most of the national debates from 1817 through at least the first decade of the July Monarchy centered on extending the franchise, not universalizing it. Into the early 1840s, serious pleas for universal manhood suffrage remained at the radical republican fringe.[109] As the Doctrinaires defended some standard of capacity, even ones that fell short of Guizot's stringent rule of reason, against mounting opposition, their political rivals had no choice but defer to capacity as the electoral baseline. It became the common term for responding to the suffrage question. At least through the 1842 national debate, each side agreed that the laws ought to be adjusted incrementally to keep pace with shifting capacities in society.[110]

They continued to disagree about where to draw the ever-shifting line between society's capable and incapable members.

Capacité beyond the Cens

Although he helped to draft the 1817 law, Guizot also took his own advice when it came to judging its effects: he looked on its property qualification with the same "legal suspicion" that he urged all modern legislators to exercise. Defenses of *le suffrage censitaire* relied on a political logic that pre-dated the Restoration and could be traced as far back as the seventeenth century, one that Guizot thought deserved to be reconsidered. Constant outlined a version of this logic in his 1806 *Principles*. Later, he used it to balance his vehement objections to the Ultras with laudatory comments about the virtues of proprietorship for a functioning representative system.[111]

Guizot did not simply reaffirm the property-centric perspective from Constant's *Principles*.[112] With Constant, he acknowledged that the owners of large estates enjoy leisure "to devote themselves to the cultivation of their intellect . . . and the study of general interests."[113] Consistent with his own sociology, Guizot went on to declare that property ownership could not serve as a permanent sign of *capacité*; nothing could, after all. Landed property served as a sufficient sign of *capacité* in simpler ages "when order, security, and education were lacking." No one could deny that France had since matured into a "developed and complicated" nation.[114] Within its "advanced" society, the new democracy, legislators needed to identify more numerous and more diverse signs of *capacité* than land alone. Although Constant articulated a similar conclusion by the end of the Restoration, when he expanded the category of property to include industrial property, he never renounced the claim that proprietors alone are fit for citizenship.

In his 1826 "Élections" essay, Guizot added shades of detail to the image of a middle class, of the kind that Constant had begun to sketch two decades earlier. He wrote of an emergent social "middle" between landed elites and wage-earners. Its members are characterized by the *work* through which they "enrich themselves and assure at the same time the subsistence of a certain number of individuals whom they employ." Large proprietors grow capable by virtue of their *leisure*, the middle class by virtue of their *work*. Certain occupations "compel" individuals to acquire "knowledge and ideas that elevate them equally to *l'intelligence des rapports* (relational or social intelligence) and to knowledge of the social interest. At the very least, their work renders them *capable* of accepting a superior intellect when it presents itself to them."[115]

This was true of those in the "industrial and liberal professions," business owners, lawyers, notaries, doctors, tradesmen, teachers, university professors—all whose professions prompted them to acquire the reason and independence that confers the franchise. Yet even as he listed the liberal professions, Guizot claimed that he would never draw firm boundaries around the middle class. He deliberately "abstained" from doing so, he told the deputies in the first year of the July Monarchy. "Have I assigned the limits of the middle class? Have you heard me say where it started? Where it ended? I carefully abstained from it . . . I simply expressed the general fact that there is a class which is not devoted to manual labor, which does not live on wages . . . which can devote a considerable part of its time and faculties to public affairs."[116] This upwardly mobile, capable aristocracy for nineteenth-century France emerged out of a commercial and a democratic social order in which work (*industrie*) rather than leisure alone signaled *capacité*—placing the franchise within the reach of a larger portion of society than ever before.

Guizot therefore questioned whether the *cens* ought to remain the sole sign of capacity, since it reflects property alone. "Who would say that a lawyer, notary, doctor well-established in their profession has any less enlightenment or independence than the man who pays 300 francs taxes on his fields?" he asked.[117] And while he never came close to calling for the end of the *cens*, he suggested that a *suffrage censitaire* was not without flaws. It may exclude some capable individuals under democratic society, precisely when a fledging representative government would most benefit from their *capacité*. It was not long before Odilon Barrot, voice of the dynastic Left opposition to the July regime, would deliver similar arguments to stage (unsuccessful) attempts at national reform—at a time when Guizot stood on the other side of the issue.[118] The seed of the idea had already been planted in the liberal consciousness before the reform-minded Barrot addressed the Chamber. It was Guizot who implied that liberals should take up their search for the capable *beyond* property, roughly a decade before the opponents to his ministry would contest the July Monarchy's unmodified *cens*.

Guizot's vision of "variable *capacité*" has been interpreted as a smokescreen to shield a middle-class electorate. Of course, there is some truth to the contention that Guizot acted as the guardian of his nation's social middle when he served as minister to King Louis-Philippe.[119] But when he later reflected on the Doctrinaires' Restoration agenda, he confessed to having found unique virtues in the middle classes even then. Following "a line of policy clearly indicated by the facts and opinions" of the time, the Doctrinaires supported the rise of the middle classes and granted them a voice in electoral politics with the 1817 law, a voice loud enough to break through the Ultras' electoral stronghold. In Guizot's retelling, however, the Doctrinaires were much more sensible about the standing of the middle class than their rivals supposed. They exalted the virtues of a moderate middle class in a society struggling to shed the remnants of its recent revolution, he conceded. At the same time, Guizot believed that the Doctrinaires never celebrated anything like the un-questioned superiority of any single part of society, middling or otherwise. In his *Memoirs*, he answered his contemporaries who denounced *capacité* as nothing more than electoral security for bourgeois interests. He deemed the thought of a "newly privileged" middle-class order "strangely ignorant and insane."[120]

Those who know of Guizot as the architect of the July Monarchy are sure to doubt his post hoc defenses of the Doctrinaires' political priorities. As we will learn in Chapter 3, Tocqueville was among those who blamed Guizot for nurturing such a monolithic and bourgeois *le pays légal*, the "legal country" of the enfranchised, that it emptied the whole of France of what little public spirit it had left. But Guizot had begun with the qualities of individuals: reason, independence, and an awareness of the general interest. Still, he had no choice but to view capable individuals in terms of the socio-economic class to which they belonged. Entire classes, not particular men, were able to be folded into the franchise with the *cens*. What originated as an attempt to find capacity in the individual voter evolved into a contentious debate over a society's capable classes. Such a practical shift away from an in-dividualist notion of *capacité* toward a class-based view stirred controversy in the Chamber during the July Monarchy. It was then that Guizot garnered a reputation as the guardian of the *haute bourgeoisie*.[121]

Despite the legislative controversies it introduced and the revolution it later incited, a class-based notion of *capacité* nonetheless fulfilled an impor-tant purpose within a democracy, at least as far as Guizot thought. By opening the franchise to the middle classes, Guizot believed that France could enliven its "real and active" parts of the nation concealed in what Royer-Collard first termed the *société en poussière*, the atomized society.[122] Guizot mourned the wasted potential of "scattered, isolated" men who lacked the opportunity to shape public affairs in a society without the local freedoms or intermediary bodies that dotted the pre-revolutionary social landscape. Men "who could have done many things" under different circumstances, "in reality were nothing" after the Revolution. Out of necessity, they turned to private commercial pursuits. Identifiable by their professions, these "small proprietors, lawyers, notaries, capitalists, manufacturers, and tradesmen, place themselves far from public affairs in order to devote themselves to their own business."[123] Even so, they could not help but exert some "natural influence" over their communities. To "give life to [that] influence," Guizot intended to see *all* capable individuals enfranchised.[124] A more inclusive political sphere, one that enfranchised as many capable individuals as the law could be amended to incorporate, was also a more vibrant one. It matched government to *capacité* scattered throughout society, wherever and in whomever it now happened to exist. And by bringing once-excluded, enervated but capable *individuals* into public life all at once by enfranchising entire *classes*, France could begin to mend the tattered, politically apathetic nation that Bonaparte had left behind. Although he would later be accused of having dampened a vibrant public sphere with a lifeless government of his own, Guizot once hoped to reanimate local liberties by means of a capable franchise. "The true way to infuse political life in all directions and to interest as great a number of citizens as possible in the affairs of the state is not to make them all combine to perform the same acts, since they may not all be equally capable of performing them; but to confer upon them all of the rights which they are capable of exercising."[125]

Guizot made the same point elsewhere in different terms. A "government of facts," or the distribution of power, should match the "government of minds," the real *capacité* in society.[126] Or simply, capable "minds," wherever they are, ought to hold power. This "governing of minds," or the issue of how to oversee the intellectual and moral development of an entire nation, captured Guizot's attention throughout his entire adult life.[127] He published essays on pedagogy and education during the Restoration. With his first wife Pauline de Meulan, he edited the *Annales de l'Éducation*, and in 1832 was appointed minister of public instruction. His greatest success came with the passage of the 1833 "Guizot Law" that established a national system of primary schools. The following section frames his lifelong interest in education, in "minds," in terms of the features of the new democracy and the new aristocracy that would guide it.

Democratic Education

Scholars have alluded to the parallels between Guizot's philosophy of education and his sociology of democracy and between education and *capacité*, but they have not gone much beyond allusions to locate where exactly his interests intersect.[128] Still, we need not search high and low to find those points; Guizot's educational recommendations flowed directly from his depictions of democratic society. And much like his suggestions for representative government, his proposals for educating the young had to strike a careful balance: to uphold equality in society without undermining nature's inequality in politics.

Just as a society's irrefutable "facts" would determine its form of government, the appropriate educational system for nineteenth-century France was one which best fit the social state as it was transformed after 1789. Most of the scholastic and religious *corps intermédiaires* that once educated children had been abolished by the Revolutionary Le Chapelier and d'Allarde laws against guilds and corporate bodies. The dissolution of such institutions left a void in providing education that the state had to fill. The Catholic Church, which once played a significant role in educating children of the poor, had been left too weak to do so.[129] Because education had become "more secularized and more free" since the Revolution, Guizot pushed the French state to take up the task of providing it.[130]

More than a decade before the publication of Tocqueville's *Democracy in America*, it was Guizot who observed how the Revolution's secularizing, democratizing effects reached so far beyond material conditions that they rearranged the human psyche. Democratic individuals imagine that they are more powerful and more free than any other population in human history, he judged. They believe that "personal merit," not noble birth, "is the first controlling influence and the primary condition of success in life." Emboldened by this conviction, men now act in ways that were once unthinkable under the *ancien régime*. So powerful and universal was this conviction, this "ardent and universal movement of ascent," that Guizot dubbed it "*democracy itself.*"[131]

Guizot's evaluations of such democratic transformations, as we might expect, were not entirely positive. On the one hand, this conviction lent legitimacy to rule by a capable aristocracy, an aristocracy of merit, over a hereditary one. On the other, what originated as confidence in personal merit gave birth to a "violent and perpetual confusion of places and persons," an image that Tocqueville later used to dramatize the most unruly features of American democracy.[132] Democratic society tends toward disorder; for Guizot in particular, it disrupts nature's hierarchy of superiors and inferiors. Ennobled by civil equality, democratic people expect equality everywhere. They espouse deceitful doctrines such as popular sovereignty and exalt plebiscitary democracy, even when it gives rise to tyranny. Such democratic confusion, such profound ignorance about the order of nature, also leaves minds susceptible to the "spirits of faction," or those "unnatural," unreasonable outside influences that troubled Guizot in his discussions of the voters' independence.[133] Given the misunderstandings about rank and hierarchy that plague a democratic society, the state must regulate—*govern*, to repeat Guizot's word—the mind of untethered democratic individuals, though without eclipsing the value of merit entirely.

The responsibility of educating children could not be left to households or local communities. The risks of variation in the quality of education were too costly to leave to chance.[134] Education serves "as much the interest of the State as that of individuals."[135] And a state-directed education "must include the precepts of religion and morals and of the general duties of men in society" along with "the elementary knowledge that has become useful and almost necessary." Guizot's educational plan is one example of what Lucien Jaume typifies as Doctrinaire "liberalism through the state," an ideology in which freedom is realized *through* state power rather than in opposition to it.[136] Even so, Guizot complained that the French state was not always the wisest purveyor of education. During the First Empire, Napoleon distributed educational opportunities to make subjects dependent on his patronage. He diverted state funds from teachers' salaries to grant university scholarships to poor families, a decision Guizot denounced as a political ploy to raise "an adoptive family" among the poor, its present and future generations indebted to the emperor.[137] Guizot devised a plan to remedy the deficiencies of private instruction on the one hand and to thwart the tyranny of centralized administration on the other.

In order to avoid the administrative failures of the First Empire, the 1833 law established a uniform primary education system but entrusted its administration to prefects of the *commune*, including mayors and local clergy, and to teachers (the Protestant Guizot, we will note, agreed to involve local priests of the Catholic Church in public education).[138] Guizot addressed a letter to the nation's teachers to accompany the new law:

The law is for the state at large and for the public advantage; and because liberty neither can be assured nor regulated except with a people sufficiently enlightened to listen, under all circumstances, to the voice of reason, universal elementary education will become henceforward a guarantee for order and social stability. As all the principles of our government are sound and rational, to develop intellect and propagate light is to confirm the empire and durability of our constitutional monarchy.[139]

In his letter, Guizot tied the law of instruction to the elements of *capacité* that he outlined elsewhere. Education predisposes the mind to follow reason. It fortifies young minds against numerous "reason-conquering" influences to cultivate *capacité* in the young, enabling reason to rule in the souls of future citizens.

In his 1816 *Essay on Public Instruction,* Guizot developed the philosophy of education that would later inform the 1833 law. Education ought to develop reason in each individual and, by extension, in society at large. Furthermore, the lessons imparted by primary schools should aid the citizen in improving his livelihood, thereby raising the economic floor for children born to lower or middle-class parents. In this way, the Guizot Law reinforced democratic equality; it gave the next generation of middle and lower-class Frenchmen the opportunity to enhance their material well-being, or to become more like their fellows. All the while, it supported the continued ascendance of the capable middle classes.

At the same time, the law was also intended to have an anti-revolutionary effect, akin to that of a capable electorate. An electoral system based in *capacité* guarantees order in politics. A uniform system of primary education likewise imparts order to society by eliminating ignorance, that which "makes a people turbulent and ferocious" and leaves the public susceptible to "error and seduction" by false ideas. Denied a basic education, Guizot worried that the lower classes would develop a "disgust for their situation" and a concurrent "thirst for change."[140] For evidence of the violent consequences of ignorance among the lower orders, he claimed that his countrymen need only remember who manned the barricades in 1789.[141]

Guizot's state-led system of primary education would accomplish two goals at once. First, it would shepherd democratic France out of the aristocratic age when primary education was limited in practice. Second, it would diminish the threat of another revolution born out of ignorance. To this end, Guizot advised that education should celebrate merit over privilege, though without promoting too much ambition in the wrong places; that is, it should stop short of awakening the "ambition of intelligence" among the inferior classes, or too much of that ardent desire for upward mobility that Guizot termed "democracy itself." Nothing proves more "injurious to society, or more hurtful to the people themselves than the small amount of vague, ill-directed popular erudition" that fills the mind of "the industrial classes."[142]

To suppress the violent ambitions of the lower orders, Guizot's educational plan was engineered to stifle some of that ambition in the first place. Not all children would hear the same lessons.[143] Areas "of the humblest social conditions," rural areas or those populated by the industrial classes, received an "elementary" curriculum with lessons in reading, writing, arithmetic, French, and religious and moral instruction. "Superior" lessons were reserved for towns and cities whose inhabitants "have to deal with necessities and tastes of civilization more wealthy, complicated, and exacting." Their curriculum also included physical science, history, geometry, and geography.[144] In practice, every commune with a population over six thousand had a superior primary school. Guizot's *Essay* of 1816 contained a similar teaching about the proper distribution of secondary education, which included courses in Greek and Latin, history, natural science, and literature. If it is imprudently extended to members of the lower classes, secondary instruction will foster "deceptive superiority," he wrote. The lower classes may confuse their rudimentary knowledge for the real, natural superiorities of those suited for a higher station.[145] Such a false sense of superiority will no doubt incite contempt among the lower orders, who will demand political rights (among other things) without possessing the *capacité* to bear them. Too much education, or instruction carelessly distributed, gives rise to the same restlessness as widespread ignorance.

By contrast, a well-organized scheme for public education elevates democracy's lower and middle classes intellectually, morally, and materially. It gives the faint promise of a future with *capacité* dispersed across every rung of the social ladder, of "light" shone on the minds of children of wage-earners and proprietors alike. At the same time, Guizot cautioned that public education should not act as the catalyst for social change. As he told France's teachers in 1833, public education was as much a tool for order as for progress, its lessons tailored to different classes and *communes*. An ignorant population was a turbulent one; but too much education, at the other extreme, upsets the delicate balance that Guizot believed already existed between the parts of France's equalizing society. For the moment at least, education had to cement social facts, not encourage pupils to concoct an imaginary world independent of them. "The object of laws," educational and otherwise, "is to provide what is necessary, not to step in advance of what might become possible; their mission is to regulate the elements of society, not to excite them indiscriminately," Guizot wrote.[146] Educational and electoral laws alike had to reinforce equality in society while denying it a place in politics.

Conclusion

Admittedly, this chapter has covered a lot of ground. But that is because Guizot himself did—in his intellectual life and in his public-facing roles. As a historian of European civilization, an eccentric theorist of political representation, an educational reformer, and a notorious politician, Guizot went from playing an oppositional role during the Second Restoration to leading the liberal government under the Orléanist monarch. And yet as this chapter has shown, a consistent if exacting vision of *capacité* and a single (re)definition of democracy underlie all of these endeavors. This theory and this definition gave shape to France's electoral laws and to its parliamentary deliberations about the size and scope of the electorate.

Today, Guizot is perhaps best remembered for resisting political democracy to such a degree that his ministry was upended by popular violence. But it was even before 1848 that his stance on French democracy and its new capable aristocracy put him at odds with one of his most celebrated contemporaries from within the liberal party. In the 1840s, Tocqueville would raise liberal challenges to the legitimacy of a capacitarian franchise and to the position of staunch *résistance* held by his former teacher, the same figure who first introduced France's most famous foreign traveler to the perils and promises of the democratic age.

3

Tocqueville's Other Democracy

On the Franchise in America and France

It should come as no surprise to find Alexis de Tocqueville's name at the center of this book—a book about liberals' reactions to democracy.[1] His *Democracy in America* (1835/40) is still widely credited as the finest work on the subject. And Tocqueville admitted to having written it while in the grip of "a sort of religious terror" about what the egalitarian revolution would bring to Europe.[2] If my readers already recognized the definition of democracy as a social state, it is most likely from Tocqueville's observations about the Anglo-Americans.[3] Whether he is portrayed primarily as a theorist of civil society, displaced aristocrat, prescient foreign observer of the United States, or even ardent French imperialist, the many interpretations of the liberal Tocqueville intersect with his thoughts on the democratic age.[4]

But if Tocqueville understood democratic society as few others have, he also knew that the word "democracy" traditionally meant something else: political rule by a sovereign people. Nevertheless, his interpreters have shown little interest in reconstructing his position on this, what I call Tocqueville's "other democracy": a political order rather than a social condition.[5] When scholars do focus on the political dimensions of *DA*'s democracy, it is to amplify what they hear as its author's calls for civic engagement and local participation, as in the New England township.[6] Yet Tocqueville introduced his famous text with questions that merged the social with the political. How should the democratic social state, the society of equals, be governed? Or to quote *DA* directly, what kind of "new political science is needed for a world entirely new"?[7] Tocqueville certainly wished to know "democracy itself," or the *moeurs* and "generating facts" that have fascinated generations of his readers.[8] At the same time, he grappled with one of modern democracy's central issues: the suffrage question.

With this fact in mind, this chapter pursues two aims. First and foremost, it uncovers Tocqueville's overlooked insights into democracy as a political phenomenon as well as a social one. If this topic has received scant

Democracy Tamed. Gianna Englert, Oxford University Press. © Oxford University Press 2024.
DOI: 10.1093/oso/9780197635315.003.0004

attention from Tocqueville scholars, it has warranted even less from those intellectual historians who have chronicled the history of the vote in France. In Rosanvallon's masterful trilogy, Tocqueville figures only as a minor player. In Kahan's parliamentary history of political capacity, we rarely hear Tocqueville speak at all.[9] And yet, Tocqueville carefully scrutinized a wide array of responses to the suffrage question from both American and French sources—so carefully, in fact, that was never content to accept a single one. He studied the "extreme democracy" of universal suffrage in Andrew Jackson's United States, where he documented its benefits without ever endorsing it outright. Years later, he found himself entangled in the contentious politics of the franchise in Louis-Philippe's France.

This brings us to the chapter's second aim. By reconstructing Tocqueville's views about electoral design across *two* nations, this chapter sheds light on his conclusions about democracy in *his own*. Thanks to Aurelian Craiutu's careful reconstruction of the Doctrinaires' political thought, we have come to appreciate the affinities between Tocqueville and Guizot as revealed through their "hidden dialogue."[10] But this chapter underscores just how dissimilar they became. To be more specific, it tells the story about how their initial affinities spurred lasting disagreements. For despite setting out from a common democratic point of departure, the two figures were pulled in opposite directions. Beyond their political quarrels during the July Monarchy, Tocqueville and Guizot adopted conflicting positions on the nature of equality, and these manifested in their respective attitudes toward political democracy.[11] Tocqueville, for his part, was reluctant to support even a weak capacitarian argument for the franchise, let alone Guizot's more exacting, metaphysical *capacité politique*. Tocqueville expressed his reservations about capacity across portions of the early drafts of DA, in the published text, and later in the Chamber of Deputies. As early as the 1830s, he began to forge a solitary path on the issue of political democracy, a path that led away from the Doctrinaires and eventually left him without obvious allies from any point along the political spectrum.[12]

Nevertheless, Tocqueville's idiosyncratic approach to the suffrage question had a principled purpose. For most of the 1840s, he actually hoped to transcend the existing debates about the extent of the franchise. He urged his countrymen to remedy the systemic ills of corruption that infected their government instead of quarreling over the composition of their electorate. Tocqueville made his intentions quite clear: as long as he lived under a corrupt and lifeless bourgeois regime, he would not seek a "more democratic" electoral law but a "more moral" one.[13]

As revolution approached, however, Tocqueville's quest for a more moral France steered him toward political democracy after all. By 1847, just as Guizot reaffirmed his commitment to a capable suffrage by rejecting a universal one, Tocqueville called on the deputies to broaden the franchise. He grew convinced that *more* democracy would inject much-needed energy into the languid and debased liberal government that endured for nearly two decades. As this chapter charts Tocqueville's departures from Guizot and from many of his contemporaries, from the liberal opposition parties to the radical republicans, it also brings to light his overlooked judgments about France's two democracies: its social state and its political institutions.

The bulk of this chapter maps Tocqueville's views on the suffrage during his parliamentary career in the 1840s. But my analysis begins earlier and elsewhere: in the final years of the Restoration and then across the Atlantic. In the first section, I argue that even if Tocqueville owed his theoretical *point de départ* to Guizot, their differences are apparent within the first volume of *DA*. The second section provides additional evidence for this thesis. It tracks Tocqueville's mixed reactions to universal suffrage in America, reactions which he expected would satisfy exactly no one on the Continent. In the second half of the chapter, we move from the Tocqueville of American democracy to the French statesman and reform-minded deputy who never quite found his place among France's liberals—in part for his peculiar interpretation of democracy in France.

Tocqueville, Guizot, and the New Democracy

A few years before the two travelers departed France for America in April 1831, Tocqueville and Gustave de Beaumont sat attentively in Guizot's course on European civilization. Inspired by Guizot's unique approach to history, the students were fascinated by the notion that democracy could appear in society even before they set foot in the New World to see the American example firsthand.[14] And Guizot continued to act as an informal teacher of sorts upon their arrival. The travelers hoped to "know the opinions that prevail at home" so as to find apt points of comparison on foreign shores, and to this end, Tocqueville asked his friend Ernest de Chabrol to send copies of Guizot's histories to America.[15] Tocqueville added these transcripts to the books by Montesquieu, Pascal, and Rousseau that made the journey with him.

Using language reminiscent of Guizot's, Tocqueville characterized democracy as an "accomplished, or nearly-accomplished *fact*," the work of Providence that "escapes every day from human power."[16] He, too, questioned whether France could avoid democracy's most devastating outcomes, social atomism and political servitude among them. "What will the probable consequences of this immense social revolution be?" he asked in an early draft of *DA*, before admitting that he, as of then, had no definite answers. Tocqueville echoed the Doctrinaires more broadly when he depicted democracy as "the waters of a flood," the same image that both Royer-Collard and Hercule de Serre evoked to undermine the Ultras during the 1820s.[17]

As he compiled his notes from America in the early 1830s, Tocqueville lamented that the Old World had already failed to channel the first waves of its democratic revolution. Hence his interest in studying equality as it had manifested elsewhere—in a faraway republic. Despite having experienced two recent *political* revolutions, the first in 1789 and the second in 1830, "the most powerful, most intelligent, and most moral classes of the nation"—his own nation—were caught unaware by this more elusive *social* revolution, such that they "did not take hold of democracy in order to direct it."[18] The result was a social state "abandoned to its wildest instincts," its anxious people still "unaware of the good that [democracy] can give" because they had seen only its vices.[19] By adapting examples from America, Tocqueville wished to bolster the French capacity to navigate the democratic revolution. The aim, after all, was to avoid the darkest possible future in despotism. It is clear that Tocqueville internalized Guizot's warnings about the absolute rule of one.[20] But he also foresaw that despotism could wear a democratic face: a "more extensive and milder" form of rule than what Constant called usurpation, or a despotism that "degrades men without tormenting them."[21]

For all their underlying similarities regarding the social state and their shared curiosity about a modern democracy, Tocqueville placed far more faith in the potential of a democratic social state than Guizot ever would.[22] This was because he never feared equality to the degree that Guizot did. In broad terms, both thinkers aimed to tame democracy's base instincts, including the ever-present desire to attain complete equality at the expense of all else. Guizot offered one answer: as we know, he championed *capacité politique* (political capacity) to eliminate equality from the electoral sphere. By contrast, Tocqueville hoped to discover a constructive political science, not only a restraining or tempering one.[23] Far from rendering democracy merely palatable by restraining its reach, Tocqueville endeavored to "see the

means to make [it] *profitable* to men."[24] He advised his countrymen to resist the Doctrinaire impulse to raise "impotent dikes" against the democratic
swell. "Let us seek rather," he urged, "to build the holy ark that must carry the
human species over this ocean without shores."[25]

Teacher and student had clearly parted ways by the time Tocqueville was
elected to the Chamber of Deputies in 1839, if not before. As we will remember from Chapter 2, Guizot chose recent publications by the Doctrinaire
polemicist Alletz and the republican Billiard to represent the state of French
discourse over democracy in 1837—and neglected to mention the widely
acclaimed first volume of *DA*.[26] But it was after his election to the Chamber
that Tocqueville emerged as an outspoken antagonist of the July Monarchy.
He made no secret of his personal disdain both for Guizot in the ministry
and Adolphe Thiers and Odilon Barrot in the opposition parties.[27] Guizot,
for his part, was puzzled that he and Tocqueville so often found themselves at
odds, and not just in the Chamber. "You deal with the greatest questions and
you understand all of their greatness," he wrote to Tocqueville in 1842. "Why
do we not think alike? I see no good reason."[28]

Even so, the cracks between their respective visions of the democratic had
begun to show as early as the first volume of *DA*. It was there that Tocqueville
first conveyed his reservations about offsetting equality in the social state
with *capacité* in the electoral system. Most importantly, it was also where he
turned the very teachings he retained from Guizot's histories against the minister himself. Looking back on the Restoration, Tocqueville denounced those
"imprudent" strategies employed by European reactionaries, who set out
to "destroy [democracy] instead of trying to instruct it and correct it."[29] He
thus restated some of the same arguments that the Doctrinaires developed
more than a decade earlier. And yet Tocqueville could not ignore an obvious
detail. The "imprudent" strategies that the Doctrinaires once attributed to
the Ultras now bore a striking resemblance to Guizot's liberal electoral plan.
When Tocqueville denounced those heads of state who refused to "teach
[democracy] to govern" and "thought only about pushing it away from government," he could easily have been describing members of the liberal *parti
de la résistance* who spearheaded the law of 1831, just as he and Beaumont
set sail for America.[30] Furthermore, Tocqueville deployed Guizot's premise
about the inevitability of democracy to criticize the latter's conclusions. "It is
impossible to think that equality would not penetrate the political world as
it has elsewhere," Tocqueville reasoned. "You cannot imagine men, equal in
other ways, forever unequal to each other on a single point."[31]

As we will learn throughout this chapter, Tocqueville's seeds of doubt about any attempts to contain equality blossomed into full-fledged objections to the July Monarchy's narrowly tailored franchise. To invoke Tocqueville's imagery, we can number *capacité politique*—particularly Guizot's metaphysical *capacité*—among the "dikes" built in vain to hold back democratic waters. Tocqueville aspired to build an ark.

Between Good and Evil: Universal Suffrage in America

When reread in the context of French debates over democracy, and particularly in light of the 1831 electoral law, Tocqueville's comments on American popular sovereignty seem to speak directly to his home country. He identified the Americans' attachment to popular sovereignty as one of the most remarkable phenomena he encountered abroad, in part because it was so different from how Europeans approached the same doctrine. Though often "buried" in the institutions of European countries (and denigrated by the liberals in his own), the sovereignty of the people is "recognized by [American] mores, proclaimed by the laws" and heralded openly as one legacy of their own Revolution.[32]

Fascinated by the quasi-divine nature of American popular sovereignty, Tocqueville also reflected on the scheme of universal white male suffrage that it supported. But as he put pen to paper on the subject, he sensed that he had already tread on "fiery ground." Anything he had to say on the matter would no doubt "offend" each of the parties dividing France, all of whom made their respective positions quite clear in parliamentary deliberations over the national and municipal suffrages.[33] Even so, universal suffrage, the subject that occupied Tocqueville in America, was not weighed as a viable proposal for France in 1831. By and large, the deputies agreed that it was premature. They deliberated within the parameters set by liberal-engineered (though defunct) 1817 electoral law. This is not to imply that there was no reformist opposition.[34] Still, the deputies spent their sessions in the spring of 1831 recalibrating the *cens* rather than entertaining radical proposals to abolish it. In the end, they agreed to a marginal increase in the size of the electorate.[35]

By giving serious thought to universal suffrage at all, then, Tocqueville's was a lone liberal voice in the 1830s, relaying lessons about electoral equality in the New World to the statesmen of the Old. His conclusions set him apart as well. Universal suffrage in America "was far from producing all the good and all the evil that are expected in Europe . . . in general, its effects were other than those supposed."[36] At home, Guizot reminded the deputies that the violence and tyranny of the Terror and the Empire sprung from the root of universal suffrage, which was no more than "an instrument of political demolition."[37] Around the same time, Tocqueville experienced it as a pacifying force abroad. Because every man has the vote in the United States, the majority makes itself known at the ballot box.[38] No association or party can therefore claim to be underrepresented in the legislature and incite unrest on that basis.

From his observations of the American system, Tocqueville drifted further away from Guizot's long-held position on the franchise. Above all, he learned how a democratic *society* could be managed by means of democratic *politics*, if only under certain conditions. Given the right circumstances and "in the immense complication of human laws, sometimes extreme liberty corrects the abuses of liberty, and extreme democracy prevents the dangers of democracy," including civil unrest and minority tyranny.[39] This statement, however qualified it was by Tocqueville's caveats about circumstances and complications, would have earned him no admiration from his Doctrinaire contemporaries, who continued to extol the protective functions of a capable suffrage.[40]

Although he acknowledged the advantages of electoral "extreme democracy" in the United States, Tocqueville's assessment of universal suffrage struck a balance between its "good and evil" consequences. At the very least, he was skeptical about the quality of the representatives who would be elected by a franchise of all.[41] While universal suffrage discouraged factional violence, preventing perhaps the worst fate that could befall popular government, Tocqueville unmasked one of the principal arguments in its favor as a "complete illusion." It is simply not true, he asserted, that there is ample wisdom in the multitude, or that "one of the greatest advantages of universal suffrage is to call men worthy of public confidence to the leadership of public affairs."[42]

To make his critical case, Tocqueville identified the unquenchable passion for equality as the people's driving desire, one that governs human behavior in elections as well as in everyday life. Entranced by equality and disdainful of hierarchy no matter where it may appear, democratic citizens will rarely elevate the best among them—a modern-day *aristoi*—to the seats of power, even if it means sacrificing the common good.[43] America put these democratic tendencies on display. There, despite having recognized "common merit" dispersed among the governed, the nation had a dwindling "race of statesmen and few outstanding men in public office."[44] The democratic penchant for equality thus became a barrier between a society and its government that prevented merit in the electorate from producing capacity in the government.

The Limits of a Capable Suffrage

But in the same breath, Tocqueville cited the American example to challenge justifications for a capable suffrage. Before we delve into these sophisticated challenges, we should make no mistake about Tocqueville's position on the "best" (that is, the most fitting) form of government. With the Doctrinaires, he argued for a representative government in which "the most enlightened and most moral classes of society lead."[45] Universal suffrage, despite its social advantages, could not guarantee the enlightened and moral assembly that Tocqueville imagined. Yet, crucially, neither could the capacitarian alternative. In the pages of *DA*, Tocqueville dismissed the suggestion that an electorate of the capable would necessarily produce the enlightened, moral government that an electorate of (virtually) all could not.

Unlike other contemporaneous critics of capacity who attacked the concept as either exclusionary or poorly defined, Tocqueville built his case upon a peculiar premise. The inherent *capacité* or *incapacité* of the voter was hardly the central difficulty confronting democracy, he declared—a point that, as we will discover in this chapter, he would later restate to address a distinctly French series of problems. "It is not always the *capacité* to choose men of merit that democracy lacks," he admitted while observing the Americans, "but the *desire* and the *taste*" for doing so.[46]

In order to feel the full force of this statement, we have to reexamine Tocqueville's portrait of the democratic individual. A democratic social state enflamed two human passions at once: envy and the desire for equality. Compelled by each, democratic citizens tend to resist the rule of *any* superior of merit. And this fact holds true whether those citizens were ever capable of identifying merit in the first place. While Guizot assumed that "every superior" will pull relative inferiors into his orbit, in society as well as in nature, Tocqueville implied that natural superiority is more often an object of revulsion than attraction for democrats. Looking at the world through envious eyes, "everything that is in some way beyond them seems an obstacle to their desires, and there is no superiority, however legitimate, that they do not grow tired of seeing."[47]

On the issue of political capacity, then, Tocqueville actually did track Guizot's arguments up to a point in *DA*, only to renounce them. He too treated *capacité* as a moral and intellectual quality in the individual and mulled over the same problems about encouraging enlightenment and education that captured Guizot's attention. On capacity and the vote, however, their differences are more striking than their similarities.[48] For Tocqueville, an individual's political capacity (assuming he had it) was easily overtaken by those "natural instincts" that "lead the people to keep distinguished men away from power."[49] Capacity could never function as the *guarantee* for rational government that Guizot proclaimed it to be.[50] To organize the vote around such a comparatively weak human faculty was to underestimate the overwhelming effect of desires, instincts, and tastes on the voter's decision-making. Hence Tocqueville's claim that the *capacity* to choose well is not necessarily lacking within a democracy—simply the *desire* to follow where it leads. What Guizot decried as "reason-conquering" authorities were, to Tocqueville's mind, humanity's inherent, ineradicable tendencies, which were now intensified under democratic conditions.

As he looked on "democracy itself," Tocqueville arrived at a conclusion about the franchise that, as he anticipated, neither seemed to satisfy nor convince anyone in France. Neither a universal nor a capable suffrage can *guarantee* moral and enlightened government; and universal suffrage, despite the Doctrinaires' misgivings, does not always portend instability and upheaval either. If many French liberals wished to close the book on universal suffrage, America gave Tocqueville quite a few compelling reasons to keep it open. His qualified optimism alone put him out of step with the more stalwart, undemocratic Doctrinaires.

Tocqueville also amassed some empirical evidence against a capacitarian suffrage. After cataloging suffrage laws across the individual states of the Union, he predicted that any restricted franchise, whether limited by *capacité* or some other principle, would not remain so for long. Here, once again, Tocqueville borrowed from Guizot's refutations of the Ultras in order to undermine the Doctrinaires' claims. Just as European countries struggled (unsuccessfully) to contain equality within *moeurs* and social relations, no polity could forever insulate the political sphere against democracy. If the state suffrages were any indication, any nation that modified its electoral qualifications toward more democracy (as France had done since the end of the Restoration) had already, if unknowingly, started down the road toward universal suffrage. Calling this phenomenon "one of most invariable rules" of societies, a rare declaration for a thinker who was always attentive to particular circumstances, Tocqueville foresaw that equality would progress in the electoral sphere as in the social one. "As the limit of electoral rights is pushed back, the need grows to push it further; for, after each new concession, the forces of democracy increase and its demands grow with its new power."[51] Tocqueville anticipated that the democratic torrent and, to import one of the insights from his later *Ancien Régime and the Revolution* (1856), the "revolution of rising expectations" that swept in alongside it, could not remain confined to the social state.[52] It was an invariable rule, after all, that "the ambition of those left below the electoral qualification is aroused in proportion to the greater number of those who are found above."[53]

Tocqueville supplemented his empirical predictions with numerous philosophical objections to capacity. Across a series of notes in which he interwove comments from family and friends with his own, he articulated his first impressions of popular sovereignty and universal suffrage. And as he had done so often, he began with certain premises drawn from Guizot's histories.[54] "I cannot acknowledge the absolute right of each man to take an active part in the affairs of his country," Tocqueville asserted, striking a Guizotian chord, "and I am astonished that this doctrine, so contradictory to the ordinary course of human affairs, could be proposed."[55] He likewise restated the Doctrinaires' rationale for denying the suffrage to the many: If a society can revoke civil liberties from anyone who abuses them, why not the right to political participation as well? If an individual cannot exercise judgment over his personal affairs, why should he be trusted to judge political affairs that pertain to everyone? And in a passage that could have been copied verbatim from Guizot's lectures, Tocqueville continued: "All questions of democracy and aristocracy (aristocracy as a ruling body) . . . are not questions of right but questions of fact, or rather the question of fact always precedes the other." To substantiate this connection between fact and right, he imagined an entire society without any capable individuals at all. Despite his reservations about absolute power, he conceded that despotism befit a society composed "in fact" of the incapable.[56] Personally, though, Tocqueville would "take care to live elsewhere."[57]

Because of the conversational style of Tocqueville's notes and early drafts, which layer revisions atop opinions and rebuttals, we are privy to the internal dialogue of a student who refused to accept his teacher's conclusions out-right. Later in that same exchange, Tocqueville expressed his ambivalence regarding capacity as a limiting condition for the vote. Immediately after describing political participation as a matter of "fact, not of right"—Guizot's distinction—Tocqueville distanced himself from the logic behind a capable suffrage. Arguments for capacity raised practical questions that they could not be used to resolve, at least not to Tocqueville's satisfaction. If *capacité* confers the right to vote, then how can the incapable ever hope to become capable? How can one who has been denied the right to take part in govern-ment ever develop the capacity to do so? Can existing defenses of capacity offer any guidance about how to ascend out of incapacity? Moreover, can a government claim to be of "the people" if one part of the people, perhaps the majority in some instances, is excluded from it? For "if you remove some from this choice, it is no longer the people who choose."[58]

With these questions still lingering, Tocqueville settled on a final com-plaint against capacity. What's more, he spun out some of the more worri-some ramifications of Guizot's reasoning to do so. As soon as you admit the incapacity of *any part of society*, however small, you acknowledge the possi-bility that *whole societies* may be incapable and therefore unfit to choose their governments at all. Tocqueville entertained that very possibility just a page earlier—where he convinced himself of despotism's legitimacy. But with this new claim about the inbuilt dangers of capacity, Tocqueville was not only decrying despotism once and for all. He also implied that any distinction between "extraordinary" lawmaking in moments of constitutional creation and the "ordinary" politics of elections held no real weight.[59] The right "to choose a government" and the right "to take part in a government" were two sides of the same coin—two "analogous products of human judgment," he concluded. It was impossible to uphold the first while denying the second. The principle of *capacité*, a test of the individual's fitness to vote, had the po-tential to undermine foundational, national claims to self-determination. At the very least, the enemies of liberty could sanction despotism from within a liberal framework. With that prospect in mind, Tocqueville issued a final warning that, given the substance of his note, seemed to be aimed at his earlier self, the writer who had briefly entertained the benefits of a capable franchise. "You are moving even further from the maxim that all people have the right to choose their government"—in his view (and despite his imperi-alist leanings), wrongly so.[60]

Political Capacity and Political Corruption

Tocqueville's misgivings about capacity resurfaced in his commentaries on the social and political state of France during the July Monarchy. Elected to the Chamber of Deputies in 1839, he participated in debates over the size of the national electorate and the qualifications of those eligible for election to the Chamber. On the latter issue of eligibility, he insisted that France should "call forth the most capable and the most disinterested men" to serve in its legislature, a statement consistent with his stance on representative government (and, as we will soon learn, his crusade against political corruption).[61] There is little doubt that Tocqueville intended to protect the salutary influence of enlightened and moral representatives, or that he invoked the ideal of the "capable" and "disinterested" deputy. On the matter of the franchise, however, his attitude toward a capacitarian suffrage was rife with ambivalence. His statements on the franchise throughout most of the 1840s tend to mirror his sentiments in *DA*, where he emerged neither as a defender of a capable suffrage nor as its vehement critic. In America, Tocqueville had the luxury of behaving as an attentive bystander, classifying the suffrage schemes of a faraway place while maintaining some distance from the happenings at home. After 1839, he occupied a role at the center of French politics.

Whichever reservations he harbored about either a weak or strong version of *capacité*, Tocqueville never abandoned the goal to foster a capable nation, that is, one that could manage the transition from aristocracy to democracy without descending into extremism. This was *DA*'s *raison d'être*, after all.[62] And in an 1836 letter to Eugène Stöffels, Tocqueville spelled out his ideal state of affairs for France, which included this discussion of a capable nation. At first glance, he seems to have adopted the Doctrinaires' outlook on political rights in that letter as well. As Guizot maintained, the individual's political participation was justifiable insofar as it was useful to society; this meant that the voter had to possess the *capacité* to recognize superior reason in his choice of a representative. Tocqueville appeared to continue that line of reasoning for himself: "I wish that citizens were introduced into public life to the extent that they are believed capable of being useful in it," he remarked.[63] But Tocqueville's letter to Stöffels ought not be read as an apology for a capacitarian franchise. In fact, Tocqueville clearly differentiated his "wish" for a capable citizenry from an electoral status quo delineated by the principle of capacity. He did aspire to introduce citizens into politics according to their utility, but this was "*instead of seeking to keep them away from public life at all costs.*"[64] If Tocqueville hoped to tie political participation to utility, then, it was because the Doctrinaire alternative—exclusion from public life on the basis of incapacity—was unacceptable. A year earlier in the Introduction to *DA*, Tocqueville accused "European statesmen" of working to "push [democracy] away from government," a strategy he now hoped to thwart.[65] To his initial "wish" for a capable citizenry from the 1836 letter, Tocqueville added two more hopes: first, that "the majority of the nation itself can be involved with its own affairs, that political life can be spread almost everywhere," and second (and *contra* the Doctrinaires) that "the direct *or indirect* exercise of political rights can be quite extensive."[66]

Given the tone and substance of Tocqueville's letter, it is necessary to separate his idealized vision for a *capable* citizenry from the Doctrinaires' uses of *capacité*. Tocqueville certainly saw the value both in a citizenry that could further the public good and in a representative assembly led by enlightened men. At the same time, he had little regard for *capacité politique* as Guizot and the liberals of the regime deployed it—that is, as an electoral barrier to keep the "incapable" away from public life. Although Tocqueville sought to develop the *political capacity* of entire nations to weather the democratic storm, he did not believe that either an electorate or a government anchored in *capacité* offered the appropriate means to reach that end.

Still, Tocqueville did not come out as a staunch opponent of a restricted franchise per se. It is telling, for one thing, that he did not include plans for a wider suffrage among his campaign promises in 1839. Once elected, he never joined the radical Left in the 1840s to agitate for universal suffrage. Nor did he participate in the banquet campaign for electoral reform led by Thiers and Barrot. Nor, most surprisingly, did he vote to lower the national *cens* and therefore broaden the franchise in 1842.

To reconcile Tocqueville's qualms about *capacité* with his perplexing 1842 vote against modest reform, we have to understand his political priorities in this period. His evaluations of *capacité* and the *cens* were interwoven with his wider disapproval of the regime under which he served as deputy but in which he saw little to admire. Having disparaged the government as a "bourgeois pot of stew," Tocqueville found it responsible for pettiness that could find no remedy in the "merchant-monarch" Louis-Philippe d'Orléans. The regime's bourgeois spirit trickled down to the people.[67] As witnesses to the homogeneity of their "shameless, materialistic," middle-class government, "the people fall more and more into indifference; it seems as if the rights which have cost them a dear price have ceased to be precious to them."[68] Since the private interests of the ministers and deputies guided policy, it was no surprise that the rest of the nation mirrored the materialism so openly displayed by its leadership.[69]

Beneath the regime's many vices, Tocqueville exposed the "great evil" of political corruption. He had long suspected the regime of engaging in bribery and patronage, going so far as to campaign (unsuccessfully) on an anti-corruption platform in Valognes in 1837. Now that he had won his seat in the Chamber, he could observe from the inside-out just how deep the regime's degeneracy ran. From this vantage, he saw that the narrowness of the middle-class government—the result of the *cens*—was but a symptom of a graver illness he diagnosed as "political demoralization," a term he coined to capture the regime's materialism, its reliance on patronage, and the disturbing civic apathy that resulted. It was an almost certain sign of corruption, in fact, that the regime had roughly the same number of bureaucratic positions (approximately 200,000) as France had national voters.[70] The ministers held the power to distribute these positions among the deputies, who distributed their share to voters who were also supporters and friends. With patronage-run-rampant, Tocqueville lamented that the voters, who were simply imitating their leaders in the ministry and parliament, confused "the particular interest for the general interest."[71] They treated politics exactly as their politicians did: as the means to further private interests, or in their case, to gain bureaucratic offices.

Faced with the reality of a spoils system that began with the ministry and reached the *moeurs* of the French public, Tocqueville chose not to direct his efforts toward resolving the suffrage question—the issue of *who* could vote—during most of the 1840s. Nor did he channel his energies to attack *capacité* head-on. Instead, he sought the cure for a "demoralization" with sources far deeper than the *cens*. In these years at least, he set his sights much higher than the incremental suffrage reforms spearheaded by the men of *mouvement*. His goals were more radical. Indeed, they steered him dangerously close to far-Left republicans, closer than either party cared to acknowledge.[72] So long as wealth and patronage greased the wheels of the French political machine, Tocqueville plotted the trajectory of his career in response. Stirred by the ills of corruption he saw all around him, he worked to destroy an entrenched system that rewarded personal loyalty with offices and disgraced the entire nation in the process.

The Dangers of Direct Elections

Even if the *cens* was not the fount of the countless political evils that Tocqueville identified, he believed that the electoral system of his day fed into them. "Among the causes within us which have produced this political demoralization of the country by the positions of power, the most energetic, the most continuous, allow me to say it, is found in the electoral law," he told the deputies in 1842, just before voting "*non*" on a measure that would have given more men the vote.[73] To wage what he saw as his private war against government corruption, Tocqueville zeroed in on direct elections of the kind that had been instituted under the 1817 law and reintroduced in 1831.[74] Both Guizot and Constant, we will recall, upheld direct elections against the Ultras, praising them as vital instruments for representative government that place electors in direct proximity to candidates. For Constant, the unbroken tie between voter and deputy would translate into a representative parliament that encompassed an array of particular interests; for Guizot, it strengthened the chain of political capacities that propelled superiors to positions of power.

What Guizot and Constant (and most other liberals) commended as the system's cardinal virtue, Tocqueville targeted as the source of its vices. The system's depravity stemmed from the unmediated attachments between voter and deputy—the same attachments that Guizot and Constant celebrated. Taking an alternative perspective on direct elections from his fellow liberals, Tocqueville complained that elections had grown so parochial as to verge on personal. He experienced some of this parochialism firsthand; in his district of Valognes, approximately 700 men possessed the vote when he won the election in 1839.[75] Under such conditions, "all local interests become, in the minds of citizens, in the minds even of the deputies, stronger than the general interest."[76] The *directness* of elections reinforced the self-interested tendencies of the government. Voters chose their deputies for the promise of private gain rather than any perceived political good. Moreover, electoral directness incentivized patronage. With the "realm divided into an infinite multitude of small plots" (districts), each of which held direct elections to the legislature, voters demonstrated little interest in issues of national or even political significance. Instead, they spent their days serving their private advantage: clustered around their deputy, "annoy[ing] him unceasingly" for favors.[77]

If the electoral system intensified the regime's reliance on corruption, it did so, ironically, through the very mechanisms that Constant deemed essential to a truly representative assembly. Motivated to gain support from his neighbors, who expected to receive favors in return, the deputy carries their narrow interests into the Chamber, "demoralizing" politics from electorate to legislature and back again. In sharp contrast to what Constant argued, Tocqueville implied that politics had grown so corrupt that its particular interests could *never* negotiate among themselves—and furthermore, that they had no motivation even to try. In their feverish materialism, the people lost all sense of the general interest or common good. Against his contemporaries in the Chamber, Tocqueville contended that the *real* problem of French politics had no direct connection to the size or scope of the electorate or even most immediately with the nepotistic government that had been elected by such a small slice of French society. The problem was in the *incentives* produced by patronage and reinforced by the system of direct elections. As of 1842, Tocqueville was explicit about the evils stemming from the electoral law: "I do not think that the electoral law should be attacked as an instrument of monopoly"—that is, as a law (and consequently, an electorate) that was too restrictive by design. "It is as an instrument of political demoralization that I attack it."[78]

Tocqueville's disapproving comments about direct elections in France invite comparisons with his romantic, almost lyrical remarks about indirect elections in America. Tocqueville sang the praises of indirect elections because he stood in awe of the legislature that they produced. Struck (and somewhat repulsed) by vulgarity in the US House in Representatives, Tocqueville made his way to the Senate chamber, where he heard deliberation among "eloquent lawyers, distinguished generals, skilled magistrates, [and] known statesmen."[79] What could account for the crude composition of one chamber and the evident dignity of the other? Tocqueville concluded that any differences sprang from the mode of election: the House was chosen directly by the people, the Senate indirectly. As the popular will passes through the state legislatures, which function as electoral intermediaries to choose the senators, it emerges "clothed in more noble and more beautiful forms." The popular voice still resounds, Tocqueville insisted. But the men it calls forth via its intermediaries "represent only the elevated thoughts that circulate in its midst, the generous instincts that animate it, and not the small passions that often trouble it and the vices that dishonor it."[80] If, as he predicted, the complete equality of universal suffrage would soon reach all democracies, then indirect elections would have to become the standard. Moreover, if a nation hoped to reap the benefits of a universal franchise (peace over violence) while retaining noble elements in its government, it would need to adjust the mode of elections.[81]

This final point is worth emphasizing, because it reveals a great deal about Tocqueville's stance on the *suffrage* question—which for him, as we've learned, was of secondary importance. The matter of *who* or *how many* could vote paled in significance to the intricacies of electoral design. Constant and Guizot turned to the suffrage question because they found indirect elections wanting. With their plans for direct elections in place, the popular will had to be regulated at an earlier stage of the electoral process, whether by a censitary suffrage (Constant) or a capable one (Guizot) that distills the capable from society before any ballot is cast. But Tocqueville approached the problem of electoral filtering from the other direction. Assuming universal suffrage to be the status quo, as in America, he held that most of its dangerous outcomes could be mitigated by the proper (that is, indirect) electoral scheme. With his final word on the virtues of second-order elections in America, Tocqueville stressed that the existing parties in France, as usual, discounted the mean in their pursuit of extremes. "Those who hope to make [indirect elections] the exclusive weapon of one party," like the Ultras, "and those who fear this means," like most liberals, "seem to me equally in error."[82]

When he addressed the Chamber in 1842, Tocqueville again accused his listeners of promoting error. It was then that he dismissed complaints about the *incapacité* of individual voters. "We still complain that it happens too often that the voter, in his choice of deputy, has paid more attention to the services rendered to him than to the political acts of the deputy he appoints," he began. Yet, to blame the individual for his incapacity was to miss the glaring issue. Because it pitted the voter's strong personal interests against an enfeebled common good, the whole system encouraged the voter to act with his personal interests firmly in mind. We will remember, too, that elections took place in each district (as Guizot intended), where the whims and interests of a relatively small number of voters held sway over the deputy, who needed the backing of his neighbors.[83] Under such conditions, Tocqueville asked rhetorically how any voter, no matter how capable he was, could be expected to think of anything else:

> How do you expect it to be otherwise, in a situation where a very small number of voters are stationed around a powerful man who they have appointed deputy, whose fortune they hold in their hands, are able to approach him at any moment, are able to annoy him unceasingly, a situation

from which he cannot escape? How do you expect this small number of voters to resist the temptation to obtain for themselves a satisfaction, for which they are only asked for their political opinion in return?[84]

With these rhetorical questions, Tocqueville reaffirmed the point about electoral design he offered in his commentary on the Senate in *DA*, though it was now adapted to suit distinct circumstances in France. To give one's undivided attention to suffrage reform—to modifying the *cens* based on the perceived *capacité* or *incapacité* of entire classes—was to underestimate the depth of political demoralization. Remarkably, the same thinker who saw how universal suffrage could inoculate politics against what James Madison called the disease of factionalism resisted more democracy in his home nation. The remedy for French demoralization could not be found, as of the early 1840s, in a wider franchise, let alone a universal one. "I do not want a more democratic electoral law," he specified, "but a more moral one . . . an electoral system that renders corruption by patronage more difficult."[85] The "extreme democracy" that moderated America's democratic social state would not confer the same advantages elsewhere—or under all conditions. At this stage, more democracy in France would bring more demoralization. It would put *more* voters in proximity to their deputy, increasing competition for offices and fanning the flames of patronage. With this in mind, Tocqueville declared that democracy in France had, for the moment, reached the appropriate pitch: "at present, in matters of electoral law, we have given enough, but not too much to democracy."[86] When he voted against those measures in 1842 that would have expanded the national electorate, Tocqueville was fulfilling the promise he made to himself when he took office: to put morality before democracy, in order to save both.

During most of the July Monarchy, Tocqueville believed that he was confronting dire national problems and proposing noble solutions—more noble, at least, than anything that ever materialized out of the deputies' stale deliberations over the *cens*. On the electoral law, he intended to redefine the terms of debate to disrupt parliamentary patronage-as-usual, eschewing liberals' language of *capacité* in order to correct for the defects of their regime. By stepping outside of the established modes of discourse, Tocqueville distanced himself from all of the parties of the period, with whom he claimed to have nothing in common.[87] At the same time, he never lost sight of the ideal, energetic France he imagined in his letter to Stöffels in 1836, in which most citizens could devote their attention to national affairs. Indeed, an entire literature has emerged detailing how Tocqueville pursued empire abroad as a common venture to unite an atomized and apathetic domestic citizenry.[88] As the political situation grew increasingly volatile, even before the slow burn of working-class resentment erupted into outright revolution in 1848, Tocqueville abandoned empire and initiated the search for that energy anew—and at home.[89] This time, he discovered it in political democracy.

Tocqueville's Other Democracy

In the year or so leading up to the 1848 Revolution, Tocqueville hoped to rewrite the electoral law so as to institute indirect elections. But by then, circumstances had changed just enough to allow him to recommend another kind of legal revision too: a broader suffrage. In 1847, he predicted revolution in two brief draft manifestos.[90] Portions of these drafts reappeared in a speech he delivered in January 1848, roughly one month before the overthrow of Louis-Philippe. In both the written texts and subsequent speech, Tocqueville embraced the reformist solution he had spent most of his parliamentary career dismissing. He located one source of the country's redemption in *suffrage* reform. We will recall that an alliance comprised of republicans and Left-liberals failed to revise the *cens* in 1842, leaving in place the laws that had been passed during the first year of the new regime.[91] By 1847, Tocqueville urged the deputies to approve the reforms they (and he) rejected once before. "Slowly extend the circle of political rights, so as to go beyond the limits of the middle class; make public life more varied and more fruitful, and involve the lower classes in public affairs in a regular and peaceful manner." He took care to specify slow reform and avoided using the phase "universal suffrage." But in calling for the franchise to extend beyond the liberal middle classes, he mounted an obvious challenge to the regime. Deeming this proposal "necessary and prudent" for the "present situation," he expected that it would have two effects. First, it would rouse the French people from their bourgeois-induced slumber; second, it would pacify a discontented, politically-estranged population that had long been denied the vote.[92] When joined to the electoral and administrative reforms he had recommended for years—the first to change the mode of election, the second to professionalize the bureaucracy so as to divorce it from politics—Tocqueville believed that a broader franchise would break the cycle of political corruption.[93]

In their attempts to explain Tocqueville's sudden *volte-face* on the franchise, scholars have interpreted his statements from 1847 to 1848 alongside two subsequent and related themes that appear in his *Recollections* (1850): the first on the status of the lower classes, the second on the triumph of socialism.[94] Drawing from this later text, they conclude that Tocqueville demonstrated minimal interest in the lower classes, specifically the plight of the urban workers, for most of his career, only to be disgusted by their actions in the streets of Paris.[95] When read in the condemnatory light of his depictions of class warfare and socialist materialism, Tocqueville's proposals for suffrage reform have been dismissed as temporary, even insincere concessions to circumvent violence rather than genuine calls for political incorporation.[96]

There is no doubt that Tocqueville often had multiple aims in mind for a single argument. In this instance, avoiding violence was one of them. Nonetheless, there are good reasons to conclude that his calls for suffrage reform were genuine. For one, he repeated the same lines about extending the franchise to the lower orders in his *Recollections*, and affirmed his confidence "in the usefulness of electoral reform and the urgency of parliamentary reform." He also linked the two projects of reform, electoral and parliamentary, to his wider goal to revive a lifeless nation: "for great events come not from the mechanism of the law but from the spirit of government. Keep the laws if you wish . . . But for God's sake, change the spirit of government."[97]

But why exactly, after resisting even modest alterations to the suffrage for so long, did Tocqueville come to believe that a wider franchise, one that incorporated the long-excluded lower classes, would help to solve the problem of political demoralization? What kind of benefits could a franchise that included *les classes inférieures* possibly confer that the existing franchise could not? For one answer to both questions, we ought to examine the social standing of the lower classes, who were neither bourgeois nor aristocratic, that is, neither responsible for what Tocqueville disparaged as the enervating national life of the last eighteen years nor, consistent with the Doctrinaires' sociology against the Ultras, the exemplars of a bygone age. Instead, Tocqueville associated the lower orders with political estrangement. This separation or political alienation from the ruling bourgeoisie defined them as a class. Moreover, they embodied alternative opinion. In this new form of class antagonism, Tocqueville saw glimpses of the clash between the feudal aristocracy and the bourgeoisie at the end of the *ancien régime*, when the two were divided by "diversity of conditions . . . diversity of interests, of passions, and of ideas" that led to open disagreement. Under such conditions of separation—indeed because of them—there were great debates and great parties, for "there had to be."[98] Tocqueville waxed nostalgic for the "fertile reawakening of the public spirit" during the Bourbon Restoration, when liberals such as Royer-Collard, Guizot, and de Serre challenged the restored aristocracy. That was also the time when *le parti libéral*, though oppositional, had "the greatest influence in the country," by which Tocqueville meant that it exerted influence on the greatest matters and the greatest events.[99]

The middle-class victory during the July Revolution of 1830, as we now know, had the opposite effect. It ushered in a political class unfit for a nation already so "self-interested and vain" that it could never flourish under the government of *any* single class—especially a class that insulated itself with a narrow franchise and then dispensed offices to friends who also came from the same exclusive strata of society.[100] The lower classes were valued as *an* alternative, a social antithesis to the bourgeoisie (themselves once the alternative, and more dynamic when they were). The bourgeoisie and the aristocracy clashed over the authority of property during the Restoration; Tocqueville predicted that property would again serve as the "great battlefield" between the next clash of parties, now represented by those who possessed property against those who did not.[101]

Still, the lower classes were more than just "not bourgeois." Tocqueville knew what the bourgeoisie had become and of what they were capable— which, he insinuated often (and against Guizot), was not much. The lower classes, by contrast, represented experiment and possibility, their energies described by Tocqueville as "muffled" for being expressed outside of politics proper but still perceptible and active.[102] If there were any pockets of political vibrancy in France, Tocqueville found them in what he called lower part of society by 1848. While those tasked with governing abandoned the common good for commercial pursuits and rent-seeking, "in the lower part [of society] . . . political life had begun to manifest itself in the form of sporadic fevers."[103] This feverish politics manifested at times as disorder, a sight that disturbed Tocqueville. But it also appeared as the exercise of judgment. "Can you not hear [these classes'] endless refrain, that those above them are incapable and unworthy of governing; that the present division of the goods of this world is unjust, and that the basis of property is unfair?" he asked in the *Recollections*.[104] He confessed to feeling unease at hearing such demands. At the same time, he was hopeful for what they represented. In their expressions

of injustice and indeed in their recognition of the incapacity of their ministers, the lower classes had begun to reawaken the political.

Contra Guizot and the lifeless, small parties that surrounded him, the
lower classes had the potential to act with great passion for principled political rather than private ends. Following along with Tocqueville's reasoning,
we can see how the return of principled politics may bestow two related
advantages on the demoralized country. First, a broader franchise would
weaken the monopoly of middle-class rule by injecting diversity into the homogenous and inert deliberations of parliament. Second, by taking a share
in politics for the first time, the enfranchised lower orders would no doubt
break the informal rules of the bourgeoisie's private political game. Coupled
with his proposal to change the mode of elections—to pursue *electoral* rule
change for the sake of *parliamentary* reform—Tocqueville sought to reap the
"moral" rewards of a wider franchise. At the same time, his plan would protect society against its characteristically "democratic" dangers with a system
of indirect elections.

This was precisely where socialism had failed, in his eyes. For Tocqueville,
the challenge was to redirect the lower classes' latent energy *through* politics rather than against it and to "involve [them] in a regular and peaceful
manner."[105] He wished to restore passion to politics while avoiding popular
uprising, toeing the thin line between a more dynamic, even agonistic political sphere and an unstable society. Channeling growing public spirit toward the end of ruling rather than revolting was the next step in realizing
true political debate instead of class warfare. The socialists, in Tocqueville's
view, never grasped the necessary distinction between class-based political
energy and class-based social violence. As they united the Parisian workers
under the banner of material-driven "envy," the socialists ensured that "the
two principal parts of society had finally separated" so that "no bond or sym-
pathy remained."[106] Their revolution also began to resemble the commercial-
ized bourgeois regime it overturned. Having transformed revolutionary goals
into economic goals, the socialists created what Tocqueville described in *DA*
as "rival nations," further dividing a society already under strain after eighteen
years of inward-looking bourgeois rule. He accordingly wrote of the 1848 revolution as a "class combat" instead of a "political struggle," likening many of its
features to the deep divisions that characterized the *ancien régime*.[107]

Tocqueville's agenda of reform differed from that of the socialists both in
its ends and in its means. In his view, the socialists dangled promises of material gain, of economic benefits for the poor over the rich, in front of the

people in order to initiate revolution.[108] Popular violence was their means; the abolition of private property their end.[109] Though he once predicted that property would serve as the "great battlefield" for party disagreements, Tocqueville endeavored to differentiate his moderate, "moral" purposes from the socialists' materialistic extreme.[110] His plan to envelop the lower classes into the franchise capped off a three-pronged agenda of reform in administration, elections, and the franchise, all of it geared toward curing the body politic without killing it, that is to say, without overthrowing the monarchy and plunging Paris into disorder. This trio of efforts would hollow out the government at its corrupt core while keeping its monarchal foundations intact. It would also use more democracy to inject energy into a country that had been dispirited by a self-interested middle-class—the class that deemed itself "the capable."

Conclusion

Tocqueville served on the committee charged with drafting the Constitution of the Second Republic in 1848, which established universal male suffrage.[111] When he was elected to the Constituent Assembly as the representative from Manche that same year, an estimated 160,000 voters participated—a far cry from the mere 700 eligibles in Valognes who cast their ballots a decade earlier. Even if Tocqueville felt personally rejuvenated as he launched his own campaign before such a relatively large electorate, a fact that he admitted in the *Recollections*, universal suffrage was never his principal goal as a politician. And yet it was also not the "instrument of political destruction" that Guizot claimed it to be. As this chapter argued, Tocqueville reflected on the extent of political democracy in France in order reach a higher goal for the nation; under the right conditions, channeled and moderated through the proper modes of election, he thought that more democracy could promote morality in the government and vitality in society.

Tocqueville also regarded universal suffrage as the *inevitable outcome* of the egalitarian revolution. The same transformative social forces that leveled the old aristocracy could not be kept out of politics for long—and certainly not by laws based in *capacité* that, to Tocqueville's mind, raised more problems than solutions. In fact, if well-directed, the forces of *political* equality could serve morality and democratic society rather than posing a threat to either.

Since he ultimately came down on the side of universal male or at least near-universal male suffrage even prior to 1848, we might assume that Tocqueville did indeed abandon one of his original priorities: what he called his "wish" to see a capable citizenry engaged in public affairs. Put otherwise, it seems that Tocqueville *did* side with equality over capacity in the end. But for Tocqueville, who saw a combination of both at work in America, the choice between political equality and political capacity was never zero-sum, as it was for Guizot. While he took issue with Guizot on *capacité* and the limited franchise the concept created, Tocqueville retained the belief that democracies need capable citizens and capable, disinterested legislators alike. By 1848, he arrived (if implicitly) at a distinct understanding of what it meant to be politically capable in his own country, a country that had been lulled to sleep by plutocratic politicians and shaken awake by violent revolution. For Tocqueville, the capable for France was not a "new aristocracy," comprised of men most outstanding in rationality or distinguished by their admirable professions. Instead, they were the principled and the political across all tiers of the social order, those who could mediate between their particular interests and the general interest. At the very least, he tried to teach his country's fledgling democracy that capacity in a government did not have to come at the expense of either morality or equality.

In the decade after Tocqueville's death, his most devoted student in France, the jurist and constitutional scholar Édouard Laboulaye, would reach a similar conclusion about combining capacity with political democracy. He, too, salvaged some of the Doctrinaires' arguments from the Restoration only to put those arguments to use in creative and undoctrinaire ways. Laboulaye weaponized Guizot's approach to history and society in order to create the platform for a unified oppositional *parti libéral* during the Second Empire. But this was a liberal party whose agenda bore little resemblance to that of the Doctrinaires' centrist cadre of the 1820s. Nor did it have much in common with the liberal July Monarchy that preceded it. Instead, Laboulaye's new liberal party welcomed the democratic status quo of universal suffrage. It also undertook a new, Tocqueville-inspired task: to enlighten political democracy, beginning within civil society and with the working classes, those who had been denied the vote in the nearly two decades of France's liberal government.

4

Édouard Laboulaye's
Enlightened Democracy

From June through November 1848, Tocqueville sat alongside seventeen other delegates on the committee to frame a republican constitution. The final draft instituted universal male suffrage for the election of the president and for members of the Second Republic's unicameral assembly.[1] With its passage, the national electorate swelled from the 240,000 "capable" Frenchmen of the July Monarchy to more than 10 million, only to shrink once again with the passage of a liberal-backed electoral law in 1850. Louis-Napoleon Bonaparte seized power in December 1851, and later reintroduced universal suffrage in the constitution for the Second Empire (1852–70). The newly titled Napoleon III professed to have founded a regime unlike any other in European history, a true democracy that surpassed even the *grandeur* of his uncle Napoleon Bonaparte's First Empire.[2] For "never has a people proven in a more direct, spontaneous, and unanimous fashion its determination to free itself from concerns about the future by consolidating its power in a single hand."[3]

Liberals struggled to find their political footing under Napoleon III's imperial democracy. They failed to coalesce into a unified parliamentary opposition through at least the first decade of the empire. Faced with universal suffrage and racked with anxiety over the rise of socialism, liberals were also forced to rebuild their case against political democracy from the ground up. Chapters 1 through 3 have shown how Constant, Guizot, and Tocqueville each reacted to the death of the *ancien régime* and the subsequent birth of a democratic order, and how Guizot and Tocqueville, in particular, wrestled with the prospect that democracy may soon permeate the political world. The arguments in this chapter grew out of different circumstances, when universal suffrage became the status quo and liberals contested Napoleon III's plebiscitary democracy. The same elites who staunchly refused to lower the *cens* now posed variations on the suffrage question. Once universal suffrage was written into the nation's constitution, could it ever be scaled back? Was

Democracy Tamed. Gianna Englert, Oxford University Press. © Oxford University Press 2024.
DOI: 10.1093/oso/9780197635315.003.0005

there any remaining role for liberals, many of whom were committed to a capacitarian franchise, under the Second Empire? How, if at all, could the French manage equality once it had spread beyond the boundaries of the social state? Was it possible to cultivate political capacity in a national assembly elected by all Frenchmen, capable and incapable alike?

Some of the richest responses to liberals' democratic dilemmas appeared in the widely circulated writings of Édouard Laboulaye (1811–83), a key player in the opposition to the Second Empire and one of the founders of the Third Republic.[4] A legal historian at the prestigious Collège de France, Laboulaye entered public life following the workers' June Day Uprisings in 1848.[5] His first political pamphlet, which contained a series of suggestions for writing a republican constitution, appeared that same year.[6] As an avowed discipline of both Tocqueville and Constant, whose ideas had rarely been brought into conversation across their own century, he encouraged the statesmen of his generation to retrace their liberal lineage—and not only in France.[7] So genuine was Laboulaye's fascination with "the real and living republic" of the United States that he was dubbed "America's greatest friend" during his lifetime.[8] His passionate pro-Union and anti-slavery tract, "The United States and France" (1862), found its way onto Lincoln's desk at the height of the Civil War.[9] Eager to forge lasting ties of friendship across the Atlantic, Laboulaye organized the gift of the Statue of Liberty from the French. It was finally unveiled to a waiting crowd in New York Harbor in 1884, one year after his death.[10]

It is striking, then, that one of the sincerest allies of American democracy abroad is virtually unknown today in the English-speaking world.[11] And although both Anglophone and Francophone scholars have acknowledged Laboulaye's contributions to mid-century French politics, it is fair to say that he remains among the history of political thought's forgotten figures.[12] For some intellectual historians, Laboulaye was a victim of bad timing. He immersed himself in French national politics at a low point in the lifespan of its liberal party, historians note.[13] For French liberalism had become no more than a "stilted and contradictory" ideology in the waning years of the July Monarchy, or so scholars have claimed.[14] Even Laboulaye's illustrious reputation as an architect of the Third Republic, it seems, was not enough to lift him out of relative obscurity beyond his lifetime.

Ironically, Laboulaye would have likely agreed with these later appraisals of liberals' political fortunes. He produced what would become his best-known political tract, *Le Parti libéral, son programme et son avenir* (1863), to resolve the contradictions that bedeviled liberalism as a political creed. By blending features of Constant's pluralist liberalism and liberal Protestantism with Tocqueville's American-inspired political science, Laboulaye aimed to shed the "illusions and disappointments" that marked the regimes of the recent past (including the July Monarchy, which he supported) and to reshape the liberal party of the 1860s into "a program for modern democracy."[15] Breaking out of the Doctrinaires' mold, he spoke (if unofficially) for a reconstituted opposition party that "sincerely embraced universal suffrage."[16] Instead of screening for signs of political capacity among the proprietors or in the middle-class professions, as his Doctrinaire predecessors had done, Laboulaye took notice of the bourgeoning signs of self-government elsewhere: in the communal and associational activities of the working classes, the so-called "incapable" of the July years.

As it revisits Laboulaye's liberal political vision, this chapter casts new light on the jurist's intellectual debts to Constant and Tocqueville. It argues, furthermore, that he anchored his justifications for universal suffrage on a third and rather unexpected collection of arguments. Laboulaye appealed to the Doctrinaires' premises about equality's unceasing advance in order expose their political errors.[17] In particular, he deployed the Doctrinaires' historical method—what Guizot had sometimes called "philosophical history"— for two purposes: first to understand the features of France's l'état social in the latter half of the nineteenth century, and later to uphold democracy as that society's fair and appropriate electoral scheme. Laboulaye thus took up the suffrage question from a novel perspective. His reformed liberal party was designed to enlighten (éclairer) universal suffrage. In this role, it would summon Christian morality along with public education and local, civil associations to redirect equality's rising tide that now reached the electoral system, in spite of the Doctrinaires' efforts to contain it. While he retained some of his forerunners' anxieties about mass politics, Laboulaye refused to dismiss either of France's *two* democracies, social or political. The working classes had become the wellspring of a "new democracy" that realized equality everywhere—a democracy that, as we will learn, bore little resemblance to Guizot's la démocratie nouvelle.

The first section of this chapter surveys liberals' reactions to universal suffrage in the Second Republic. It paints a clear (but by no means complete) picture of liberals' electoral priorities after the end of the July Monarchy, and in so doing, aims to bring Laboulaye's contributions to the debate over democracy into relief. The remaining parts of the chapter illuminate the various dimensions of his enlightened democracy, which borrowed from liberals' post-1789 origins to speak to a post-1848 France.

Bringing Capacity Back In

In the aftermath of the Revolution of 1848, liberals who once split into the factions of *résistance* and *mouvement* during the July Monarchy reached a temporary consensus on the franchise, if only to repel their common enemy: socialism.[18] Once an outspoken rival of the Guizot government, Pierre Jules Baroche became so consumed by the threat of socialism that he shifted toward the political Right. From this more conservative vantage point, he claimed to have unmasked universal suffrage as a plot to secure "the triumph of those appalling ideas that are called socialism."[19] The same Adolphe Thiers who addressed large crowds at the reformist banquets from 1847–8 railed against the republic's "vile multitude" only three years later. Once empowered, that multitude would "deliver over to every tyrant the liberty of every Republic," he alerted the assembly, as all mobs had since the days of republican Rome.[20] A universal franchise was an incapable one, and it was through the votes of the incapable classes that the socialists would ascend to power. "Everything must be done for the poor and the needy," Thiers granted, "except, however, to grant them the power to decide the big questions facing the future of the government and the country. Yes, everything for the poor, except the government."[21]

The remaining capacitarian liberals, Thiers included, set out to find creative ways to reinsert political capacity into legislation for the infant republic. This was no small task. The 1848 constitution mandated direct, universal suffrage for all Frenchmen over twenty-one years of age and forbade property requirements for the vote. At the same time, it contained a loophole that liberals would soon exploit. "The electoral law shall ascertain the causes that may deprive a French citizen of the right to elect and to be elected," read its 27th article.[22] As they strategized to subvert the republican mandate with such an electoral law, liberals also had to achieve two practical electoral objectives. First, they aimed to disenfranchise the socialists' electoral base in the urban working classes, and second, they had to ensure that liberals' poor supporters in the countryside retained the vote—all without reinstituting the *cens* or resorting to a multi-tiered electoral scheme.[23]

To strike their preferred balance between rural and urban elements, liberals recommended a three-year residency requirement that could be proven either by direct taxes or by a certificate from one's employer confirming three years' continuous residency in a single home. The 1850 legislation stopped short of violating the letter of the constitution while nonetheless undermining its spirit, even if Thiers would continue to insist otherwise in his speeches in the assembly. Those poor urban voters who moved from town to town in search of public relief or temporary employment—*les vagabonds*, in Thiers' words—would not meet the three years' standard.[24] By contrast, the rural, stationary poor, a population that traditionally favored liberal candidates and causes, would keep the vote. The law hit the cities hardest of all, where mobility was high and housing temporary. Approximately 60 percent of eligible voters in Paris were disenfranchised; in the more rural Moselle, by contrast, the law excluded 15 percent of the eligible population.[25] When one member of the assembly asked just how many voters would lose the right they held, the law's supporters retorted that any worries over sheer "numbers"—over voters lost or gained—were irrelevant to the needs of the country.[26]

Through the 1850 law, liberals retook control of a capacitarian franchise, and they carved out an electorate that would at least forestall the socialists' political rise. At minimum, the residency standard served as a guarantee of personal self-sufficiency, since anyone entrusted with the vote had to prove personally capable of keeping a permanent residence. More importantly, the law screened for what Constant once described as the cultivation of public patriotism through personal interest, though it did so without explicitly reinstituting a propertied franchise. More than forty years after the first *Principles of Politics*, the architects of the 1850 law put forward a similar justification for their residency standard. Attachment (proven by residency) to a particular place and community signaled that the individual had a vested interest in the public good, or to quote the deputy Ferdinand Béchard, that one belonged to an "organized body that lives its life in common."[27] Although Guizot would later remark in his *Memoirs* that the principle of capacity prevailed in one form or another until 1848, liberals' strategies to reinstate a capable suffrage post-insurrection were more clever than even he may have realized. In the face of mounting socialist sentiment and under a constitution that mandated direct universal suffrage, liberals smuggled capacity into law.

Still, this version of capacity differed from any that came before. Whereas Guizot and the *résistance* liberals celebrated a capable bourgeoisie (although, as we have learned, they were reluctant to define the "bourgeoisie" with any precision), those who authored the 1850 law avoided explicit references to a rational or virtuous social middle altogether. In order to make any electoral headway, liberals needed to strike the classist language of an ascendant bourgeoisie from their deliberations.[28] Thiers, for one, tried to convince the assembly that liberals harbored no classist prejudices at all. He insisted that the law carefully distinguished between society's poor, who kept the vote, and the smaller class of vagrants, who had no ties to any community and therefore no claim to the franchise.[29] Liberals' willingness to concede the point about social class allowed them to recover capacity (if temporarily) by proposing that "residency," rather than profession or taxation, serve as its outward sign. Their law did produce a much wider franchise than the liberal-backed legislation of the July Monarchy allowed.[30] Nonetheless, it denied the vote to approximately 3 million men who participated under the November constitution.[31] Despite their tolerance for modest reform, the majority of liberals refused to entertain the thought that universal suffrage could ever be made legitimate. By the time capacitarian liberals agreed to entertain further reform in 1851—to adjust the domicile standard in the hope of gaining a larger share of the working-class vote—their opponents succeeded in portraying them as enemies of the republic.[32]

The liberal party fared no better in the wake of Napoleon's *coup d'état* in December of that same year. For roughly a decade, the new emperor reigned as an autocrat. Keen to emulate the *grandeur* of the Consulate and the Empire ruled by his uncle Napoleon I, the new emperor pursued aggressive policies of military and commercial expansion abroad.[33] At home, he banned most newspapers and strictly censored the few that continued publishing, outlawed political meetings, and sought to expunge France of his republican enemies. Tocqueville was arrested; Laboulaye was exiled for delivering subversive lectures on the history of the United States.[34] These were hardly the worst fates that befell Bonaparte's rivals: some Orléanists were deported to penal camps in the Algerian colony. While the regime reinstituted universal suffrage and organized plebiscites, Napoleon's heavy-handed interference in elections fictionalized the democratic components of his imperial democracy. He compiled an official list of candidates for the *Corps législatif* and appointed and dismissed ministers at his discretion.[35] Liberals were indeed forced to retreat. Banned from the press, muted in the assembly, even exiled from their country, they could garner very little popular support, even with universal suffrage.[36]

But Bonaparte's regime took its first steps toward liberalization beginning in 1859, and liberals managed to regain power in the press and influence in the academy.[37] In lectures at the Collège de France beginning in 1862, Laboulaye outfitted his criticisms of the empire as lessons in the public law of the faraway republic of the United States, employing some of the tactics that Guizot pioneered to evade censorship during the Restoration.[38] The liberal party achieved modest success in the 1863 legislative elections. In reaction, Laboulaye saw flashes of life in the listless liberal party.[39]

Yet Laboulaye knew better than anyone that this reemergent liberal union was plagued by infighting.[40] Many liberals were dismayed by state centralization; many more distrusted the emperor's early promises to liberalize and decentralize the French state. But their disagreements lie in the details. Liberals clashed over just how centralized the French state ought to be, over the regime's economic and foreign policies, and on the necessity of a state religion, among other issues.[41] If the Revolution of 1848 forced liberals to reach a provisional compromise on the suffrage, old disputes soon resurfaced.[42] The elites who governed the July Monarchy and even those who led the opposition parties against Guizot—including Thiers, Barrot, and the younger of the Restoration's Doctrinaires de Broglie and Rémusat—joined the *résistance* against universal suffrage. The succeeding generation of liberals, many of whom felt compelled to enter national politics in 1848 as Laboulaye had, glimpsed political equality on the horizon.[43] In the chaos and confusion of the June Days and especially after the formation of the Empire in 1852, liberals lost sight of the values that once bound them together. More often than not, they described their political positions only as critical alternatives to the policies of Napoleon III.[44]

Liberalism as a "Universal Church"

In the opening pages of his liberal manifesto, *Le Parti libéral*, Laboulaye made it clear that he would neither ignore nor discount the existing rifts among those who identified as liberals. On the contrary, he envisioned a political association that could accommodate an array of opinions along a wide ideological spectrum, so as to bridge the pre- and post-1848 generational divide. Ideally, the party ought to act as "a universal church," he claimed, "where there is room for anyone who believes in liberty and wants to enjoy it."[45] Laboulaye himself was well positioned to provide this perspective. It is true that his political sympathies lie with the more hopeful, more democratic cohort. But as a former supporter of the July Monarchy, Laboulaye kept one foot in the Orléanist camp. If his more ecumenical liberalism enveloped a multiplicity of views, it was also held together by a single creed. Its common principles were "those of 1789," which were identical to the principles "recognized by all modern constitutions" and to the "common patrimony of civilization."[46] Laboulaye regretted that the French had abandoned principled politics shortly after the Revolution, lamenting that he lived in a country "that speaks often about freedom but hardly uses it."[47] Yet the spirit of 1789 endured elsewhere, he believed. One could see it at work in the great modern constitutions of Belgium, Holland, Great Britain, Switzerland, and especially the United States.

The basic tenet of Laboulaye's liberal party was straightforward and familiar. "What we ask is the enjoyment of those liberties" that allow "each citizen the care and the conduct of his own life."[48] To make this case, he subdivided liberty into two categories: individual (a category he elided with social liberties) and political. Rooted in human nature, individual liberties constrain state action. They enable "the individual to become the master of his destiny."[49] Unless charged with a crime, for example, citizens ought to live without fear of police power, and if charged, remain innocent until proven guilty by jury trial.[50] Inspired by Constant's multi-volume *De la Religion* (1826–31), Laboulaye wrote that the individual is "born to search for the truth on his own," rendering religion "an individual matter, a right which belonged to each person."[51]

Laboulaye's choice to reconstruct liberals' platform atop the foundation of natural, individual liberty was a strategic one. He endeavored to see beyond the party's internecine disputes, and thus to expose whichever agreements still existed below the party's fractured surface. When Laboulaye himself broke with the liberal orthodoxy on democracy, then, he claimed to do so out of respect for the values that informed the liberal party since its inception in the pamphlets of Constant and de Staël. To a familiar list of three "essential political liberties" that included a free press, an elected assembly, and an independent judiciary, Laboulaye added a controversial fourth: universal suffrage.[52] Such an addition no doubt set off alarm bells for at least half of his readers. As we learned in Chapter 2, Guizot associated universal suffrage with tyranny and anarchy; *capacité* alone, the Doctrinaire believed, balanced liberty with order, a refrain that his fellow liberals were wont to repeat. In an evident repudiation of Guizot's words, Laboulaye declared that "a nation of truly free people must possess a fairly widespread electoral suffrage for the entire nation, or the vast majority of the nation, to take part in public affairs."[53] The imitable "free countries" of Belgium, Holland, Britain, and the United States, where liberal principles continued to reign, enshrined such "a widespread electoral suffrage" in their laws.[54] Laboulaye exalted these examples from afar to reimagine liberals' agenda at home—and to shed some of their long-held antidemocratic baggage. Few Frenchmen from any party could doubt that the Americans enjoyed true freedom, he contended.[55] "To attack universal suffrage, to try to reduce it or eliminate it by the deceptive tactic of two-tiered elections, these are views unworthy of a statesman, and completely foreign to the liberal party," by which he meant the new liberal party of the 1860s.[56]

Laboulaye's message about the two types of liberty was ultimately tailored to reach a wider audience beyond those politicians who already identified with the loosely-organized *le parti libéral*. Far from segregating one type of liberty from the other, he reminded the French people that political liberty, of the kind Bonaparte offered them, meant little in the absence of constitutional restraints on power.

> All [liberties] are necessary; but the hallmark of the new liberal party is to have finally understood that political liberties are nothing by themselves, and that the people tire of them as empty and deceptive conventions if they do not have behind them those individual and social rights that are the fount and the very substance of liberty. It is because they misunderstood this truth that, from 1814 to 1848, two governments, animated by good intentions, could not manage to establish in *moeurs* the liberty that would have saved them.[57]

Oddly like Bonaparte, Laboulaye distinguished his proposed program from the governments of the Restoration and the July Monarchy. But very much unlike the emperor, he insisted that even the most well-intended heads of state missed the mark when it came to protecting individual freedom. "The July Monarchy has done more for freedom than any other government . . . but has it weakened or actually strengthened centralization?" Laboulaye questioned, implying that he, too, recognized the weaknesses of Guizot's so-called "liberal" government.[58] Laboulaye's more scathing indictments of the current Second Empire lie just beneath his rather tame criticisms of past regimes. The principal takeaway from his critiques was unmistakable: universal suffrage alone cannot liberate people from despotism once and for all, a hard truth that the liberal party alone—and neither Bonaparte nor his loyal partisans— had come to grasp.

As Laboulaye already knew, Constant had issued a similar warning about the allure of political liberty earlier in the century. "Individual liberty is the true modern liberty. Political liberty is its guarantee," Constant told his audience during a lecture at the Athénée Royal in 1819, which was later given the title of "The Liberty of the Ancient Compared with that of the Moderns." "But to ask the peoples of our day to sacrifice, like those of the past, the whole of their individual liberty to political liberty, is the surest means of detaching them from the former and, once this result has been achieved, it would be only too easy to deprive them of the latter."[59] The memories of Jacobinism and the Terror weighed heavily on Constant. More than half a century later, Laboulaye saw those patterns of history repeated in the reign of Napoleon III, particularly in the emperor's pronouncement that universal suffrage and plebiscitary democracy fulfilled the people's demands for freedom.[60] For Laboulaye, Constant's predictions about the abdication of personal for political liberty had fallen on deaf ears once again, leaving the whole of France doomed to relive its despotic past.

Yet Laboulaye's Constant-inspired point about the limits of political liberty seems to introduce a tension into his own arguments for democratic liberalism. On the one hand, he amended the standard list of liberal freedoms to include universal suffrage. On the other, he warned that universal suffrage, however attractive, would not necessarily set the necessary limits on absolute power. Nor could universal suffrage guarantee the individual liberties celebrated by le parti libéral. And yet Laboulaye combined these two points to recast Constant's 1819 distinction anew: political rights, no matter how widely they extend, amount to mere "demi-libertés" without the institutional protections enshrined in a stable constitution. "Complete, frank, sincere freedom has existed for a long time in Holland, England and America, but in France we have only ever had demi-libertés. Our administrations have always been half-hearted about our rights."[61] With this claim, Laboulaye piled layers of nuance upon the insights of the Restoration liberals, Constant among them, who segregated political from civil or individual rights in order to underscore the inevitable trade-offs between them. As a student of Constant's political theory and a witness to the "faux freedom" of universal popular participation under Napoleon III, Laboulaye was no stranger to the notion that one type of liberty may come at the expense of the other.[62] While searching outside of France, however, he found evidence that a nation could hold on to both. Universal suffrage ought to be counterbalanced with liberal attitudes, in particular, with liberals' suspicions of unchecked power. But under Laboulaye's watch, the liberal party would not deny the significance of political liberty—or the need to universalize it. "Political liberties are of supreme importance; they are the rampart and the shelter of civil liberties," the majority's "defense[s] against the ambition, intrigue, and greed" of the few or the one.[63] "There is neither industry, nor commerce, nor arts, nor letters, nor sciences where the person and property of subjects are at the mercy of a master," he reasoned.[64] Laboulaye thus set out to overturn the Doctrinaires' most basic teachings about freedom. If the new liberal party hoped to restore liberty after more than a decade under illiberal government, its members had to embrace political democracy.

Democracy as Self-Government

Fully aware of the difficulties he faced in transforming a broken liberal party into a more democratic "universal church," Laboulaye set out to define "democracy" with as much analytical precision as he applied to the term "liberty."[65] One of his (and also Tocqueville's) frequent correspondents in the United States, the jurist and legal theorist Francis Lieber, pressed his French contemporary on exactly this point. What did Laboulaye mean by referring to "democracy's rise" on the Continent? The Frenchman sent a detailed reply:

> In France today the word [democracy] is a translation of self-government. It does not mean the power of numbers, but free government. This kind of democracy is making progress in France, especially among urban workers. This is where the life of the nation is at this time. The bourgeoisie, the small merchants, the minor property owners, have never recovered from the failure of 1848, but the workers are educating themselves, forming associations, founding public libraries, establishing public classes, and if war or government errors do not interrupt this progress, we will soon notice a considerable and happy change in the ideas of the people.[66]

The differences between Laboulaye's elevated democracy as self-government and the Doctrinaires' "new democracy" jump out immediately from this passage. But before we explore them, we may be just as struck by the similarities between the two definitions, which were separated by four decades and four different regimes. In a passage that could have been lifted from the parliamentary record of the 1820s, Laboulaye remarked that "if there is one striking visible fact that imposes itself on all eyes, it is the advent of democracy."[67] Yet his democracy was neither Guizot's leveled society, the egalitarian social state that rose out of the dust of revolution, nor was it the "world quite new" that Tocqueville glimpsed in the 1830s. While the "prophetic" proclamations of Royer-Collard and de Serre rang true forty years after they were first articulated—democracy *had* overflowed its banks, Laboulaye agreed—the matter of how to respond to democracy's rising tide had changed dramatically since the Restoration.[68] "Not only is there no longer an established Church in France, not only is there no nobility and no privileged corporations," Laboulaye explained, so far in full agreement with his forerunners about the nature of the democratic age. "But there are no longer any bourgeois or peasants. Those are old names for things long dead," he continued, noting the effects of equality in places where his fellow liberals, past and present, never felt them.[69] So equalized was the France remade by the upheavals of 1848 that the lines between social classes had been erased almost completely. Those social distinctions drawn by virtually all liberal statesmen from Constant to Tocqueville—distinctions between the bourgeoisie and the laboring classes, for one—no longer existed. Or at least, Laboulaye indicated, they ceased to be meaningful for politics.

Laboulaye encouraged his fellow liberals to view the democracy of their day in this new light. "The whole question today is how to organize democracy, not by imprisoning it, but by breaking the bonds that chain it, and in habituating it to live its own life," he wrote.[70] Gone was Guizot's derisive definition of democracy as the illegitimate "supremacy of numbers." The term had come to mean "self-government" since 1848, or the ability of individuals and groups to act, think, and organize without (and often against) the tutelary power of the state.[71] In an ironic turn, Laboulaye himself invoked the traditional categories of social class to sharpen his point about equality's far-reaching effects. It was the urban workers who engaged in the art of self-governing following the bourgeoisie's dramatic fall from power, and who took advantage of the incremental liberalization of the Empire in recent years, he argued.[72] Members of the working classes already founded mutual aid societies and public subscription libraries of the kind that Laboulaye's literary Société Franklin would spread throughout Paris in the 1860s.[73] They established fraternal groups, unions, and cooperatives, filling the administrative space left open by Bonaparte, who by 1860 had agreed to relinquish his firm control over local affairs.[74]

Through this novel account of democracy as self-government, Laboulaye hoped to correct liberals' cynical interpretations of the collective (in)capacity of the people. This new democracy, he believed, would also dispel the belief that universal suffrage was nothing but a vehicle for socialist revolution. It is true that socialism "was born from the sufferings of certain classes, rightly or wrongly."[75] But this did not mean that the urban workers were the passive agents of a wider socialist agenda. After all, as Laboulaye reminded his readers, the English working classes survived even though Chartism, the working-class reformist movement in mid-century England, could not.[76] "The workers have an extreme desire to live in peace and to exert control over their rights," he explained, and as in England, they will not look blindly to the spokesmen of an ideology or to the heads of a "despotic" organization to lead them. "The worker is no longer socialist and revolutionary," Laboulaye went so far as to declare, "*il est individualiste et libéral.*"[77]

Laboulaye's stance on the workers' potential and their role in a modern democracy set him apart from capacitarian liberals past and present. Even so, it is remarkable that his justifications for universal suffrage shared much in common with the thoughts of the most capacitarian among them: the Doctrinaires. For Royer-Collard, Guizot, and de Serre in the 1820s as well as for Broglie and Rémusat in the present-day Second Empire, the Revolution of 1789 rendered the conventions and institutions of the *ancien régime* obsolete. For Laboulaye, the violent 1848 Revolution wrought similar consequences; it toppled outdated institutions and *moeurs*, disrupting bourgeois politics-as-usual for a social condition so leveled that it blurred the social lines separating the urban workers from the bourgeoisie.[78] Those who once existed outside of Guizot's democratized France now gave "life" to this radically transformed *l'état social*, the culmination of three major revolutions: 1789 (the intellectual point of departure for Guizot and Tocqueville), 1830, and finally 1848. Laboulaye followed the path charted by Guizot as the Restoration's foremost historian and, as Chapter 2 demonstrated, one of its most thoughtful theorists of democracy. Having set out from the same starting line, Laboulaye followed the Doctrinaires' logic to its inevitable, egalitarian conclusion: "In France there is only one order and only one people. We are all citizens and to the same degree . . . Many are frightened by this democracy, which is rising unceasingly, and they only accept it out of resignation. *Moi, je l'aime.*"[79]

What some of the leading liberals after 1848 denounced as the corrupted source of socialism and hence of tyranny—an enfranchised multitude— became the symbol of Laboulaye's new democracy. To turn a blind eye to the realities of this reformed *l'état social* was to ignore the basic social facts upon which freedom depends—the same message that Guizot once delivered to his students at the Sorbonne. In reaction to this new France, the France of the second half of the century, of a subsequent revolution, republic, and empire, Laboulaye envisaged a liberal party whose political platform complemented the changed social order. Accordingly, "the liberal party sincerely accepts universal suffrage as a guarantee of freedom, as a means of government, as an instrument of political education. Far from seeking to weaken it, the liberal party would like to strengthen universal suffrage, by enlightening it."[80]

One key point is worth emphasizing. Laboulaye did not believe that liberals ought to accede to universal suffrage solely to keep themselves afloat in electoral politics. Of course, we cannot deny the basic fact that liberals campaigned to win legislative seats. But there is good reason to think that Laboulaye "sincerely" accepted universal suffrage, or that his politics indeed flowed from his principles. Instead of separating political from civil rights, he discussed them together as the harmonious elements of liberty and devoted equal parts of his *Le Parti libéral* to each. Moreover, to his mind, the working classes exemplified self-rule, local liberty, and collective action, so much so that he need not take the time to justify their enfranchisement. The content of his chapter on "Universal Suffrage" bears little resemblance to similarly ti- tled publications from earlier in the century, which tended to fall into one of the two molds cast by either the Doctrinaire Alletz or the republican Billiard. Unlike the Orléanist masterminds behind the 1850 electoral law, Laboulaye approached political democracy as a system that could be integrated within the standing framework of liberal politics, rather than an electoral scheme concocted to displace liberty with socialist ideals.[81]

At the same time, Laboulaye sought to improve upon the liberal tradi- tion that he inherited. One of his innovations was to recognize that the first shoots of political capacity had to be cared for within the social soil where they had naturally taken root. Earlier liberals were content to codify the signs of political capacity where they existed, and they wrote their laws to pre- serve the influence of the already-capable classes. But as we will remember from Chapter 3, Tocqueville worried that capacity was an insufficient tool for strengthening democracy; the standard of capacity could direct the legal search for the capable, Tocqueville noted, but it alone would not tell liberals *how* to make capable citizens out of incapable subjects.[82] Laboulaye's agenda gave liberals the means to augment capacity that the Doctrinaires' plan for a capable electorate, in his view as well in Tocqueville's, failed to supply. In other words, liberals would intervene in the democratic social state in order to enlighten it. "To enlighten the people" (the whole people, we should note) "this is the big question of the future," Laboulaye announced in his chapter on universal suffrage.[83] The French should not resign themselves to living at the whims of an incapable, enfranchised *demos*. Nor should they succumb to the "appetites and passions" of an "ignorant crowd."[84] True to his liberal roots, Laboulaye repeated de Serre's words from the Restoration. "What is universal suffrage?" he asked and answered, "it is an unceasing tide . . . it is an almighty force." In the end, however, Laboulaye's response was more Tocquevillean than Doctrinaire. "Depending on the direction it receives, [universal suffrage] can make use of its energy for evil or for good. The popular vote may support a government, as it can overturn it; it can save the country, as it can lose it," he wrote, using words that were oddly reminiscent of the ones that Tocqueville first used in *DA*. Once a "force of this magnitude is introduced into the Constitution, it must be instructed because it is intelligent, and it must be moralized because it is sovereign."[85]

Universal suffrage, in the end, was just as Guizot had portrayed it: fickle, uncertain, irrational, dangerous. To its long list of defects, Laboulaye added one more. Universal suffrage was neither as free nor as universal in practice as it seemed to be in theory. To take just one example, French governments from the Revolutionary past up through the Bonapartist present engaged in the practice of preselecting their preferred candidates for the assembly, a move that would constrain the people's choices well before the election. Even so, the free nations of his day could no longer rely upon the "external precautions" supplied by the *cens* or by *capacité* in any form.[86] Liberals under the Empire had to give direction to universal suffrage without resorting to creative legal restrictions, such as those implemented in 1850, or to the clever tactics employed by governments in order to celebrate democracy in name but not in fact.

By reconfiguring the relationship between liberalism and political democracy, Laboulaye sought to ensure that political capacity would not fade from public debate, especially after the introduction of universal suffrage, though it would undergo transformation. Guizot insisted that a nation could organize the franchise around one of two principles, either equality or capacity. For Laboulaye, whose image of the social state grew from the sociologies first developed by Guizot and Royer-Collard, France had reached the moment when the two values could exist in harmony. His goal to realize an enlightened democracy remained liberals' North Star, their fixed point for navigating the politics of the mid-century.

Enlightening the Democratic Soul

It is worth taking a moment to clarify Laboulaye's use of terms in *Le Parti libéral* as well as his intentions as democracy's most sincere liberal advocate in the 1860s. For one thing, *capacité politique*, the term that suffused nearly all of liberals' responses to the suffrage question since the Restoration, never appears in Laboulaye's liberal manifesto. He chose the more neutral "enlightenment" instead, a word that did not carry all of capacity's antidemocratic connotations. Nevertheless, Laboulaye would continue to champion the features of capacity—rationality, independence, intelligence, and political judgment—by another name. The same questions that agitated his fellow liberals weighed on Laboulaye's mind as well: how could a free democracy be sustained? And what kind of citizens were needed to sustain it? As he set out to answer these questions, Laboulaye was captivated by the ongoing process of enlightening the French citizenry, and it was this process that gave purpose to the party association he set out to redesign. Although a capable (now an enlightened, to use his preferred term) citizenry endured as a liberal goal, it ceased to act as a dividing line for the vote. Laboulaye's shift in language, from political capacity to enlightened democracy, reflected liberals' new political aim: "to enlighten and improve the soul" of each voter.[87] In reaction, liberals would have to abandon one of the political projects that occupied their greatest minds since the Restoration: the project of partitioning the whole society into its capable and incapable parts.

Laboulaye pressed the liberals of his day to practice something like the art of political soulcraft instead. For the study of the human soul ought not be siloed in churches or contained within the academic disciplines of theology and moral philosophy, he contended. With the establishment of universal suffrage, public officials had to redirect their energies to forming souls, not exclusively to rewriting constitutions. Because the "almighty force" of popular electoral power may usher in either evil or good for a nation, democracy requires a "guarantee" for intelligence and morality. "In a country of restricted suffrage, that guarantee lie in the *cens*," Laboulaye admitted, while reiterating that a censitary suffrage was necessarily an institution of the past. Under universal suffrage, by contrast, the guarantee for intelligent, moral government lay elsewhere—within individuals, each one an organ of a universal voting body. In a democracy, "it is the soul of the voter that is the guarantee . . . it is therefore this soul that must be enlightened and improved." Although the mere mention of political soulcraft sounds more ancient than modern and also more Aristotelian than liberal, Laboulaye was unwilling to sacrifice individual freedom for spiritual perfection. Instead of habituating humankind to virtue through the laws, liberal soulcraft operated with the less corruptible and, at least according to Laboulaye, less coercive means of education. "Popular education," by which he meant the education of the whole people, "is no longer simply a question of morality," he asserted. "It is the first of all political questions; the fortune of France is attached to it."[88]

As with so many features of Laboulaye's political thought, his interest in the human soul originated with his readings of Constant. When Laboulaye reintroduced Constant to the French of the 1860s, he eulogized his Swiss-French predecessor as both an authority on religion and "the master of political science for friends of liberty."[89] Constant's once-eminent reputation as a liberal and a parliamentarian suffered at the hands of the July Monarchy's ministers and in the pages of Guizot's *Memoirs*. For Laboulaye, Constant's posthumous disrepute was certainly undeserved. More so than any other theorist of the modern era, Constant understood that liberty needs "essential conditions" to flourish, including religious sentiment, "civic energy" on the part of citizens, and morality.[90] By uniting Constant's religious and political writings, Laboulaye reaffirmed the former's maxim that "liberty is the soul in action," and held that "freedom is nothing but the complete development of the human soul."[91] In order to safeguard the two halves of freedom for the sake of the whole, liberals should look well beyond the details of institutional design.[92] A free democracy is reinforced by free *souls* alongside stable institutions—souls free not only to exercise their rights to worship, act, speak, and publish as citizens of a particular nation, but also to participate in the human search for truth free from external impediments. In the lengthy *De la Religion*, Constant tied this unfettered search for truth to self-development. Both, he argued, were antidotes to the egoism and materialism that poisoned the modern age.[93] Laboulaye drew upon the spiritual dimensions of Constant's liberalism—and as we will soon discover, he called them to the aid of liberal democracy. "The most elevated goal a man can propose here below is to develop the whole of his faculties," Laboulaye asserted.

"To improve himself, even at the cost of suffering, this is the task of a man, a Christian, a citizen."[94]

When he recast democracy as self-government, then, Laboulaye was not only drawing attention to the workers' visible, external displays of collective action or their exercise of associational freedom. He was also referring to the self-governing soul, or to the individual's well-regulated inner life—in a word, to what earlier figures may have called the *capacity* for self-governance. The strands of Constant's Protestantism were woven throughout both Laboulaye's religious and political writings. It is no surprise, then, that the latter leaned on Christian morality—though morality without the need for a theology, as he indicated elsewhere—to regulate human action.[95] Morality differentiates an "ignorant and revolutionary democracy" from a "Christian, enlightened, industrious democracy" that reflects the well-ordered souls of its people. Educated by Christianity, the individual soul becomes the "guarantee" of an enlightened democracy, since "each individual learns from childhood to govern himself, and by governing himself learns to respect the rights of each."[96] A self-governing, moral democracy therefore has no need for an exclusionary *cens* to assure its enlightenment.

A "Perpetual Education" for America and France

After calling religion to the aid of modern democracy, Laboulaye said little about which particular academic lessons would elevate the souls of men, Christians, and citizens alike. But it is worth noting that his educational ideal encompassed two potentially contradictory elements. He aimed to educate human beings by means of Christian morality; at the same time, he subscribed to a liberal—in this sense, a free and in the tradition of Constant, a pluralist—ideal of education and its purposes. "Education is but preparation for life; it opens the mind, it does not fill it," he wrote, implying that the capacity-enhancing or enlightening effects of education were more valuable than any particular academic lessons it may impart.[97] And while Laboulaye had nothing but admiration for American schools, where pupils studied subjects as varied as geometry, writing, and their nation's constitutional history, it was the "perpetual education" that took place within society that set the United States apart. Having pored over Tocqueville's *DA* and other French accounts of American life, he stood in awe of the dynamic image of a healthy civil society that his countrymen painted.[98] More teachings circulate outside of the classroom than within it, he marveled; "this is the immense service rendered to society by churches, newspapers, popular libraries, public courts, public meetings, and by the thousands of associations that always keep religion, science, and opinion awake in free countries." Laboulaye appreciated the ways that civil associations combat individualism and atomism. But he went further than Tocqueville, in fact, to laud their educative and enlightening functions. Associational life, more so than formal instruction, wages the "fight against ignorance" to "stifle" revolutionary passions in the soul before they can ever see the light of day.[99] And yet it was not enough to cultivate a peaceful soul and city. The educated citizen, the human being who is exposed to a multitude of opinions in his daily life, also understands when resistance to authority is justified. He alone walks the fine line separating senseless revolution from defensible defiance.[100]

Laboulaye did not seem to notice any potential tensions between his concurrent calls for a Christian democracy and for a pluralist civil society. In his mind, Christianity and liberty walked hand-in-hand. As he added new arguments to support the maxims first expressed by Constant, Laboulaye wrote that "religion is the friend and necessary companion of liberty." Because religious liberty is the "first" of all other liberties, it supports the proliferation of ideas and associations that enable the individual to pursue the truth free from interference.[101] According to both Laboulaye and Constant, it is the true Christian philosopher who supports "complete religious freedom" and the separation of church and state.[102]

Along the same lines, Laboulaye also pressed for the separation of schooling and state. Just as he glorified civil society as the primary site of democratic education, he endeavored to break the state's control over the provision of education altogether. Yet he also applauded what a well-organized educational system could accomplish. An admirer of the educational writings of Horace Mann and William Ellery Channing in the United States, Laboulaye possessed intimate knowledge of America's primary and secondary schools.[103] Very much unlike the French, he claimed, the Americans understood that education was "a matter of life and death" for their republic, the same lesson that Laboulaye tried to impart to his fellow citizens. The Americans organized their public schools to ensure the safety of their precious freedoms.[104] As a result, they lived in a nation where ignorance was the exception rather than the rule. In Mann's home state of Massachusetts, for one, "there is nothing rarer than a citizen who cannot read."[105]

Laboulaye formulated his recommendations for democracy's education in France with an eye toward American successes. But his proposals were colored by French liberals' fears of despotism and centralization. Laboulaye, for his part, feared intellectual centralization just as much as administrative centralization, or the uniformity of thought and opinion that a "state-imposed" educational program would induce, or a program for schools that regulated both their organization and the lessons taught within them. "The state may offer instruction, but it may not impose it on anyone," he clarified. Although the citizen owed his obedience to the state's laws, his conscience should remain his own. "Does not it feel as if the government managed to stifle every dissenting voice, that would be the end of French civilization?" Laboulaye asked, speaking more broadly of the dangers of censorship and uniformity just as Constant had. "The country would be dead." He contrasted the lively "variety" of American civil society with the "dead uniformity" wrought by centralized power, in schooling as well as in administration.[106] "How can we not see that unity is the opposite of freedom, and moreover, is a chimera?" he asked, channeling Constant's admonitions from the first Bonapartist empire.[107] In light of the dual dangers of centralized power and uniform minds, "nothing can therefore justify a monopoly over education, either in the hands of the Church or in the hands of the State."[108]

Writing at two very different moments in the nineteenth century, the two very different liberals Laboulaye and Guizot both extolled education as a pillar of the liberal party and of a free government. But the two parted ways when it came to the details concerning its delivery. Guizot believed that a state-directed, centralized program of primary education was the surest means for social progress, though he too left a role for local organizations and associations to oversee the administration of schools. Guizot's faith in a state-led system of education troubled Laboulaye, who imagined that eventually uniformity and backwardness would follow from such a program, however well-intended it was. In this spirit, he aimed to see public education decentralized. Inspired by Mann's writings from New England, Laboulaye favored a system of free primary schools, with each school controlled by a local school board instead of the national government.[109] Furthermore, Laboulaye suggested that the requirements of the 1833 Guizot Law for education, "which still brings so much honor upon its author," had not truly been met in the thirty years or so since its passage.[110] In contrast to America, where a visitor would be hard-pressed to find a child who cannot read or write, "the number of men, women, and children in France who know how to read or write does not exceed half of the population." More distressing still is that such ignorance extends from "children to their fathers and mothers."[111] The two French liberals held different opinions on the relationship between education and social class as well. In their pursuit of a self-ruling citizenry, the Americans "have everywhere established schools of different degrees that allow even the poorest individual to receive solid and varied instruction" in subjects ranging from geometry to geography to physical education, Laboulaye wrote with admiration.[112] While the 1833 Guizot Law did succeed in universalizing primary education across every district, its architect suggested that lessons ought to vary between localities, some of which were populated predominantly by the middle classes and others by the urban laboring classes. Consistent with his account of a thoroughly equalized France after 1848, a nation where the boundaries between a bourgeois class and all others had been blurred by revolution, Laboulaye did not draw such class-based distinctions regarding the provision of education.

It is no exaggeration to say that Laboulaye lived out his principles. He devoted his life to providing each citizen with a "perpetual education," beginning with the creation of public subscription libraries. As one of the founding members of the Société Franklin, Laboulaye encouraged the public libraries to host open lectures, on subjects as far-ranging as science, history, government, even the importance of education itself. He delivered some of these public lectures throughout France in addition to his regular academic and later administrative duties at the Collège, and his audiences included women as well as working-class men.[113] A collection of these lectures was published as *Discours populaires* in 1869.

The Popular Vote as Popular Education

Laboulaye's proposals for popular education revealed his faith in human perfectibility, or to borrow the from the favored language of other liberals, his faith in the *capacity* of individuals to develop their souls within a climate of free thought and action. But exactly how deep did Laboulaye's belief in human development run? Could engagement in politics through the act of voting exercise an educative influence over the electorate? Could voting function as a form of soulcraft? Or would the lessons in responsible political practice have to be grasped elsewhere, outside of the electoral sphere?

A number of now well-known answers to very similar questions appeared in the writings of Laboulaye's canonical British contemporary John Stuart Mill, who called for the radical expansion of the Victorian franchise by extolling the social and psychological benefits of the vote—just before putting forward his scheme for plural voting.[114] In his "Thoughts on Parliamentary Reform" (1859) as in his *Considerations on Representative Government* (1861), Mill contended that the act of voting expands the moral and intellectual faculties of those who engage in it. Laboulaye did not share Mill's confidence in the ennobling effects of the vote, or at least not as expressly as his English counterpart.[115] In fact, the themes that occupied Mill (and Tocqueville before him) about the individual and social utility of an expanded franchise were absent from Laboulaye's discussion of the topic. This is no doubt in part because the Frenchman had already accepted universal suffrage. Unlike Mill, who agitated for further reform in a democratizing Britain, Laboulaye had no reason to legitimate the electoral status quo for anyone but the hardline liberals who refused to accept it. More importantly, Laboulaye knew that political participation was rarely exercised under Mill's idealized conditions, in which individual minds are elevated, in the Englishman's words, "to weigh large interests and contemplations"—all within a progressive society that operates according to the principles of *On Liberty* (1859).[116]

If Mill looked forward to reaping the social rewards of universal political participation, Laboulaye surprisingly homed in on some of its most disastrous and despotic outcomes. However, he did not merely restate the Doctrinaires' objections to universal suffrage as "the destructive instrument" that displaces order with anarchy. Instead, Laboulaye warned that the franchise was easily co-opted by a centralized government, whose heads of state tended to manipulate the choices of voters rather than to expand their minds in the Millean sense. So pervasive were such acts of electoral interference in France that the subjects of the Second Empire took them "as articles of faith." The people had come to expect that the ministers would attempt to regulate the outcomes of elections—a fact that, as Laboulaye reminded his readers, would have dismayed at least one of the Restoration's prominent Ultras, who condemned such governmental meddling as "political heresy" half a century earlier.[117] In addition to compiling an official register of candidates, the imperial government circulated pamphlets and "special instructions" in the days prior to elections, intent on helping the people "discern who are their friends and who are their enemies."[118] The government recruited its nearly

116,00 civil servants to act as agents of the regime. The historian Roger Price recounts one particularly memorable story from the city of Blois, whose academic rector instructed teachers to "prove their devotion" to the state not simply by casting a vote for approved candidates but by leaning on their friends to do the same.[119] At the very least, these maneuvers on the part of the state muddied the waters that separate persuasion from compulsion.

For Laboulaye, such efforts to sway the minds of electors were emblematic of the French instinct to impose "unity of thought" from the top down. He regretted that his countrymen had not yet internalized valuable lessons about the dangers of accepting political despotism for the sake of an imagined unity. "How can we not see that . . . the world lives and advances through the diversity of opinions?" Laboulaye asked, hearkening to Constant's *Principles* with a question that also resembled some of those recently articulated by Mill across the Channel. Laboulaye not only took up the mantle of Constant as France's liberal defender of diversity. Writing also as one of liberalism's most outspoken advocates of political democracy, he tied diversity to the essence of the new democracy, the democracy after 1848.[120] Uniformity and democracy will always be at odds, he suggested. For "to believe that the will of a single power and its agents is better than the general will of society is to deny the very right of a democracy. If we do not listen to the nation, what is the point of attributing an illusory sovereignty to it?"[121] If the partisans of democracy expected it to endure, they had to call upon all citizens to lead the struggle against uniformity wherever it manifested, from the despotism of thought to the manipulation of elections. Only an enlightened citizenry, their minds opened by virtue of living day-to-day within an active and pluralist society, will produce a capable, self-sustaining, and self-governing democracy.

Conclusion

With some recent exceptions, much of Laboulaye's thought has been lost in the intellectual landscape of France's nineteenth century. His post-1848 insights were eclipsed both by the failures of the liberal July Monarchy that preceded them and by the disagreements that his own liberal cohort never exactly resolved amongst themselves. Ironically, Laboulaye once lamented that a similar intellectual "eclipse" had obscured the genius of his personal heroes, especially Benjamin Constant. He hoped to remedy the defects of the liberal present by looking back toward what he imagined as its more illustrious past, toward a tradition that incorporated not only the pluralism of Constant or the Americanism of Tocqueville but also the incomplete egalitarianism of the Doctrinaires, the foremost theorists of the social state.[122] When his work has been discussed by specialists in French history, his conclusions about liberalism and democracy are cited as evidence of liberals' "adaptations to exigency," their reluctant surrender to "the inevitable"—a regime of universal suffrage.[123] Along with his contemporaries, liberal figures such as Thiers, Barrot, and Rémusat, he represents concessions and losses, the final years of a waning political tradition in France that would soon give ground to republicanism and socialism.

This chapter has shown that most of these existing interpretations conceal the novelty and depth of Laboulaye's contributions to a debate over democracy that raged well after the institution of universal suffrage. Rather than conceding to an equalized status quo, Laboulaye folded universal suffrage into liberals' political philosophy. Along the way, he hoped to imbue the liberal party with a more spiritual purpose: to locate democracy's guarantee in the souls of its truth-seeking members rather than in the elitist institution of a limited suffrage. The goal, then, was to enlighten souls rather than to restructure elections.

Writing in the waning years of the Empire, Ernest Duvergier de Hauranne would reopen the suffrage question in search of another guarantee for a capable democracy, though he would not abandon the theme of education that ran throughout Laboulaye's work. In the spirit of Laboulaye and Tocqueville before him, Duvergier de Hauranne reasoned that France needed strong, competitive associations—a proliferation of major political parties, to be exact—to shelter the mean of a capable democracy against the extremes of mob rule on one side and absolute power on the other. By merging some familiar French liberal tropes about the "incapable" with examples gleaned from studying America's social state and Britain's electoral debates in the 1860s, Duvergier de Hauranne wrote to free the French of their skepticism toward pluralism and their antipathy toward political parties in particular. And he did so for the purpose of finally bringing liberalism and political democracy together.

5

"The Regular Representation of Opinion"

Ernest Duvergier de Hauranne and Democracy's Spirit of Party

Laboulaye's popular *Le Parti libéral* was reprinted in eight different editions in the decade following its initial publication. Even then, the author's dream of a "universal church" for liberal politics, with universal suffrage as one pillar of its newfound democratic faith, ruffled feathers within the liberal ranks. Laboulaye gave too much ground to political democracy and looked too far outside of France for his inspiration, or so some of his critics alleged. In a review of *Le Parti libéral*, the well-known linguist Antoine Isaac Silvestre de Sacy complained that Laboulaye's reverence for the United States blinded him to the republic's pathologies. Sacy was quick to remind his readers that the so-called land of liberty was also the land of "slavery and civil war." Amid his criticisms, Sacy also restated at least one of liberals' longstanding claims against political democracy. In America, "excessive political liberty is paid for by the sacrifice of personal liberty," precisely the outcome that liberals most feared for France. Sacy was unmoved by Laboulaye's Americanism. "For myself, I declare, I have not the least desire to exchange my identity as a Frenchman for that of an American."[1]

However unpalatable to certain figures within the liberal camp, the French fascination with the New World persisted well after Tocqueville's death in 1859.[2] And it was not limited to Laboulaye's writings, either. From June 1864 to February 1865, a barely twenty-one-year-old Ernest Duvergier de Hauranne (1843–77) spent eight months traveling throughout the United States in what would be the final year of the American Civil War. Across twelve entries published in *Revue des deux mondes* and given the title *Huit mois en Amérique*, he depicted a democracy under duress, its Constitution tested by secession, war, and the evils of slavery. Yet he was steadfast in his admiration for the war-torn republic. Even at its most troubled moments, American democracy shone forth as a sterling example for Second Empire

Democracy Tamed. Gianna Englert, Oxford University Press. © Oxford University Press 2024.
DOI: 10.1093/oso/9780197635315.003.0006

France, whose citizens—like Duvergier de Hauranne himself—had regrettably acquired "the habits and tastes of living under despotism."[3]

Of his numerous impressions of mid-century America, the young traveler's entries on the 1864 presidential election are the most relevant for our discussion of democracy. As he watched the two campaigns unfold with great interest, Duvergier de Hauranne reimagined how *political* democracy might take shape across the Atlantic. He would continue to propose American-inspired answers to French problems in the years following his voyage. As this chapter will argue, Duvergier de Hauranne also applied Tocqueville's (and by extension, Laboulaye's) reasoning about the merits of associations to one type of political association. And in his 1868 *La démocratie et le droit de suffrage*, he reproduced some of the arguments in defense of political parties that he first developed in the charged atmosphere of 1864 Chicago, the site of the Democratic Convention that would nominate George McClellan as its candidate.[4] The political party could be tasked with making political democracy useful, he claimed. Political parties would ensure that the many interests and opinions that circulated throughout society also received representation on the national stage, a goal he adopted from reading Victorian theorists of the franchise. Parties also provided the answer that liberals had been looking for; they would retain political capacity within a political democracy.

By celebrating the party system at all, Duvergier de Hauranne was forced to swim against the political current in France. As we learned in Chapter 1, the French harbored a lasting distrust of all things parochial and particular, which scholars have traced first to the ethos of the French Enlightenment and later to the intentions of the 1789 revolutionaries. Their distrust extended to political parties.[5] When Duvergier de Hauranne praised the party organization during the 1860s, he had to erase almost a century of mounting prejudice against it. Despite all appearances, the party was a unifying organization at its core, he insisted. It was also an obstacle to administrative centralization and despotism, a bridge between local affections and national interests, and a school for popular education, augmenting and enhancing many of the functions already performed by a free press. Above all, the party could accomplish what once seemed impossible to the Doctrinaires: to preserve the authority of the capable without denying the legitimacy of universal suffrage.

The son of Prosper Duvergier de Hauranne (1798–1881), a Doctrinaire and later an outspoken Orléanist critic of the Guizot ministry, the young Duvergier de Hauranne seemed destined to walk in Tocqueville's famed footsteps. He grew up in the company of his father's Americanist friends, imbibing their first-hand recollections of life in the New World.[6] But Ernest Duvergier de Hauranne never quite left his lasting mark on French politics or on the mid-century intellectual scene. While his entries from America were well-received by contemporaneous readers of *Revue des deux mondes*, they never rose anywhere close to the venerable status of *Democracy in America*.[7] In studies of French liberalism, he is sometimes mistaken for his more famous father, who outlived him.[8] The bibliography to Louis Girard's monograph on French liberalism, to cite one example, attributes the writings of both father and son to the elder Prosper.[9] According to Lucien Jaume, Duvergier de Hauranne's "pioneering" 1868 essay on democracy and the party had no "direct effect" on public debate.[10]

How heavily, if at all, should we weigh the insights of a forgotten Frenchman in the century's controversies over democracy? Apart from Chapter 4 on Laboulaye, the previous chapters of this book showcased the contributions of canonical liberals on the democratic question; and even Laboulaye's star continues to rise among scholars. By introducing a relatively unknown writer alongside these liberal luminaries, I do not mean to imply that Duvergier de Hauranne's reflections on the state of French democracy (or his articles on America) swayed his contemporaries. Nor do I wish to suggest that he was the sole theorist to consider the merits of the party in this period, as we will learn later in the chapter.[11] Instead, he is included here for two reasons. First, although Duvergier de Hauranne took a distinctive approach to the suffrage question, he also saw himself as a participant in the decades-long conversation that swirled around it, as an interlocutor not only with the French Doctrinaires and republicans but with British Tories and Whigs. Second, if the previous chapters foregrounded some of the disputes over a capable franchise, the present one homes in on one *institutional* solution to the dilemma of upholding political capacity and political equality together. It just so happens that this solution appeared in the forgotten writings of a fringe figure in the liberal tradition.

The first section of this chapter begins with a brief overview of Duvergier de Hauranne's essay on democracy, which was authored as a review of foreign writings on the suffrage—not from the United States, but from Victorian Britain. As he inspected debates over the French suffrage question through the lens of British democratic theory, Duvergier de Hauranne noticed the flaws in virtually every existing recommendation for designing the suffrage in his home nation, from a capable to a universal solution and everything in between. If Britain's recent successes revealed French flaws, it was America that showcased how a political democracy could be made equal, capable, and free all at the same time through its major parties. The second half of this chapter brings Duvergier de Hauranne's initial observations from America together with his thoughts on democracy and the party at home.

British Lessons for French Democracy

Having made a (modest) name for himself with the publication of *Huit mois en Amérique* in 1864–5, Duvergier turned to Britain to inform his reflections on the suffrage.[12] He was certainly not the only French writer to look across the Channel in this period. The philosopher and political economist Charles Dupont-White translated John Stuart Mill's *On Liberty* and *Considerations on Representative Government* in 1860 and 1862 respectively, and as other scholars have shown, the publication of Mill's seminal political works in French prompted a flurry of responses.[13] Confronted with the novelty of Mill's arguments, his French readers contemplated the (in)justices of the working-class vote, the tyranny of the numerical majority, and the need to preserve minority voices in a majoritarian system. Some were so emboldened by Mill's insights that they called for a wholesale retooling of the electoral system. Mill stayed apprised of the conversations that his writings generated among his neighbors, occasionally weighing in from afar.[14]

Duvergier de Hauranne situated his 1868 essay on the right to vote among these recent receptions of Mill's democratic theory. He introduced the first installment of his *De la démocratie et le droit de suffrage* as a review essay of recent publications by Mill, Thomas Hare, James Lorimer, and Henry George Grey, the Third Earl Grey. By the second installment, however, it became clear that Duvergier de Hauranne's essay was far more than a book review. Its author used the writings of British theorists to reframe the debate over democracy for France's liberals, drawing on Britain's democratic and radical traditions to do so.[15] Britain's 1867 Reform Act rekindled his interest in the suffrage at home. Championed by the Conservative government of Lord Derby and Benjamin Disraeli, the Act extended the franchise to all householders in the boroughs, to lodgers who could pay 10 pounds rent, and to urban workers who met a reduced property requirement. It roughly doubled the size of the meager electorate; a mere 35–40 percent of adult men held the right to vote even after its passage. Nonetheless, the Act initiated the country's long-term shift toward political democracy, even if it was not exactly "democratic" in its intention.[16] As one historian put it, the 1867 Act sparked "the most unintentional revolution in the history of British politics."[17]

To Duvergier de Hauranne, the passage of the Reform Act was an occasion to scrutinize Britain's theories of the suffrage vis-à-vis its legislative practices, and to compare both with recent happenings in France.[18] As he studied the Act alongside tracts by some of Britain's eminent political writers, Duvergier de Hauranne pressed the French to reevaluate their assumptions about the vote, many of which had become, to borrow a Millean phrase, nothing more than dead dogma. Like those "brave persons who sing to give themselves courage while walking in darkness," citizens of the Second Empire had come to parrot state officials who declared that the nation was free because its suffrage was universal and its elections frequent. The truth, as Duvergier understood it, was more distressing. "We do not know where we are going," he lamented, "and no one dares to light the way."[19] His sentiments mirrored Laboulaye's from five years earlier and Constant's from the early part of the century. When citizens begin to equate liberty solely with the right to vote, they are destined to lose it, or so all of these figures argued in different ways and in different contexts.[20] Duvergier de Hauranne heaped another warning upon those put forward by his predecessors, and his words showcase the impact of Mill's writings on the Continent. Without open debate about the fundamental questions of freedom and equality, the suffrage question among them, "the flame of thought has come to languish and to be extinguished in the choking air."[21]

Duvergier de Hauranne accused both state officials and spokesmen for the liberal opposition of lapsing into unthinking rhetoric when it came to the suffrage.[22] Officials continued to reassure the public by reciting the same empty lines about combining universal popular participation with beneficent power in the person of Napoleon III. Liberals were just as guilty of ignoring reality. Well into the 1860s, many of them spurned universal suffrage without offering a viable alternative in its place. While generally critical of the Empire, Duvergier de Hauranne also chastised his fellow liberals for their tired theories and weak attacks on political democracy. His analyses were familiarly Tocquevillean. In the opening pages to *Democracy in America* in 1835, Tocqueville advised his cautious, antidemocratic comrades to make democracy "useful to humankind." In the same vein, Duvergier de Hauranne now recommended that liberals strive to see the advantages in universal suffrage. "Instead of vainly groaning over the defects of universal suffrage," he counseled, "instead of looking for reasons to despair about our future and for pretexts to abandon our affairs, let us learn what this form of the suffrage is worth, which conditions are required for its successful practice, and how we might use it so as to take advantage of it."[23] In this passage at least, Duvergier de Hauranne stopped short of "sincerely embracing" universal suffrage as part of the liberal platform, as Laboulaye had. All the same, he did indicate that universal suffrage was "worth" something and that liberals could recognize its value—all without giving in to aimless, disordered politics.

On this score, Duvergier de Hauranne believed that the French had much to gain from studying the British debate over political democracy and its alternatives. There was a reason why French tracts and treatises on the vote, Left, Right and Center, had been so unsatisfying across since the days of the Revolution, he asserted. Their authors were consumed with attaining "metaphysical perfection" instead of practical results.[24] Duvergier de Hauranne no doubt had Guizot, his father's liberal ally-turned-enemy, in mind when he denounced the "reckless metaphysics" that motivated French theorists of the vote.[25] Liberals, for their part, spent their time bemoaning the *abstract* defects of universal suffrage instead of looking ahead to its practical results. The radical democrats were no better. Since they upheld universal suffrage on the grounds of human personhood and abstract equality, they fixed their gaze on the same "metaphysical heights" as their capacitarian rivals.[26]

The British, by contrast, tended to avoid abstractions. They deliberated as if "each social theory is at the same time a political act . . . when [they] want to judge a new idea, the first and most important question they ask is not whether it is in line with certain abstract doctrines, but how it works and what the positive results will be."[27] Britain's "sage" electoral reforms revealed its people's penchant for practicality.[28] Unlike the French, especially the metaphysically minded Guizot, the British were not wedded to any "symmetrical or beautiful" electoral arrangements. Nor did they treat electoral systems as "works of art." Instead, they considered the consequences of any given theory. According to Duvergier de Hauranne, this attitude suffused the Victorians' written works as well as their parliamentary debates.[29] If a broader suffrage was to be preferred, as with the Second Reform Act, it was because the British predicted that such an arrangement would advance liberty and promote utility. French writings therefore paled in comparison to their British counterparts. In an evident critique of everyone from Guizot to Alletz and even to Laboulaye, Duvergier de Hauranne declared that "our modern political literature has nothing to compare either to genius treatises of Mr. Stuart Mill on representative government, nor to the solid work of Mr. Hare on the representation of minorities, nor to the impartial exposition of principles of Professor Lorimer on the right of suffrage."[30]

Duvergier de Hauranne claimed that such prudence also crossed party divides across the Channel. Referring to the debates surrounding the Reform Bill, he marveled at how the Whigs, Tories, Radicals, and Conservatives could have all taken a common, consequentialist approach to the issue of an extended franchise.[31] Very much unlike their French neighbors, the English could all agree that the best government is not one that "satisfies either aristocratic or democratic theories; it is the one that best guarantees respect for private rights and public freedoms, that which most favors the progress of well-being and enlightenment."[32] Duvergier de Hauranne's version of British history glossed over the contentious constitutional debates over the vote, which had begun at least fifteen years before the Act's passage and stalled at least seven previous attempts to expand the franchise.[33] But it was meant to illustrate a specific point. Britain's success raised the possibility that party politics could also be productive politics, a conclusion that, as we will see, would have struck Duvergier de Hauranne's French readers as improbable.

While Duvergier de Hauranne contrasted the reasonable assumptions that drove British politics with the defects of French political theory, he also claimed that the English approach was not as foreign as it may seem.[34] If one looks closely enough, the Victorian democrats should look quite familiar. "Do we dare to say it finally? They are *only doctrinaires of a new species*," he declared, before extending this strange comparison further. "This name, which has introduced so many quarrels among us and is so repugnant to French democracy, could apply today to men who bear the flag of equality in England."[35] This point is striking, as it was intended to be. What could England's partisans of political equality possibly have in common with the French Doctrinaires, the guardians of the new aristocracy? Were not the Doctrinaires in fact the most guilty of promoting a "reckless metaphysics" when it came to regulating the vote? Why link present-day defenses of political democracy to, of all traditions, Doctrinaire liberalism, a name that by the author's own admission stirred so many repugnant feelings in both countries?

The two schools represent opposite extremes: universal suffrage versus elitism, complete political equality versus narrow political capacity. And still, Duvergier de Hauranne deftly claimed to have walked on the common ground between them. Both British democrats and French Doctrinaires were committed to representative government as the best possible regime type, and both aimed to govern according to the standards of reason, truth, and justice.[36] One needed only to study the writings of the protean John Stuart Mill for evidence of these similarities, since Mill himself upheld both equality and rationality as the principles of representative government and joined parts of the theories of Tocqueville and Guizot.[37] Even the so-called irresolvable tensions between democrats and Doctrinaires seem to disappear when viewed in a different light. For one, English democrats were not nearly as devoted to the doctrine of popular sovereignty as their French detractors assumed. "They are less attached to the sovereignty of the people than to the people's freedom and happiness, which they do not separate from justice and reason," those same standards that informed Guizot's entire theory of sovereignty. Insofar as any theorist in England venerated popular sovereignty, it was because he saw the principle as "an expression of justice and a necessary condition of freedom," rather than a political good in itself.[38] On this reading, the Victorian democrats bore a greater resemblance to Guizot than to Rousseau.

With this comparison, Duvergier de Hauranne sought to close the gap between France's capacitarian past and Britain's more democratic present. His goal was also to make the foreign more familiar or at least more acceptable to his French readers.[39] If the principles of reason and justice could support an extended franchise elsewhere, then they might be marshaled to reinforce the status quo of universal suffrage at home. In other words, accepting universal suffrage did not have to mean abandoning recognizably liberal values, reason and justice the first among them. Nor did it require the remaining Doctrinaires or capacitarian liberals of any kind to forsake their commitments to a rational and just representative government.[40] Put otherwise: if even the most intransigent, indeed the most "Doctrinaire" principles could lead to democratic conclusions, then there was no reason that liberals of the 1860s could not also see the wisdom and worth in universal suffrage.[41]

By citing Mill as an authority who had one foot in each of the two schools, Duvergier de Hauranne laid out several arguments that both groups could find favorable. Both English democrats and French capacitarian liberals were confident that "a government of intelligence and energy" would frustrate the ambitions of a despot, he began, although they disagreed about where such intelligence and energy would originate.[42] Liberals located intelligence in a capable electorate; democrats believed that such intelligence would arise from within the electoral process, and to buttress their arguments for universal suffrage, they claimed that the experience of voting elevates the intellect and the moral sense of *every* citizen. From the other side, it was no surprise that liberals distrusted political democracy and popular sovereignty, which—as Constant first recognized and Duvergier de Hauranne later granted—often functioned as a "mask for dictatorship and a pretext for the destruction of liberties." But insofar as adherents of both schools upheld representative government as the "instrument of progress, intelligence, morality, and dignity," they must all "hope that the benefits of this government will spread among the popular classes," and with time, "recognize the great and obvious advantage for a free people to initiate the crowd of citizens into the knowledge and practice of liberty."[43] Duvergier de Hauranne thus wished to erase the Doctrinaires' hardline distinction between a representative government and a political democracy. Against Guizot, who took great pains to isolate one from the other, Duvergier de Hauranne claimed that liberals' reverence for representative government should lead toward a democratic franchise. "Whether they admit it or disguise it, true liberals [*les vrais libéraux*], if they remain consistent, are at the same time the surest friends of modern democracy."[44] Liberals did not have to sacrifice their identity to admit as much. Capacity should be retained even under universal suffrage, Duvergier de Hauranne would go on to affirm, but *only* because it promotes the public good and achieves positive results for the whole people.

This consequentialist outlook was not the only mark of British influence on Duvergier de Hauranne's work. He adopted his view of representation from the English reformers, who held that the legislative assembly ought to "mirror" the existing society, without regard for any presumed capacity on the part of its voters or its representatives.[45] Guizot once rejected a similar proposal to ensure that the assembly accurately reflected the composition of French society. He reasoned that since France had a *single* social state—the new democracy—it made no sense to insist that a multitude of classes and contingents should receive representation in the Chamber.[46] As he imported the perspective of British authors to France in the 1860s, Duvergier de Hauranne hoped to resurrect a version of the model of descriptive representation that Guizot and the capacitarian liberals were quick to discard twenty years earlier. But first, he had to revisit some of the issues that haunted liberals since they first presented their theory of a capable suffrage.

Political Democracy and Descriptive Representation

At some moments in his essay on democracy, Duvergier de Hauranne sounds like a reluctant democrat, who begrudgingly accepted the reality of universal suffrage. At others, and despite what he concluded about France's "true liberalism" and its relationship to democracy, he claimed that a restricted suffrage could be compatible with a free government and even with what he called a "true democracy." Recognizable liberal tropes resurfaced in his reflections on universal suffrage. Democracy may degenerate into the rule of "an ignorant and inexperienced mob," "the undisciplined militia," and "the illiterate."[47] As one of the few Anglophone interpreters to mention Duvergier de Hauranne at all, Kahan hears plenty of this "old liberal rhetoric" across the text's two halves.[48] As such, Kahan appreciates the originality of the young Frenchman's solution to an incapable democracy (the political party) but does not believe that the thinker sheds any new diagnostic light on that problem to begin with.[49]

Yet, even as he restated these antidemocratic tropes, Duvergier de Hauranne was quick to expose the falsehoods behind them. In fact, he was open about his intention to disentangle political democracy from the violence and anarchy that liberals so often attached to it. "We want to show that popular government does not lead invariably to despotism or to anarchy," he wrote without reservation, immediately after placing his work in the same liberal democratic tradition as Tocqueville's.[50] Most of the problems that liberals attributed to democracy were actually problems of prematurity—of sweeping changes enacted too soon, well before the dust of revolution had settled.[51] He thus relaunched some of the standing critiques of political capacity at his fellow liberals. Overall, he was an ambivalent player in the clash between a capable and a universal suffrage. Even amid his back-and-forth on the two schemes, Duvergier de Hauranne was adamant that capacity could indeed be made useful to democracy, though not on its original foundations as a liberal limit on the electorate.

This conclusion rested on two arguments. First, the problems that plagued capacitarian arguments as early as the Restoration had gone unresolved even into the Second Empire.[52] No one, Duvergier de Hauranne maintained, had settled those issues raised long ago both by liberals' political enemies and their allies alike. Who, after all, were "the capable"? How could capacity in the individual be measured and codified in the electoral law? If political participation was not a natural, universal right, then what exactly was it? The success of England's recent electoral reform revealed the flaws in liberals' timeworn responses. Second, universal suffrage was there to stay in France. It had become "one of the fundamental laws of French society."[53] Liberals' sustained opposition to it, coupled with their refusal to answer basic questions of their own making, necessitated a new approach, one that included capacity but had to be redesigned for Duvergier de Hauranne's present moment.

Building a new edifice for capacity required dismantling the old at its weakest points. To take one example, Duvergier de Hauranne accused the Doctrinaires of upholding an "illogical" and "fragile distinction" between civil rights and the privilege of the vote.[54] On what basis can a society decide who is worthy to bear that privilege of voting, and who (or which body) confers the title of *électeur*? Guizot gestured at these same issues in his Restoration lectures on European history when he tried to fortify his nascent theory of political capacity against the Ultras' onslaught. That those questions still lingered forty years later was telling. For Duvergier de Hauranne, it was further evidence of the insufficiencies and limitations that characterized French deliberations over the suffrage (especially when compared with Britain) and beset the capacitarian position in particular. Duvergier de Hauranne summarized the contradiction at the very center of liberals' capacitarian logic: "What indeed becomes of the right to be well-governed, if we do not give the people the right to choose who will govern them?"[55]

Such failures to address the suffrage question were not unique either to French liberals in general or to the capacitarian liberals in particular. The entire nation failed to make headway on the suffrage because its sharpest minds—Left and Right, liberal, socialist, republican, legitimist, and otherwise—misunderstood the basis of their dispute over democracy. Staunchly committed to their tidy and beautiful theories, each side arranged its perfect pattern for the suffrage, whether as a pure democracy (Billiard), an electorate of proprietors (Constant), a capacitarian suffrage (Guizot), or a middle-class franchise (Alletz), to name just a few. Those men who emerged as the "democrats of the last hour" were therefore just as *doctrinaire*—that is, just as inflexible—as Royer-Collard and Guizot. "These men do not want to suffer to see the slightest qualification placed on that sacred right," he noted, even if it became obvious that the public good could benefit as a result of such qualifications and limits.[56]

At the same time, the stalwarts of each view overlooked what Duvergier de Hauranne, following the path first trodden by British theorists of the vote, identified as the true purpose of any modern electoral system: to represent society in all of its complexity.

> The ideal of a system of suffrage (if it is permissible to join two words that may balk at being placed together), the ideal of a system of perfect representation is neither a pure democracy nor the government of intelligence, neither a restricted suffrage of any sort, nor even universal suffrage; it is the form of representation where each of the existences and each of the forces of society would obtain a part of power exactly proportional to its value.[57]

With this clarifying claim, Duvergier de Hauranne hoped to shift the terms of the suffrage debate in France. Until his countrymen understood that the purpose of *any* suffrage scheme was to reflect society in the legislative assembly, they were doomed to chase after chimerical theories of perfect electoral design. Instead of pursuing either a restricted or a universal suffrage, the French needed to work backwards, beginning from the *end* to represent their diverse social state.

For Duvergier de Hauranne, it came as no surprise that this theory of representation originated with the utility-minded English, who did not begin with imagined electoral arrangements but with observable political consequences. As Greg Conti has shown in rich detail, the Victorian-era controversies about organizing the suffrage revolved around the issue of how best to represent society's component parts in Parliament.[58] Texts as varied in their tone and substance as Mill's *Considerations on Representative Government*, Hare's *The Election of Representatives*, and Lorimer's *Constitutionalism of the Future* all tackled the matter of which groups and interests should be represented, to what degree, and by which means.[59] Whether they proposed a varied, plural, or graduated scheme for the suffrages, the exemplars of this British school of "mirror theory" tended to agree that the franchise was but the electoral mechanism to reach a higher representative end.[60] For Duvergier de Hauranne, it was the Scottish jurist Lorimer who captured the proper relationship between the goal of representation and the electoral mechanisms to reach it: "a perfect representative system would be one which, so to speak, photographed society—the function of the suffrage corresponding to that of a camera."[61] Although this image was quite different from any of those that captured the attention of France's liberals earlier in the century (with Constant as a possible exception), Duvergier de Hauranne once again emphasized that English ways were not wholly unfamiliar.[62] At least two of the theorists he cited, Hare and Mill, were profoundly influenced by Guizot. They, too, worried about safeguarding the opinions of an intelligent minority and cited Guizot as their authority, bringing England's mid-century democratic theory full circle to Doctrinaire liberalism, though with some obvious modifications.[63] Duvergier de Hauranne traced another connection between the two philosophies, though he had to stretch the truth in order to bring them into close proximity. So deeply engrained was the principle of descriptive representation that one could find it even in the opinions of the notorious Guizot, he insisted, before carefully excerpting a single line from the infamous Doctrinaire:

> "the aim of representative government," says Guizot, "is to publicly expose, in the face of great interests, the diverse opinions that share in society." These simple words contain more true democratic spirit than all of the subtleties that are fashionable among the official panegyrists of democracy.[64]

As we know from earlier chapters, this quotation paints not only an incomplete but an inaccurate picture of Guizot on representation. The Doctrinaire argued that reason alone, rather than opinions of any kind, merited a place in representative government. It is also a curiosity that Duvergier de Hauranne cited Guizot instead of Constant, who—as we learned in Chapter 1—did advance an argument about social diversity and political representation years before the Victorians would formulate their ideas about a mirroring Parliament. But Duvergier de Hauranne seemed to have been unaware of Constant's contributions. Either that, or his selective and strange reception of the Doctrinaire perspective was a deliberate attempt to bridge two disparate traditions. If Duvergier de Hauranne was correct, then social or descriptive representation was not a novel principle with which to upend the entire French electoral system. It was a *lost* one, a goal for representative government that the French had long abandoned (whether willfully or not) in their single-minded aim to institute an "ideal" suffrage scheme.

In fact, the imperative to represent society had been obscured by the seemingly never-ending controversies over the suffrage question. For Duvergier de Hauranne, the French had grown preoccupied with the form that their electorate would take, since they believed that its composition held the key to realizing a rational, just, or at least competent representative government. This was one of the original lines of defense for a capable franchise: by restricting the right to vote to those with the demonstrated intellect, independence, and social sense for public life, only the most capable statesmen would ascend to the positions of legislative power. Duvergier de Hauranne agreed that an intelligent and just government was most likely to uphold the freedoms of the individual, and he did not wish to discount the valuable role played by political capacity in a democracy. In his view, however, the French had pursued ineffectual means to reach this rather sensible end. In the vein of Constant, Tocqueville, and Laboulaye, Duvergier de Hauranne insisted that the *extent* of the suffrage by itself had little bearing on freedom. In light of his preference for British-style practicality, he took his version of the argument in a new direction:

> The question of whether the electoral law will have limits or if all citizens will be called to exercise it with their own hands will undoubtedly be of great importance from the point of view of political doctrine; *but the interest in it is mediocre for the practice of freedom.* There are fortunate countries where the most admirable equality reigns, and which, despite the right to suffrage, the people are not their own masters. The citizen of a free country has many other ways of making his influence felt in daily affairs than in going to the ballot box ... If political life were limited to the accomplishment of these formalities, it would not be worth preserving.[65]

Immediately after distinguishing political doctrines from the actual practices of freedom, Duvergier de Hauranne likened his nation's almost single-minded focus on the suffrage to the spiritual poverty of the individual who participates exclusively in the outward, observable rituals of "all serious religions." With nations as well as individuals, one should not confuse external actions for internal grace—or an enfranchised people for a free one.[66]

Once again, liberals were especially guilty of clinging to the wrong questions. Since the French had forgotten the real purpose behind electoral design—to represent society—their deliberations over the extent of the suffrage had become rather aimless. The suffrage question was in fact a dead question, Duvergier suggested, not because the Empire had resolved it to anyone's satisfaction, but because the right to vote could not *practically* be revoked from anyone who once had a taste of its exercise. When Duvergier called universal suffrage a "fundamental law," he implied that it had become as ironclad in the minds of the French people as in their written constitution, and that it would become a fundamental law elsewhere too. Britain's Reform Act, to take one example, was but a waystation on the road to universal suffrage. And in conveying this point, Duvergier de Hauranne sounded oddly like Guizot from the time of the Restoration: "the sole claim of [the Act's] authors is to bring the [electoral] system into harmony with the present state of society. When the time comes, the enlightened classes, in whose hands power resides, will know how to yield to the legitimate demands of the people."[67]

Even so, Duvergier de Hauranne maintained that there were certain facts about human beings that even the most fervent egalitarians could not deny. In a series of lines that could have been uttered by Guizot or Royer-Collard, he wrote to advise those countries that had not yet established universal suffrage. But he did so to remind them that *inequality* was nature's law. For any nation that may be considering the prospect of electoral reform, "the right of suffrage is never granted to classes which have not yet demanded it or which cannot enforce it. . . . The deaf and the blind also have the right to see and hear, and when their ailments are not incurable, nothing should be spared to cure them. This is not to say that humanity or justice demands that we consult the blind about colors and that we ask the deaf their opinions about music." It is the same with nations, he decided, before divulging his capacitarian sympathies. "The electoral right should be reserved for those who are able to understand it."[68] At first blush, this sounds like another attempt to resuscitate liberals' controversial claims about the incapable many, the same claims that Duvergier de Hauranne accused his forebears of failing to justify. But incapacity was for the most part a "curable" affliction.[69] And in contrast to the Doctrinaires, Duvergier de Hauranne placed the responsibility for finding its "cure"—for transforming an incapable mob into a capable electorate—squarely on the powerful. "The enlightened classes must make efforts to hasten this gradual emancipation, and they fail in their first duties when they abuse the type of tutelage entrusted to them in order to delay the education of the people in order to prolong the duration of their own power."[70] Without mentioning Guizot by name, it is clear how Duvergier de Hauranne would have evaluated the Doctrinaire's suggestion to vary primary school lessons for each district and for pupils in each social class. To his eyes, it would be another attempt on the part of the enlightened to "delay" popular education out of an interest to preserve existing hierarchies.

Despite his contention that the French had already spent too much time ruminating over the suffrage, Duvergier de Hauranne put forth two teachings of his own about the matter. First, those countries that did not have universal suffrage would no doubt one day institute it, since it was inevitably the "last stage in the progress of our political laws."[71] Not only that, but it was incumbent upon the enlightened classes, the holders of political power, to adjust their electoral laws to meet the capacities of the people (as Guizot once emphasized) *and* to raise the general level of education and morality. Second, in countries where universal suffrage had already become a fundamental and irrevocable law, it was futile to try to revert to an older, outdated electoral scheme. "Without a doubt the future belongs to democracy, without a doubt the progress which brings it is similar to the movement of a stone which falls and which is always accelerating in its fall," he concluded, equating the progress of democracy with the law of gravity and providing the French with a new image to replace their "democratic torrent" first developed in the 1820s. Nevertheless, he agonized over some of the same questions that troubled his liberal forebears: "Does this mean that this so-called progress is really nothing but *décadence*? Does this mean that modern civilization is the ruin of freedom? Does this mean that it must swallow up all superior individuality in the bosom of an anonymous and tyrannical multitude, and that it must bend all independence under the implacable yoke of this 'monster with a thousand heads'?"[72] In the end, and unlike his more famous predecessors, he refused to fuel such "senile fears" about democracy as mere mob rule.[73] This was because he had already discovered democracy's "*génie tutélaire*," its institutional guardian against the tyranny and ignorance of the multitude. As he learned in America, democracy's security lay in its political parties.

The Despotism of the Party Spirit

As Duvergier de Hauranne knew full well, any apology for the party organization in France would have to confront a long legacy of hostility toward it, the full force of which became apparent in the aftermath of the Revolution of 1789. If the France remade by the Revolution was to authorize the unanimity or generality embodied in the whole people, it had to avoid particularity in all its forms, from civic associations to trade unions.[74] This attitude was reflected both in the Revolutionary laws against associations and *corps intermédiaires*, and in the philosophical impulse toward uniformity that Constant confronted in his own time. As Rosanvallon framed it, "any organization that walled individuals off from one another" was a potential cradle of discord, and this included political parties.[75] The term *parti* thus evoked factionalism in the early part of the century.[76] In 1815, Royer-Collard alerted his fellow deputies that "the violent spirit of party [is] forming among us." For Royer-Collard, a member of the Doctrinaire cohort himself, the partisan spirit was nonetheless contrary to the impartiality of the French legislators, who traditionally refused to judge an issue on the basis of ideological affiliation and so could be persuaded by deliberation and compelling oratory.[77] The spirit of party befitting England, Royer-Collard told his audience, had no place in France.[78]

The French quest for national unity, so compelling even in Constant's lifetime, arguably reached its apex under the Second Empire, which modeled itself as a regime that transcended all particular loyalties, parties included. If it were not for the imperial state, in fact, the entire republic would have been destroyed in the "disastrous" clash between parties, or so Napoleon III alleged:

> [The people] knows that in 1852, society would have rushed to disaster, because every party was willing to risk being shipwrecked in the hope of hoisting its flag over the debris that floated. I am glad to have been able to save the ship and hoist the national flag. I admit, though, like the Emperor [Napoleon I], I have conquests to make. I want, like him, to work for the conciliation of dissident parties.[79]

Napoleon III preyed on the fear of party discord to reinforce his authority as emperor. It was only natural that supremacy should lie in the executive, who was the elect of the *entire* nation, rather than with the assembly, he claimed. The deputies, after all, represented merely a multitude of "local intrigues, rather than the expression of a general ideal."[80]

It is necessary to clarify the meaning of the party [*parti*] in this period, since nineteenth-century parties barely resembled their twentieth-century inheritors. During the Restoration, deputies with shared interests sat together in sections of the Chamber, but they cast their votes as individuals without a common platform. Throughout much of the century, "parties" lacked the centralized organizational apparatus that would merge national and local issues and mobilize voters—which should come as no surprise given the small size of the French electorate until 1848.[81] Laboulaye's noble *le parti libéral* lacked the administrative mechanisms of the modern party, and as we will recall, it sorely needed to reestablish itself on a common set of values. The modern party organization as we have come to know it emerged slowly between the end of the nineteenth and the early twentieth centuries. The historian Raymond Huard locates the earliest signs of the modern party organization in the liberalizing political climate of the 1860s, just as Duvergier de Hauranne was formulating his arguments.[82] But when the French condemned "the spirit of party" in roughly the century after the Revolution, they were attacking an institution that was a mere shell of what it would become.[83]

The Doctrinaires shared this antipathy toward party government, although their particular brand of resistance went hand-in-hand with their commitment to political capacity. Alongside Royer-Collard, who decried parties as the malignant sources of "partiality," Guizot expressed disdain for party politics in his Restoration lectures, in which he contrasted the "despotism of party spirit" with a healthy representative body comprised of capable representatives. For the representative was capable *precisely because* he was free from another's opinions; he was neither a mouthpiece for the regime nor for a more influential "master," in whatever form that mastery might take. By contrast, the party spirit was synonymous with intellectual dependence, or a willingness to follow the dictates of a given ideology regardless of its relationship to reason or justice. Guizot cautioned that the "despotism of party spirit is no better than any other despotism, and all good legislation should tend to preserve citizens from its sway."[84] Even the most capable electors and deputies were prone to those outside, "reason-conquering" influences that threatened to overtake capacity. Among these influences, Guizot named the "party spirit" among the most pernicious, since he thought that political allegiances tended to have the greatest hold over the human mind.[85]

Although Duvergier de Hauranne defended the party institution against its detractors, he did share some of his fellow citizens' reservations about the nation's existing parties. To be more precise, he disparaged those weak alliances that operated under the banner of *parti*, and which had all of the disadvantages of the obstinate and partial party spirit that the Doctrinaires decried with none of the benefits of a political association. "What is called a party," he specified in 1868, "is not a meeting of honest men guided by principles and by common convictions, it is a band of adventurers, assembled by chance under the same banner and held together by their interests more than by their opinions."[86] These words bring to mind Tocqueville's blistering appraisals of both the July Monarchy in France and the "small parties" that "swarm" Jacksonian America, all of which chased after petty interests instead of furthering the common good.[87] While recognizably Tocquevillean, Duvergier de Hauranne's disapproval was also rooted in the vision of diverse, descriptive representation that he adopted from his British counterparts. At their worst, parties reinforce the human tendency toward factionalism, and they structure a legislature that does not accurately represent the entire nation but only the views of the majority or of the minority faction in power.[88] And when a government falls prey to factionalism, a demagogue will follow closely behind.

Even so, Duvergier de Hauranne believed that much of the French aversion toward political parties was misdirected. It was one outgrowth of their dangerous attachment to administrative centralization. When the words "authority" and "centralization" bear "so great a charm . . . where there is so little defiance against the influence of government over citizens, we think we have everything to fear from the citizens' influence on one other. We would like to annihilate all local or private influences unless they occur under administrative protection or under an official character."[89] Because of this aversion to all things intermediary and parochial, the party included, Duvergier de Hauranne despaired that "secrecy and solitude [have become] the condition of our independence" with the state as the "jailer" of a cave in which each citizen lives in isolation.[90] There was good reason to disapprove of those "bands of adventurers" that masqueraded as political parties. But the entire institution could not be dismissed *tout court*.

We can think of Duvergier de Hauranne's praise of parties as a form of resistance against the totalizing influence of a centralized state and a defense of intermediary associations against administrative despotism. But if parties were also to function as sites of political resistance, they had to be distinguished from those interest-driven alliances that bore the name "party" in nineteenth-century France. His plan for major parties was aspirational, and it reflected his deep admiration for American democracy.

The Party in American Democracy

Just as Britain's slow road toward democracy inspired Duvergier de Hauranne to pose the suffrage question anew to his French contemporaries, his observations of American politics showed him the potentials of the party as a political association. Yet when he landed in New York Harbor in 1864, he carried many of the characteristically French prejudices against the party with him. In an entry dated July 1864, one month after his arrival, he chastised the Americans for bestowing political power on party "intriguers and underlings" rather than esteemed statesmen.[91] As a guest at the Chicago Democratic Convention in late August, he witnessed a partisan spectacle that would have shaken any Frenchman. To his dismay, the convention resembled "a committee of nine hundred obviously formed to overthrow the administration, an electoral meeting to usurp the attributes of the sovereign assembly that dare to propose its chosen candidate in place of the government . . . a legalized rebellion supported by half of the citizens."[92] Moreover, the party appeared to be another source of division in a country that desperately needed to preserve any remaining shreds of unity. As the critical presidential election drew near, he predicted that "the parties will bluster and lock horns [and] during this time, the general welfare will be forgotten."[93]

But it would not take long for Duvergier de Hauranne to see the good in this bizarre and divisive association. Far from the "usurpative" and revolutionary committee of "intrigue" he first described, the party was a vehicle for representing minority opinions. It operated much like a "State within a State," that is, a well-organized, public alternative to the current administration— the very kind of intermediary political body that would have been seen as a danger to the uniformity of the French state.[94] As Duvergier de Hauranne would soon note, however, the party's particularity was among its greatest virtues. For what would have been condemned as a "seditious conspiracy" in France was actually "the free and regular representation of one the great bodies of opinion to be found in the country," an associational safeguard against the tyranny of the majority. There is "no undertaking . . . whether a horse-race or a presidential election, that is not organized from the start as a political body," he continued, and thus no opinion that is denied its place in public debate.[95]

Paradoxically, such a partial institution was also one of the surest supports for national unity. What was so remarkable about American parties was their ability to stitch together local, state, and federal interests. Unlike the French, the Americans accepted (perhaps as early as James Madison in *The Federalist Papers*) that the "passions and interests of local factions" were permanent and ineradicable features of social life. Instead of extinguishing those passions, they sought to tether them to "a set of principles common to all." Each party highlights national issues as its "rallying point," pulls an array of local interests, desires, and passions into its orbit, and thus ties "the election of the executive to that of police chief or street cleaner."[96] Because of their party organizations, Americans have come to believe that "there is no issue, so local, so private, that it is not connected with the great political and constitutional questions which divide the nation."[97] In other words, the Americans drew no clear-cut distinctions between the local and the federal, or indeed the purely private and the public. It is remarkable that a foreign visitor to the United States in 1864 could have found harmony anywhere. But out of their divided allegiances, the Americans fostered "a unity more complete than under the most absolute despot" because their party system embraces the diversity of human opinions and interests within a single nation.[98] Of course, he was limiting his observations to the political temperature in the North. In the weeks following Lincoln's re-election, Duvergier de Hauranne also marveled at the sense of calmness that spread among a population that had only days earlier been "on the verge of tearing itself to pieces" but which now largely conceded the legitimacy of a president chosen by the people. For the two parties had already brought their disagreements into "the open air" via the free press and in their conventions. Although their quarrels may have interrupted day-to-day democratic life with moments of incivility and vulgarity, Duvergier de Hauranne concluded that parties were less likely to ignite the kind of revolutions that "paralyze a nation with surprise and shock," rendering it a "half-dazed captive of the next dictator who comes along."[99]

The party held the "whole secret" behind pairing liberty with ordered unity, he decided then. "What is this *génie tutélaire* that guards democracy?" he asked, "To what does she owe this spirit of order, perseverance, and wisdom, which her friends themselves have never counted among her virtues? She owes it to her party organizations."[100] This was the teaching that Duvergier de Hauranne would try to convey to his countrymen in the waning years of the Empire.[101] "There is only one way to ensure peace within a democratic society," he explained to his French readers in 1868. "That is to allow and to encourage the formation of major political parties."[102]

French Democracy and the Political Party

However penetrating his insights were, Duvergier de Hauranne was not the first of his countrymen to comment on the virtues of the party. The most renowned Frenchman to set foot on American soil, Alexis de Tocqueville, also appreciated the pivotal role played by America's parties in stabilizing her democracy. As he denounced the indolence of the July Monarchy in the 1840s, Tocqueville pled for the return of his own country's "great parties," or those that took sides in the "Great Debate" between aristocracy and democracy during the Bourbon Restoration. Their loss, he wrote, was both a cause and a consequence of the bourgeois political uniformity that infected France in the mid part of the century, for "where the laws have narrowly confined the exercise of all political rights within a single class . . . one can hardly expect to find true parties, that is to say, either variety, movement, fecundity, or life."[103] This lament accompanied his call to extend political rights to the laboring classes, which we examined in detail in Chapter 3. Yet in that same speech, Tocqueville could define great parties only in terms of their absence. Political life without them amounted to "morbid torpor" and a national "slumber." The closest he came to a definition was by association, juxtaposing "public agitations" and civic energy with the return of "great parties" to endorse the lawful, formal incorporation of the workers into politics. The great party was different in kind from the parliamentary "parties" of small ideas, petty interests, and personal intrigue that quibbled with one another during the 1840s.[104] It replaced egoism with principle and material wants with general ideas. Loyal to "ideas and not to men," the great parties that Tocqueville romanticized were meant to reawaken a slumbering population.[105]

Tocqueville's concept of great parties was tied to the regime's failures he witnessed and to the revolutionary violence he anticipated. When he called for the revival of "great parties" in 1848, he repeated some of the cautious words he first used to characterize American parties in the 1835 volume of *DA*. It was there that he wrote of the party as a "a danger opposed to another danger more to be feared" and called it one of democracy's "necessary evils."[106] In France during the 1840s, that "greater danger" came from the insular, complacent bourgeoisie who controlled the government during the July Monarchy.[107] Just as Tocqueville's comments on parties emerged in response to the bourgeois "plutocracy" that infiltrated the French state, Duvergier de Hauranne's grew in reaction to the "unifying" promise of Napoleon III's imperial regime.[108] To his mind, the party was neither a necessary evil nor an unpleasant remedy for a much graver illness, and its ability to arouse a listless, apathetic nation was but one virtue among many. By 1868 and under universal suffrage, Duvergier de Hauranne sharpened many of the arguments about the party's democratic benefits that he first developed on foreign soil. It was in America that he noticed the representative function that could be performed by major parties, a point he conveyed again to the French years later. But in the 1868 tract, he also applauded the party as an institution to elevate the capacity of the few without undermining the rule of the many, portrayed it as a bulwark against the totalizing tendencies of a despot, and even embraced the competitive nature of an American-style system in which warring parties battle for influence.

To build his case for the party, Duvergier de Hauranne returned to the issue of preserving political capacity, hoping to engage his liberal contemporaries on their own terms. "What actually happens in a free democracy when the country is called upon to give its opinion on its affairs?" he asked. "Do citizens decide in the solitude of their conscience and in the independence of their reason? Do they turn a blind eye to all advice, all the warnings, all the exhortations, all the hints of outside influences? . . . Do voters have to decide like philosophers or like moralists, who examine questions of metaphysics?" While the great metaphysician of the vote Guizot sought to shelter each citizen's reason from outside opinions, Duvergier de Hauranne believed that political capacity was not formed in isolation, but in "the exchange of opinions, the diffusion of knowledge, the contagion of beliefs, the authority that is attached to experience."[109] The party promotes these intellectual exchanges, or to rephrase its function in Guizot's terms, it links the superior few to the less-capable many. Like Guizot, Duvergier de Hauranne pointed to an example from the natural world—in his case, from the cosmos—to illustrate this relationship:

> Small planets become the satellites of large ones and let themselves be dragged into their orbit; in the same way, small existences and small interests are attracted by great powers; they gather and amass around them, develop the habit of becoming a group and sharing their opinions, and they join their destinies. There is no need for intimidation or violence for these legitimate influences to be felt in society: they are satisfied with the moral force they draw from persuasion and example.[110]

In Duvergier de Hauranne's portrayal of modern democracy, those with greater capacity pull less-capable others into their moral orbit. For those well-versed in the canon of political thought, the image of superior individuals as great natural powers might bring to mind reactionary arguments about the merits of a natural aristocracy à la Joseph de Maistre, or the novel, capable aristocracy envisaged by Guizot.[111] But unlike preexisting defenses of a natural aristocracy, whether they came from the pen of reactionaries such as Maistre or Doctrinaires such as Guizot, Duvergier de Hauranne was neither arguing for the preeminence of an aristocratic class nor defending their preordained claims to political power.[112] His "great powers" were notable not because they possess rare virtues or quasi-divine rationality, but for their moral and epistemic impact on others around them, or for a "known honesty that inspires trust, a persuasion that convinces and animates ... [these] are natural powers that act on the minds of men."[113] When Duvergier de Hauranne identified the capable or "the great," he never intended to enclose the suffrage around them. Instead, he hoped to allow those same influences to persuade and educate the many who now shared equally in the franchise.[114] The party was thus an institution to complement universal suffrage. It would enhance political capacity by diffusing enlightenment from its leadership to its electorate and back again, without having to revert to an outdated *cens* or two-tiered electoral plan.[115]

For Duvergier de Hauranne, the party also functioned as a counterweight to a strong state, as it would thwart the despot's stratagems to manipulate public opinion. To make this argument, he began much as Laboulaye did. He knew that the Napoleonic Second Empire tried to fashion an electorate in its own image and thereby foster dependency under the guise of democracy.[116] Although civil associations would ideally act as intermediaries to shield individuals from state overreach, only the political party could truly prevent the state from controlling or corrupting the electorate. To highlight the party's role in preventing despotism, Duvergier de Hauranne looked once again to America. Writing to his French audience in 1868, he repeated his 1864 description of the party as "a spare government"—or, in America, "a State within a State"—that acts as a competing fount of information for the electorate and therefore breaks the state's monopoly on political education.[117] In the absence of strong parties, he had little faith that a universal electorate could remain free and uncorrupted, or that public opinion would reflect more than the whims of the moment:

> Parties are like frames that envelop citizens in public life. Suppress them or prevent them from being born, and democracy is nothing more than dust which easily takes the imprint that is given to it, but which does not keep that imprint for more than an hour and which disperses at the first strong wind.[118]

Anchored by the moral weight of the capable and influential few, parties also act as stabilizing and unifying associations in times of political uncertainty, since they hold public opinion around a relatively fixed political center. At heart, they are "conservative powers," he declared, pockets of underlying continuity across revolutions and regime changes.[119] Without major parties, the people will be subject to one of two extremes. They will either be governed by a despot or caught in the struggle between "obscure factions, incapable of guiding public opinion, powerless to rally the public under their banner, good at most in the hour of danger."[120]

Nor should the French fear the competitive spirit that animates party politics, Duvergier de Hauranne asserted, as he drew once again from the treasure trove that was American democracy. Parties keep each other honest, and by making use of the press, they never allow a rival opinion to go unexamined.[121] Much like the free press, which keeps the entire nation from "falling asleep and remaining stagnant," political competition enables citizens to interrogate both majority and minority opinions. Although party government may appear quarrelsome, vulgar, and disruptive to French eyes, Duvergier de Hauranne encouraged his readers to look below the unsettled political surface, as he had been prompted to do during America's presidential election years earlier. Despite all combative appearances, "the party organization brings neither confusion nor tyranny . . . nor is it an organized civil war."[122] Instead, "the party organizations and the permanent struggles they wage are still the best way to ensure security, unity, and peace for a free country."[123] In a much more recent (and rare) defense of parties and partisanship, the political theorist Nancy Rosenblum captures what Duvergier de Hauranne began to envision for a fledging French democracy. The party serves "a source of political creativity," Rosenblum writes. "Someone must create the lines of division over social aims, security, and justice . . . party rivalry 'stages the battle.' "[124] Duvergier de Hauranne's call for a version of such "creative competition" in the nineteenth century was at the same time a critique of post-Revolutionary politics. For too long, he suggested, the French pursued elusive peace at the expense of political dynamism. In their quest to represent a single, national will, his fellow citizens forgot "the fact that the competition of power is the necessary condition of the game of representative institutions, and thus the soul of liberty itself."[125] But the French would not have to sacrifice either unity or order in the process of attaining liberty, if Duvergier de Hauranne's incisive observations of American democracy were any indication: "These powerful [party] associations, which from time to time, as rulers or ruled, winners or losers, engage in battle all over the country, are cemented together by the question of the national interest. They thus transmit to citizens a stronger form of solidarity than the most absolute despotism could ever achieve."[126]

Conclusion

Duvergier de Hauranne's pleas to bring parties and partisanship to the aid of an inexperienced democracy fell on deaf ears in the final years of Napoleonic rule. Nevertheless, he would continue to advance a series of arguments about the utility of party politics into the Third Republic. The publication of his *La République conservatrice* (1873) marked the author's full conversion to republicanism, as he seemed to shed whatever Orléanist prejudices he inherited from his father. He continued to insist on the advantages of an American-style party system for the French and of open and civil disagreement between major parties in the newly established Third Republic.[127] Without acknowledging the connection (or perhaps knowing about it at all), his defense of the party for the new republic brought his ideas full circle to the early liberal philosophy articulated by Benjamin Constant, who pressed the post-revolutionary generation to embrace both pluralism in society and diversity in its assembly—and to unite one with the other by instituting direct elections.[128] Duvergier de Hauranne came to the intricate theory of descriptivist representation, which bore more than a passing resemblance to Constant's plan for "representation with real force," from reading British debates. Ultimately, it was America's presidential election that showed him how plurality, democracy, and political capacity could coexist through a nation's major parties.

While Laboulaye has been regarded as Tocqueville's heir apparent in the Second Empire, Duvergier de Hauranne also put his own spin on the democratic and comparative project that Tocqueville initiated. It was Tocqueville who first noticed that the "extremes of democracy" may become a regime's most useful safeguard. For Duvergier de Hauranne, it was the democratic instrument of the party organization that would promote peace and plurality at the same time, thereby resolving one of the conundrums that vexed Guizot and the Doctrinaires and introduced tensions into Constant's polemics as he railed against uniformity while nevertheless promoting capacity.

How should we ultimately interpret Duvergier de Hauranne's conclusions about political democracy? It is tempting to read those memorable passages about the orbits of lesser satellites around great planets as just another example of liberals' engrained elitism, or as a form of paternalism conveyed in the kinder, gentler terms of moral persuasion. On this reading, Duvergier de Hauranne's argument for party politics shares much in common with what Mill described as a "government of leading-strings," a tutelary form of paternal rule that might operate under the guise of freedom.[129] However, despite any superficial similarities, we ought to resist the temptation to reduce Duvergier de Hauranne's solution to either a new brand of elitism or a softer paternalism.[130] Granted, as long as the goal is to form capable citizens, there will always be a role for guidance and education in politics and even a (temporary) hierarchy between those who teach and those who are taught—a new aristocracy, to reuse Guizot's term. Yet Duvergier de Hauranne envisioned the party organization as more than the repository of a capable aristocracy or as a cadre of wise elites.[131] The "teachers" within his essay were not meant to nudge the people toward perfect rationality or political omniscience. Instead, parties would interject an array of opinions and proposals into the political sphere, thereby fostering the conditions for voters to cultivate reason and judgment and enhancing those epistemic functions already performed by a free press. To borrow once again from Rosenblum's political theory of partisanship, political parties "stage the battle" over justice and truth in a society, and by staging those political battles in the open air, they transform points of dissension into matters for public deliberation.[132] Duvergier de Hauranne articulated a similar point about the epistemic value of party politics in the 1860s. In a competitive party system in which major parties pose an ideological challenge to the state and to one another, it is the people who stand to benefit. Parties create a climate for informed reflection on the part of citizens.

Even so, few readers would doubt that the major parties in today's Western democracies fall far short of the heights that the Frenchman had in mind. While he appreciated the competition and even perhaps some of the mudslinging that takes place within the party system, he also wished to discourage the formation of those purely interest-driven, "petty" alliances that Tocqueville observed in America and France. When do the party's battles become unproductive wars? When does the party cease to act as an engine of democratic deliberation? When does it forestall open debate instead? Duvergier de Hauranne's work may lead us to ask these questions, but he did not give us their answers. These are questions uttered by those of us who have seen the modern party system at work. However far today's parties have drifted from Duvergier de Hauranne's nineteenth-century aspirations for them, his work does give us one glimpse into how liberal goals may be joined to and furthered by democracy's more divisive institutions.

Conclusion

Nearly two decades after Ernest Duvergier de Hauranne penned his two-part essay about redeeming the party system to save liberal democracy, a piece called "The Philosophy of Universal Suffrage" (1884) by the academic philosopher Alfred Fouillée appeared in *Revue des deux mondes*. The essay's title alone was significant. Almost forty years after universal male suffrage was mandated by the French constitution, its philosophy was apparently still in need of elaborating.[1] In terms that were both clear and elegant but at the same time reflected the apprehensions of their author, Fouillée described the same democratic predicament that his predecessors had confronted. "All of [democracy's] contradictions come back to the fundamental antinomy of the *right* to vote, granted to all, and of the *capacité*, which really belongs only to a certain number," he summarized. "This is the eternal opposition of political democracy and natural aristocracy."[2]

Democracy's "eternal antinomy" between the rights of the many and the wisdom of the few, between the universality of political rights and the limits that nature has presumably placed upon the capacity to bear them, captivated each of the figures in this book. It also helped to shape debates about the character of liberal politics in France until at least the Third Republic. Does democratic government require intelligent, moral, and productive voters? Can the act of voting alone do the work of encouraging such intelligence and morality? Or is the task of governing democratically, counterintuitively, best left in the hands of the few? Does political democracy, then, need its aristocrats? Even if Benjamin Constant did not frame these problems as "democratic" contradictions as Fouillée later would, he did think deeply about how to represent an equalized and socially diverse French society while still injecting a dose of wisdom or sound judgment into the representative assembly. In the end, Constant decided that the assembly should reflect the diversity of its entire nation, and that it could so even if its members were chosen by a relatively-homogenous electorate of the propertied—by the wisdom of a certain class, though an evolving and expanding one. His Doctrinaire counterparts, who were represented by Guizot in Chapter 2, came down

Democracy Tamed. Gianna Englert, Oxford University Press. © Oxford University Press 2024.
DOI: 10.1093/oso/9780197635315.003.0007

firmly on the side of a capable government over either a diverse or a universal one, choosing the wisdom of the few over the rights of all. They also pushed the word "democracy" toward the center of public debate during the Restoration, if only to claim it for the liberal, that is to say, the anti-reactionary and electorally antidemocratic, cause. Indeed, one of the Doctrinaires' rhetorical innovations was to strip the word democracy of its universality—and of its political connotations. In the eyes of the Doctrinaires, the new (and true) democracy was the egalitarian society that grew out of the Revolution, a society whose characteristic features practically called out for capable—not equal or universal– rulership. Paradoxically, it was on the basis of this novel equality, which saturated and distinguished the new democracy, that these Doctrinaire liberals developed their antidemocratic political views. They urged their countrymen to avoid experimenting with universal suffrage or any scheme approaching it, all for the sake of preserving individual freedom. And they would continue to do so until at least 1848.

While cognizant of the potential trade-offs between an inclusive government and a capable one, two of the most influential luminaries in the French tradition would later follow the Doctrinaires' logic to what they believed was its natural and indeed politically inclusive conclusion. For Tocqueville, who occupied the no-man's land between a universal suffrage and a capable one for most of his career, the equality that the Doctrinaires ascribed to their "new France" would eventually spill out from one sphere into the next, from the social state into electoral politics, just as it had in America. By 1848, Tocqueville envisaged a nation in which capacity and democracy could co-exist and be mutually enhancing, though he was well aware of the challenges his nation would face as it tried to balance the two values. Laboulaye would take Tocqueville's instincts further. Laboulaye's *new* new democracy after 1848 possessed all of the features of the Doctrinaires' democratic society of the 1820s. But its equality had so thoroughly leveled the social order, Laboulaye maintained, that the class-based distinctions behind the Doctrinaires' sociology, those distinctions between France's bourgeois middle and lower orders, no longer reflected reality. The liberal philosophy that Laboulaye developed in reaction to such altered social conditions had both a political and spiritual purpose: it would cultivate not only reason but also morality in each individual soul by means of public and popular education. Laboulaye's contemporary Duvergier de Hauranne was well-versed in the array of answers that his countrymen, liberal and otherwise, proposed in response to the suffrage question since the Revolution of 1789. He also investigated how the

Americans and the British dealt with their specific dilemmas about the franchise, and he came away from his studies with a novel perspective about attaining equality and wisdom in the government. Along with Laboulaye, Duvergier de Hauranne operated on the Tocquevillean assumption that democracy had indeed overflowed its banks. Having revolutionized the social state, it transformed the political world in turn. Statesmen needed to respond, he urged, by establishing major parties as the organs of representation and the reservoirs of political capacity. The party, he insisted, would help to resolve the contradictions within a liberal democracy.

If I had set out to write this book thirty, twenty, or probably even ten years ago, I suspect that most of the claims put forth by the nineteenth-century authors within it would have seemed distant and disagreeable to my present-day readers. The mere suggestion that *democracies* pose a danger to the hard-won freedoms of individuals and entire groups, while maybe vaguely believable in theory, would have likely rung hollow in practice. Democracy, many of my critics would have no doubt declared, has proven to be the best of all possible systems. This is especially true for anyone who, along with Fukuyama, looked with confidence on the ascendance of liberal democracies after the end of the Cold War. Not only that, but more than a few contemporaneous readers would have balked at the suggestion that liberal democracies need saving or at least that they are self-undermining rather than self-sustaining. Quite a few others may have recoiled at the proposition that voting rights ought to depend on a notion as indeterminate and open to abuse as individual competence or, more nebulous and dangerous still, "political capacity." And given that America's dark and exclusionary electoral past was not really so long ago, they would have been right to do so. Who, after all, is capable of exercising the vote? How can we possibly detect that capacity? How can we ensure that an electoral threshold as amorphous as capacity, as necessary as it may be for good government, does not become another pretense for class or race-based political exclusions?

Even though we have yet to answer these questions and others like them, the perception that the rule of all may turn self-destructive is more widespread now than it was even a decade ago. It is this perception, in fact, that first brought the issues I raised in this book to my attention. Whether because of financial crises, charismatic politicians, or a series of other causes entirely, the fault lines between liberal values and democratic orders that the earliest European liberals could not help but feel under their feet have opened up to our view once again. In our attempts to make sense of our own "world quite new," to borrow Tocqueville's turn of phrase, today's scholars search for the means to piece our broken institutions back together. Some have nobly tried to restore our confidence in the collective. These "epistemic democrats" argue that democracies tend to outperform competing regime types on epistemic margins. Even the most anxious among us, these theorists claim, should take comfort in the fact that democratic decisions tend to be the "correct" ones, for they either conform to an independent standard of reason or mirror voters' stated preferences.[3] But we should not be shocked that other academics have resurrected old solutions in novel terms. At the extreme, today's "epistocratic" analytic philosophers ask that we at least consider the reality that, when it comes to democracy, there is nothing valuable to salvage and nothing credible to defend. On their view, liberals should entertain the option to divorce democracy—a scheme of universal and equal suffrage—in favor of rule by "the knowers."[4]

While none of the nineteenth-century thinkers in this book made much of an effort to uncover the epistemic merits of democratic rule (with Tocqueville in Chapter 3 as a possible exception), at least a few of them recognized the value in operating within a politically inclusive framework rather than trying to disassemble it piece by piece. They took Tocqueville's counsel in *DA* to heart and thus worked to make democracy "profitable" and not merely palatable to those who live under it. If these more hopeful liberal democrats, those who made every effort to drag French liberalism out of the capacitarian shadow cast by Guizot, have anything to offer readers at this present moment, it is not the old claim that democracies need to restrict their membership in an attempt to achieve smarter outcomes. Rather, it is the insight that social hierarchy and political democracy are not necessarily incompatible. Or to put their liberal case more strongly, that political democracies need pockets of hierarchy and the guidance of elites (both in electoral politics and in society, in political parties and in institutions of higher learning and secondary education) if they hope to endure. Vexed by what seemed like an unsolvable puzzle that involved fitting both democracy and capacity in the electorate, it was the *fin-de-siècle* philosopher Fouillée who summarized the most persuasive lesson that his predecessors had to offer, a lesson that now resonates well outside of the specific context in which it originated. "If universal suffrage presupposes, from below, human beings capable of choosing, it supposes above all, from the top, human beings worthy of being chosen."[5]

While the democratically inclined authors within France's liberal tradition (Tocqueville, Laboulaye, and Duvergier de Hauranne) endeavored to raise the general level of enlightenment and political acumen across the entire citizenry, it is their attention to shaping the individuals at "the top"—potential statesmen, representatives, party leaders, and leaders of thought—that should encourage us to move beyond the stale but persistent conversations about either improving democracy at the margins or casting it off altogether. While civic literacy initiatives may be laudable as ends in themselves, it is debatable whether they improve democratic outcomes. Nor is there any reason to expect that an urbane "epistocratic" franchise will solve our problems. As the historical debates featured in this book have shown and as the most committed capacitarians of the nineteenth century seemed to realize for themselves, it is likely to introduce new ones. Guizot, the capacitarian par excellence, could do no more than gesture at how capacity could be codified in laws that improve democratic institutions. He, too, worried that those same institutions, bolstered by thin appeals to capacity or privilege, may fall into the hands of unworthy oligarchs and incompetent elites.

If our attempts to redesign democracy "from below"—that is, by restricting who participates at the level of elections—so often achieve the opposite of their intended effect, then which options remain? In writings from Constant to Duvergier de Hauranne, and even from the antidemocratic stalwart Guizot, we have heard not solely about who should possess the power to *choose* in a democracy but about who should *be chosen*. These long-ago liberals insisted that the most effective assurances for the longevity of liberal democracy were never democratic at all. But nor do those assurances undermine democracy's basic assumptions about political equality. The liberal spirit displayed by many of the figures in these pages would prompt us to put aside our democratic doubts about a legitimate aristocracy, not a class of the wealthy but of the worthy few. Since our attempts to reform the *demos*—the choosers, to use Fouillée's language—have failed from the beginning, perhaps the time has come to revisit "the top," to support institutions that encourage humans beings to become "worthy of being chosen," a moral *aristoi*. There is a virtue, the liberals in this book taught us, in nurturing an aristocracy in and for democracy, an aristocracy whose boundaries are porous and whose membership is ever-changing, a new and true aristocracy from which the people—the whole people—may choose for themselves.

Notes

Introduction

1. Marc F. Plattner, "Liberalism and Democracy: Can't Have One Without the Other," *Foreign Affairs*, March 1, 1998, https://www.foreignaffairs.com/articles/1998-03-01/liberalism-and-democracy-cant-have-one-without-other. See also the summary by Fareed Zakaria, "The Rise of Illiberal Democracy," *Foreign Affairs* 76, no. 6 (1997): 22–43: "For almost a century in the West, democracy has meant liberal democracy."
2. Marc F. Plattner, "From Liberalism to Liberal Democracy," *Journal of Democracy* 10, no. 3 (1999): 121–134.
3. Francis Fukuyama, *The End of History and the Last Man* (New York: Simon and Schuster, 2006).
4. Beyond the pages of *Foreign Affairs*, a similar diagnosis appears in Steven Levitsky and Daniel Ziblatt, *How Democracies Die* (New York: Crown, 2018) and in Anne Applebaum, *Twilight of Democracy: The Seductive Lure of Authoritarianism* (New York: Doubleday, 2020).
5. Nor are today's self-identified classical liberal and libertarian opponents of democracy articulating brand new objections to majoritarian democracy. What are sometimes cast as *sui generis* arguments by modern-day "epistocrats" such as Jason Brennan have a long and sophisticated history behind them, which seems to have been generally disregarded by some of the "anti-democrats" within the academy. For a sampling of this literature, see Jason Brennan, *Against Democracy* (Princeton, NJ: Princeton University Press, 2016); Ilya Somin, *Democracy and Political Ignorance: Why Smaller Government Is Smarter* (Stanford, CA: Stanford University Press, 2013); and Bryan Caplan, *The Myth of the Rational Voter: Why Democracies Choose Bad Policies* (Princeton, NJ: Princeton University Press, 2011).
6. Norberto Bobbio, *Liberalism and Democracy* (London: Verso, 2005), 38.
7. Alan Kahan, *Liberalism in Nineteenth-Century Europe: The Political Culture of Limited Suffrage* (New York: Palgrave Macmillan, 2003), 6. See also Pierre Rosanvallon, *Le sacre du citoyen: Histoire du suffrage universel en France* (Paris: Folio, 2001) and *Le peuple introuvable: Histoire de la représentation démocratique en France* (Paris: Gallimard, 2002).
8. Helena Rosenblatt, *The Lost History of Liberalism: From Ancient Rome to the Twenty-First Century* (Princeton, NJ: Princeton University Press, 2018), 93. The notion that liberals were skeptical of popular sovereignty in the wake of the French Revolution is explored in James T. Kloppenberg, *Toward Democracy: The Struggle for Self-Rule in European and American Thought* (Oxford: Oxford University Press, 2016), 12. The Doctrinaires' animus toward political democracy, which is explored in Chapter 2

of this book, is discussed in Aurelian Craiutu, *Liberalism under Siege: The Political Thought of the French Doctrinaires* (Lanham, MD: Lexington Books, 2003), chapters 7 and 8. Annelien de Dijn contends that an "undemocratic" conception of freedom has undergirded the liberal project since its inception in the late eighteenth and early nineteenth centuries. Annelien de Dijn, *Freedom: An Unruly History* (Cambridge, MA: Harvard University Press, 2020). As Greg Conti has shown, Victorian liberals defined their theories in opposition to those articulated by the British democrats of their day. Gregory Conti, *Parliament the Mirror of the Nation: Representation, Deliberation, and Democracy in Victorian Britain* (Cambridge, UK: Cambridge University Press, 2019).

9. One notable exception is Conti's *Parliament the Mirror of the Nation*, which depicts British alternatives to a uniform and universal suffrage.

10. In *The Social Contract*, Jean-Jacques Rousseau described the right to vote as "a right of which nothing can deprive Citizens." The capacitarian liberals challenged Rousseau's premise about the inviolability of political rights, and we will explore their critical responses in Chapters 1 and 2. Jean-Jacques Rousseau, "The Social Contract," in *The Social Contract and Other Later Political Writings*, trans. Victor Gourevitch (Cambridge: Cambridge University Press, 1997), 122. For a genealogy of how natural rights were transformed into political rights in this period, see Daniel Edelstein, *On the Spirit of Rights* (Chicago, IL: University of Chicago Press, 2018).

11. And as Chapters 1 and 2 will argue, what appears as the elitist notion of *capacité politique* also grew as a liberal defense against reactionary elites.

12. The only existing study of *capacité politique* in English is Kahan's *Liberalism in Nineteenth-Century Europe*. My approach here differs from Kahan's in method and substance. Kahan studies *capacité* by combing through parliamentary records of the period to provide a comparative parliamentary history of the concept across three countries. The focus here, by contrast, is on liberals' theoretical arguments. In particular, I explore *how* liberals assembled their arguments against political democracy, uncovering the assumptions upon which they relied and the particular positions they defended.

13. Plato, *The Statesman*, ed. Julia Annas and Robin Waterfield (Cambridge: Cambridge University Press, 1995); Plato, *The Republic*, trans. Allan Bloom (New York: Basic Books, 2016).

14. Aristotle, *Politics*, trans. Carnes Lord (Chicago: University of Chicago Press, 1985), Book III.

15. Edmund Burke, *Reflections on the Revolution in France*, in *Select Works of Edmund Burke* (Indianapolis, IN: Liberty Fund, 1999), 139–140. For an explanation of Burke's "trouble with hair-dressers," see Don Herzog, *Poisoning the Minds of the Lower Orders* (Princeton, NJ: Princeton University Press, 2021).

16. Mary Wollstonecraft, *A Vindication of the Rights of Woman with Strictures on Political and Moral Subjects* (London: J. Johnson, 1792). See also Olympe de Gouges, *Déclaration des droits de la femme et de la citoyenne*, in *Écrits politiques*, tome 1, ed. Olivier Blanc (Paris: Côté-femmes, 1993), 209–215.

17. Nicolas de Condorcet, "Sur l'admission des femmes au droit de cité," *Journal de la société de 1789*, July 3, 1790, 27.

18. Some readers will notice that I did not mention the distinction between passive and active citizenship proposed by Emmanuel Joseph Sieyès during the Revolution. This is because I explore the similarities and differences between Sieyès' two types of citizenship and liberals' appeals to political capacity in Chapters 1 and 2.

19. The degree to which *capacité politique* dominated parliamentary debates, especially during the July Monarchy, is apparent from Kahan's *Liberalism in Nineteenth-Century Europe*. So pervasive was the concept that even the socialists were forced to rely upon it—or at least to respond to it. In 1868, for example, Pierre-Joseph Proudhon attempted to co-opt what was originally liberals' antidemocratic term to serve socialist goals, including uniting "the social" with "the political," or realizing social equality alongside the equality of universal suffrage. Pierre-Joseph Proudhon, *De la capacité politique des classes ouvrières* (Paris: Librairie internationale, 1868).

20. While the French revised the laws governing both national and local elections during the period I discuss here, most of my study focuses on the national suffrage laws, simply out of an interest to keep the links between chapters as clear and manageable as possible. That said, the arguments of Chapters 1–5 inevitably touch on the franchise at both levels, since the French legislature set down uniform laws for the local and national suffrages at the same time.

21. For a biography of Guizot, see Douglas Johnson, *Guizot: Aspects of French History, 1787–1874* (Westport, CT: Praeger, 1976).

22. For a sophisticated investigation into whether the liberal framework can accommodate elites, see Olivia Leboyer's comparisons between Guizot, the Austrian economist F.A. Hayek, and the twentieth century philosopher John Rawls. Olivia Leboyer, *Élite et libéralisme* (Paris: CNRS Editions, 2012).

23. On this divide between the rationalist and pluralist strands of liberalism, see Richard Boyd, *Uncivil Society: The Perils of Pluralism and the Making of Modern Liberalism* (Lexington Books, 2004) and Jacob T. Levy, *Rationalism, Pluralism, and Freedom* (Oxford University Press, 2015).

24. In addition to scrutinizing electoral procedures, liberals thought deeply about where and when elections should take place. This becomes a major theme across Chapters 1 through 3, as liberals sought to counter electoral and parliamentary corruption.

25. Rosenblatt, *The Lost History of Liberalism*, 63 and 108.

26. On treating liberalism as an "actor's category" that encompasses the wide range of thinkers, movements, and ideas that were regarded or identified as liberal at one time or another, see Duncan Bell, *Reordering the World: Essays on Liberalism and Empire* (Princeton, NJ: Princeton University Press, 2016), 5. On the more general challenges involved in delimiting political traditions, liberalism among them, see Duncan Bell, "What Is Liberalism?," *Political Theory* 42, no. 6 (2014): 682–715.

Chapter 1

1. Helena Rosenblatt, "Why Constant? A Critical Overview of the Constant Revival," *Modern Intellectual History* 1, no. 3 (October 2004): 439–453. The characterization of liberalism's "revisionist moment" comes from William Selinger and Gregory Conti,

"The Lost History of Political Liberalism," *History of European Ideas* 46, no. 3 (April 2020): 341–354.

2. Steven Vincent documents this use of "liberal" in K. Steven Vincent, "Benjamin Constant, the French Revolution, and the Origins of French Romantic Liberalism," *French Historical Studies* 23, no. 4 (October 2000): 622. For a "word history" of "liberal," see Rosenblatt, *The Lost History of Liberalism.* For an interpretation of Constant's moderate politics, see Aurelian Craiutu, *A Virtue for Courageous Minds: Moderation in French Political Thought, 1748–1830* (Princeton, NJ: University Press, 2012), chapter 6.

3. Tzvetan Todorov, *A Passion for Democracy: Benjamin Constant* (New York: Algora Publishing, 2007), 41. Other scholars who interpret Constant as a theorist of liberal democracy include Stephen Holmes, *Benjamin Constant and the Making of Modern Liberalism* (New Haven, CT: Yale University Press, 1984); Paul Delbouille, "Aux sources de la démocratie libérale: Benjamin Constant," *Revue d'Histoire littéraire de la France* 106, no. 2 (2006): 259–270; and Nora Timmermans, "Benjamin Constant, Political Power, and Democracy," *History of European Ideas* 48, no. 3 (March 2022): 246–262. Robert Alexander cites Constant's "increasingly democratic" stance with an important qualifier: "it would push matters too far to assert that [he] was a democrat." Robert Alexander, "Benjamin Constant as a Second Restoration Politician," in *The Cambridge Companion to Constant,* ed. Helena Rosenblatt (Cambridge: Cambridge University Press, 2009), 169.

4. This held true not only during the Directory and the Empire, but into the Restoration as well. And yet it was after 1820, as we will learn in Chapter 2, that the term became a battle cry of sorts for the Doctrinaires. For a conceptual history of democracy, see Joanna Innes and Mark Philp, "'Democracy' from Book to Life: The Emergence of the Term in Active Political Debate, to 1848," in Jussi Kurunmäki, Jeppe Nevers, and Henk te Velde, eds., *Democracy in Modern Europe: A Conceptual History* (New York: Berghahn, 2018), 16–34.

5. Quoted in Vincent, "Benjamin Constant, the French Revolution, and the Origins of French Romantic Liberalism," at 610. A fuller discussion of the meaning of "democrat" and "democracy" in this period can be found in R.R. Palmer, "Notes on the Use of the Word 'Democracy,' 1789–1799," in *Political Science Quarterly* 68 no. 2 (1953): 203–226.

6. Benjamin Constant, *Réflexions sur les constitutions, la distribution des pouvoirs, et les garanties, dans une monarchie constitutionnelle* (Paris: H. Nicolle, 1814).

7. Timmermans equates popular sovereignty with democracy to expose Constant's "unwritten theory of democracy." Timmermans, "Benjamin Constant, Political Power, and Democracy."

8. Holmes challenges claims that Constant was antidemocratic by analyzing his depictions of the ancient participatory *polis.* Holmes, *Benjamin Constant and the Making of Modern Liberalism.*

9. During this period, Constant was a prolific writer and he spoke quite often in the Chamber of Deputies. Excerpts of his speeches have been reproduced in Dennis Wood, *Benjamin Constant: A Biography* (New York: Routledge, 2002), 342–347;

Paul Bastid, *Benjamin Constant et sa doctrine* (Paris: Armand Colin, 1966), 324–326; Robert Alexander, *Re-Writing the French Revolutionary Tradition: Liberal Opposition and the Fall of the Bourbon Monarchy* (Cambridge, UK: Cambridge University Press, 2004), 10–11, 280–281. Constant's proposed remedies for the pathologies of parliamentarism have been documented in William Selinger, *Parliamentarism, From Burke to Weber* (Cambridge, UK: Cambridge University Press, 2019).

10. M.J.V., *Le cri d'un Ultra, ou le "vade-mecum" de l'électeur honnête homme* (Paris: Delaunay, 1818).

11. In his classic study of Constant on liberal democracy, Holmes devotes roughly ten pages to the suffrage. Holmes, *Benjamin Constant and the Making of Modern Liberalism*. The most focused discussion is Bryan Garsten, "From Popular Sovereignty to Civil Society in Post-Revolutionary France," in *Popular Sovereignty in Historical Perspective*, ed. Richard Bourke and Quentin Skinner (Cambridge, UK: Cambridge University Press, 2016), 236–269. I am grateful to Bryan for encouraging me to study Constant's reflections on electoral rules several years ago. See also Rosanvallon, *Le sacre du citoyen*.

12. The Charter stipulated a property qualification of 300 francs taxes for electors. The full text can be found in Jacques Godechot, *Les constitutions de la France depuis 1789* (Paris: Flammarion, 1995), 209–224.

13. Pierre Rosanvallon, *Le moment Guizot* (Paris: Gallimard, 1985); Rosanvallon, *Le sacre du citoyen*.

14. Rosanvallon categorizes Constant in his chapter on *l'ordre capacitaire*, but his discussion of Constant in the Restoration debates over the vote is nuanced and careful. Rosanvallon, *Le sacre du citoyen*, 271–327. Others elide Constant with the capacitarian Doctrinaires on the issue of the franchise. Craiutu, *Liberalism under Siege*, 225; Aurelian Craiutu, "The Battle for Legitimacy: Guizot and Constant on Sovereignty," *Historical Reflections/Réflexions Historiques* 28, no. 3 (2002): 471–491; De Dijn, *Freedom*.

15. De Dijn, *Freedom*.

16. Readers may have already recognized similarities between Constant's view of representation that of Britain's nineteenth-century "mirror theorists," whose electoral schemes have been masterfully analyzed by Gregory Conti. When I characterize Constant as "singular," it is meant in the context of France. In a later footnote, I draw modest comparisons between Constant's view of a diverse assembly and that of the later Victorian variety-of-suffragists. Conti, *Parliament the Mirror of the Nation*.

17. Benjamin Constant, *Principes de politique applicables à tous les gouvernements*, ed. Etienne Hofmann, vol. 2 (Genève: Librairie Droz, 1980), 395.

18. Although Lucien Jaume uses the term *individualisme* to describe Constant's brand of liberalism, he points to its pluralist dimensions as well. Lucien Jaume, *L'Individu effacé, ou le paradoxe du libéralisme français* (Paris: Fayard, 1997), 63–109; Helena Rosenblatt, "Re-Evaluating Benjamin Constant's Liberalism: Industrialism, Saint-Simonianism and the Restoration Years," *History of European Ideas* 30, no. 1 (2004): 23–37; K. Steven Vincent, *Benjamin Constant and the Birth of French Liberalism* (New York: Palgrave Macmillan, 2011); Levy, *Rationalism, Pluralism, and*

Freedom, 184–201; Jacob T. Levy, "Pluralism without Privilege? Corps Intermédiaires, Civil Society, and the Art of Association," in *Organizations, Civil Society, and the Roots of Development*, ed. Naomi Lamoreaux and John J. Wallis (Chicago, IL: University of Chicago Press, 2017); Andrew Jainchill, *Reimagining Politics after the Terror: The Republican Origins of French Liberalism* (Ithaca, NY: Cornell University Press, 2008); Arthur Ghins, "Benjamin Constant and Public Opinion in Post-Revolutionary France," *History of Political Thought* 40, no. 3 (2019): 484–514.

19. In 1814, Constant turned away from republicanism and toward a constitutional monarchy modeled on England. Constant, *Réflexions*.

20. Benjamin Constant, *De la force du gouvernement actuel de la France et de la nécessité de s'y rallier* (Paris, 1796); Benjamin Constant, *Des effets de la Terreur* (Paris, 1797).

21. Helena Rosenblatt, *Liberal Values: Benjamin Constant and the Politics of Religion* (Cambridge, UK: Cambridge University Press, 2008), 122. Both Etienne Hofmann and Marcel Gauchet claim that Constant was "maturely" liberal by 1806. Etienne Hofmann, *Les "Principes de politique" de Benjamin Constant: la genèse d'une oeuvre et l'évolution de la pensée de leur auteur, 1789–1806* (Geneva: Droz, 1980); Marcel Gauchet, "Constant," in *Dictionnaire Critique de La Révolution Francaise*, ed. François Furet and Mona Ozouf (Paris: Flammarion, 1988).

22. Benjamin Constant, *The Spirit of Conquest and Usurpation and Their Relation to European Civilization*, ed. Biancamaria Fontana, *Constant's Political Writings* (Cambridge, UK: Cambridge University Press, 1988); Benjamin Constant, Speech on Bonaparte, in "Journal des débats politiques et littéraires," March 19, 1815, 1–2.

23. Constant, *Conquest and Usurpation*, 88.

24. Constant, *Conquest and Usurpation*, 95, 89.

25. *Principes*, 2:30.

26. *Principes*, 2:37.

27. The thesis that Constant developed his liberalism in contrast to Rousseauean "pretexts" belongs originally to Holmes. See Holmes, *Benjamin Constant and the Making of Modern Liberalism*.

28. The Declaration of Rights which prefaced the new constitution stated that each male over the age of twenty-one had equal right to participate in elections. In practice, however, this was not quite a universal suffrage, as the historian Serge Aberdam notes. Serge Aberdam, *Démographes et démocrates: L'oeuvre du Comité de division de la Convention nationale* (Paris: Société des études robespierristes, 2004).

29. For a detailed and contextualized analysis of Constant's response to the Terror, see Stefano de Luca, "Benjamin Constant and the Terror," in *The Cambridge Companion to Constant*, ed. Rosenblatt (Cambridge, UK: Cambridge University Press, 2009), 92–114.

30. Bryan Garsten highlights the degree to which Constant aimed to combat legislative usurpation along with the usurpation of a single ruler. Bryan Garsten, "Representative Government and Popular Sovereignty," in *Political Representation*, ed. Alexander S. Kirshner et al. (Cambridge: Cambridge University Press, 2010), 90–110. On the aristocratic and economic faces of usurpation in Constant's thought, see Gianna

Englert, "Usurpation and 'The Social' in Benjamin Constant's *Commentaire*," *Modern Intellectual History*, 17, no. 1 (March 2020), 55–84.

31. *Principes*, 2:400, 399.

32. *Principes*, 2:399.

33. In his work on public opinion, Ghins meticulously maps Constant's calculated attacks on popular sovereignty. Arthur Ghins, "'Popular Sovereignty That I Deny': Benjamin Constant on Public Opinion, Political Legitimacy and Constitution Making," *Modern Intellectual History* 19, no. 1 (2022): 128–158.

34. *Principes*, 2:38.

35. See also his Benjamin Constant, *Fragments d'un ouvrage abandonné sur la possibilité d'une constitution républicaine dans un grand pays* (Paris: Aubier, 1991), which was authored concurrent to the first *Principles*.

36. See the editor's note 1 to *Principes*, 2:19.

37. *Principes*, 2:40.

38. *Principes*, 2:39.

39. "The existence of public spirit is a danger for [usurpation], while the appearance of one is a necessity." Constant, *Conquest and Usurpation*, 95.

40. *Principes*, 2:400; Some of the same passages appear word-for-word in Constant, *Fragments d'un ouvrage abandonné sur la possibilité d'une constitution républicaine dans un grand pays*, 290–303. Up until the passage of the liberal-backed Lainé Law in 1817 that instituted direct elections with a property qualification, Constant continued to argue that "the right to freely elect national deputies" in France was "sometimes incomplete and sometimes illusory." Benjamin Constant, *Considérations sur le projet de loi relatif aux élections, adopté par la Chambre des Députés* (Paris: Delaunay, 1817), 5.

41. *Principes*, 2:22, 404.

42. *Principes*, 2:398–399, 401.

43. A fuller picture of Necker's influence on Constant can be found in Henri Grange, "De l'influence de Necker sur les idées politiques de Benjamin Constant," *Annales Benjamin Constant* 2 (1982): 73–80.

44. To be more specific, the new constitution abolished the censitary (property tax) requirement for the vote that had been in place since the Constitution of Year III. Rosanvallon notes that the term "universal suffrage" appeared for the first time in France in this period, in an article outlining the provisions of the new constitution. Rosanvallon, *Le sacre du citoyen*, 256.

45. Jacques Necker, *Dernières vues de politique et de finance* (Paris, 1802), 2.

46. The details of this system are described in Jean Yves Coppolani, *Les élections en France à l'époque napoléonienne* (Paris: Albatros, 1980). See also Malcolm Crook, *Elections in the French Revolution: An Apprenticeship in Democracy, 1789-1799* (Cambridge University Press, 2002), 190–196; Malcolm Crook, "The Uses of Democracy: Elections and Plebiscites in Napoleonic France," in *The French Experience from Republic to Monarchy, 1792-1824: New Dawns in Politics, Knowledge and Culture*, ed. Máire F. Cross and David Williams (London: Palgrave Macmillan UK, 2000), 26. Constant served in the Tribunat until he was purged by Napoleon in 1802 for voicing his critiques of the administration.

47. Necker, *Dernières vues de politique et de finance*, 10.

48. Necker, *Dernières vues de politique et de finance*, 7.

49. Constant often expressed his misgivings about the indirect system in this way, citing the degree to which it separated first-order voters from outcomes. For one such instance, see Constant, *Considérations sur le projet de loi relatif aux élections, adopté par la Chambre des Députés*, 7; Constant also took issue with the 1799 system in *Fragments d'un ouvrage abandonné sur la possibilité d'une constitution républicaine dans un grand pays*, 305–315.

50. Not all of these schemes sprung from the same motivations, however. Condorcet developed his network of assemblies to enable the direct exercise of popular sovereignty. Nicolas de Condorcet, *Plan de constitution présenté à la Convention nationale, les 15 et 16 février 1793* (Paris: De L'imprimerie nationale, 1793).

51. Benjamin Constant, "Principles of Politics Applicable to All Representative Governments," in *Constant: Political Writings*, ed. Biancamaria Fontana (Cambridge, UK: Cambridge University Press, 1988), 201.

52. Necker had earlier outlined a system that gave the people the final choice from among a curated list of candidates. Jacques Necker, "Sur l'élection des membres des assemblées provinciales," in *De l'administration des finances de la France*, vol. 2 (Paris: Jean-Pierre Heubach, 1784), 292–296. Constant demanded more directness instead. See Constant, *Principles of Politics Applicable to All Governments*, 203.

53. *Principes*, 2:393.

54. *Principes*, 2: 393.

55. For the intriguing suggestion that Constant shared more with the tradition of French rationalism than we might assume, a thesis that differs markedly from my own in this chapter, see Arthur Ghins, "Benjamin Constant and the Politics of Reason," *History of European Ideas* 44, no. 2 (2018): 224–243. Rosanvallon makes a passing reference to Constant's place in the political rationalist camp of the Thermidorians in Pierre Rosanvallon, "Guizot et la question du suffrage universel au XIXe siècle," in *François Guizot et la culture politique de son temps*, ed. Marina Valensie (Paris: Gallimard, 1991), 132.

56. Constant, "Principles of Politics Applicable to All Representative Governments," 205.

57. Pierre Rosanvallon, "Political Rationalism and Democracy in France in the 18th and 19th Centuries," *Philosophy & Social Criticism* 28, no. 6 (November 2002): 689.

58. Michael Sonenscher, "Introduction," in *Sieyès: Political Writings: Including the Debate Between Sieyès and Tom Paine in 1791* (Cambridge, MA: Hackett Publishing, 2003), xxxi–xxxiii.

59. Emmanuel Joseph Sieyès, "Constitutional Observations," in *Emmanuel Joseph Sieyès: The Essential Political Writings*, ed. Oliver W. Lembcke and Florian Weber (Leiden: Brill Academic Pub, 2014), 187.

60. Pierre-Jean-Georges Cabanis, *Quelques considérations sur l'organisation sociale en général, et particulièrement sur la nouvelle constitution* (Paris, 1800), 27.

61. Cabanis, *Quelques considerations sur l'organisation sociale en général*, 28.

62. Constant was well-aware of the Idéologues, who moved in and out of Mme de Staël's orbit. As Cheryl Welch has shown, figures such as Destutt de Tracy and Pierre Daunou

joined the broad coterie of the *Indépendant* Left, in which Constant was a key player. Cheryl B. Welch, *Liberty and Utility: The French Idéologues and the Transformation of Liberalism* (New York: Columbia University Press, 1984), 154–187.

63. Rosanvallon, "Political Rationalism and Democracy in France in the 18th and 19th Centuries."

64. Pierre Rosanvallon, *Le Modèle politique français: La société civile contre le jacobinisme de 1789 à nos jours* (Paris: Seuil, 2004). As Rosanvallon notes, Guizot, too, subscribed to the culture of generality and imbued it with new meaning. As we will discuss in Chapter 2, Guizot put it to different uses. In his hands, the drive toward uniformity had to be realized through restrictions on who could vote and hold office, not through an indirect scheme for elections.

65. Adam Smith, *The Theory of Moral Sentiments* (Indianapolis, IN: Liberty Fund, 1982). Constant referred to the spirit of system without attributing the idea to Smith elsewhere in his discussion of uniformity, though we know that he was well versed in the ideas of the Scottish Enlightenment. Constant, *Conquest and Usurpation*, 73–74.

66. A more thorough discussion of Sieyès on representation is beyond the scope of his chapter. Nonetheless, Sieyès' proposals for elections grew more elitist over time. Sewell makes this point in William H. Sewell Jr., *A Rhetoric of Bourgeois Revolution: The Abbe Sieyes and What Is the Third Estate?* (Durham, NC: Duke University Press, 1994), 195–196. Nadia Urbinati analyzes Sieyès' theory of representation to argue that it "excluded directness." Nadia Urbinati, *Representative Democracy: Principles and Genealogy* (University of Chicago Press, 2006), 140. Most recently, Lucia Rubinelli shows that Sieyès put forward a novel understanding of the power of the people as "constituent power" rather than popular sovereignty. Lucia Rubinelli, *Constituent Power: A History* (Cambridge, UK: Cambridge University Press, 2020).

67. Constant, *Conquest and Usurpation*, 73.

68. Constant, *Conquest and Usurpation*, 73–74.

69. Cabanis, *Quelques considérations sur l'organisation sociale en général*, 22. Bonaparte came to renounce any association with the Idéologues, and they with him.

70. Alan B. Spitzer, "Restoration Political Theory and the Debate over the Law of the Double Vote," *The Journal of Modern History* 55, no. 1 (March 1983): 54–70.

71. Using social choice theory, Breton and Lepelley observe that the Double Vote did not necessarily have its intended effect, that is, it did not double the power of the wealthiest voters. Michel Le Breton and Dominique Lepelley, "Une analyse de la loi électorale du 29 juin 1820," *Revue économique* 65, no. 3 (2014): 469–518.

72. That same year, Constant published a pamphlet against the Double Vote. Benjamin Constant, *De la proposition de changer la loi des élections* (Paris: Poulet, 1819).

73. Constant raised (and then promptly rejected) this point in Constant, *De la proposition de changer la loi des élections*, 3–4.

74. Constant relayed this argument, which he attributed to the far Right, in Constant, *Considérations sur le projet de loi relatif aux élections, adopté par la Chambre des Députés*, 7.

75. Benjamin Constant, *Des Motifs qui ont dicté le nouveau projet de loi sur les élections* (Paris: Béchet aîné, 1820), 9–10.

76. More extensive discussions of this theme can be found in Jeremy Jennings, "A Note on Freedom of the Press in Restoration France," *Journal of Modern Italian Studies* 17, no. 5 (December 2012): 568–573 and Fabian Rausch, "The Impossible *Gouvernement Représentatif*: Constitutional Culture in Restoration France, 1814–30," *French History* 27, no. 2 (June 2013): 223–248.

77. Lucien Jaume has uncovered a surprising intellectual *rapprochement* between Guizot and the Ultraroyalist Bonald. The discussion here of the free press only scratches the surface of their similarities. Jaume, *L'Individu effacé*, 128–130.

78. Guizot's hesitancy to experiment with a free press after the initial fall of Bonaparte is clear from his claims in François Guizot, *Quelques idées sur la liberté de la presse* (Paris, 1814).

79. This facet of Guizot's stance on the press is nicely articulated by Craiutu, who otherwise takes a much more charitable (and in my view, too liberal) interpretation of Guizot's attitude toward press freedom. Craiutu, *Liberalism under Siege*, chapter 9.

80. The liberal stance on press freedom and censorship receives careful analysis in Jaume, *L'Individu effacé*, 407–444. Jaume, too, addressed the parallels between the *cautionnement* as proof of rationality among editors, and a census suffrage, or proof of capacity for the would-be voter.

81. *Archives parlementaires de 1787 à 1860: Recueil complet des débats législatifs et politiques des chambres françaises*, Deuxième Série (1800 à 1860), ed. M.J. Madival and M.E. Laurent, vol. 24, (May 3, 1819), 164–7. Constant's response immediately follows.

82. Kahan, *Liberalism in Nineteenth-Century Europe*; Aurelian Craiutu, "Guizot's Elitist Theory of Representative Government," *Critical Review* 15, no. 3–4 (January 2003): 261–284.

83. While Constant emerged as the guardian of press freedom, he only arrived at that position in the context of Restoration politics. For an overview of Constant's shifting opinions on freedom of the press, see Ghins, "Benjamin Constant and Public Opinion in Post-Revolutionary France." K. Steven Vincent concludes that Constant's liberalism complicates the image of French liberalism as political rationalism offered by Rosanvallon; see Vincent, "Benjamin Constant, the French Revolution, and the Origins of French Romantic Liberalism."

84. Constant, *Des Motifs qui ont dicté le nouveau projet de loi sur les élections*; *Second Discours prononcé par Benjamin Constant sur la loi des élections* (Grenoble: Barnel, 1820); Constant, *Des élections de 1818* (Paris: Béchet, 1818); Constant, *De la proposition de changer la loi des élections*.

85. Constant, *De la Liberté des brochures, des pamphlets et des journaux, considérée sous le rapport de l'intérêt du gouvernement* (Paris, 1814), 19.

86. Constant, *Conquest and Usurpation*, 77.

87. And a proliferation of religious sects as well. See Rosenblatt, *Liberal Values*.

88. The themes of self-development and self-knowledge can be found throughout Constant's multi-volume *De la Religion*, ed. Tzvetan Todorov and Etienne Hofmann (Arles: Actes Sud, 1999).

89. This is due in large part to work by Lucien Jaume.

90. *Principes*, 2:397, 150.
91. *Principes*, 2:401, 396.
92. *Principes*, 2: 390.
93. *Principes*, 2:391.
94. Garsten, "From Popular Sovereignty to Civil Society in Post-Revolutionary France," 254; Levy, "Pluralism without Privilege?"
95. *Principes*, 2:391.
96. Constant, *Conquest and Usurpation*, 77.
97. Constant, *Conquest and Usurpation*, 77. "The whole nation is nothing separated from the parts that compose it."
98. Constant, *Conquest and Usurpation*, 74–76; 155. Constant praised the pluralism of Great Britain and its unreformed Commons.
99. Welch, *Liberty and Utility*, 45–59.
100. *Principes*, 2:391.
101. *Principes*, 2:392.
102. Constant was himself attuned to the dangers of minority faction in the legislature, but he defined the problem as the domination of one single interest, rather than as the diversity of the deputies. Selinger very clearly outlines Constant's recommended safeguards against legislative factionalism. Selinger, *Parliamentarism*, 128–143.
103. *Principes*, 2:394.
104. Selinger, *Parliamentarism*, 118–120.
105. *Principes*, 2:391.
106. *Principes*, 2:395; Constant repeated this same line or some variation of it throughout his writings on elections during the Restoration. For only one example, see Constant, *Considérations sur le projet de loi relatif aux élections, adopté par la Chambre des Députés*, 11–12.
107. At this point, it is worth distinguishing Constant's views of the vote from those of the Victorian mirror theorists. While the two perspectives spring from a similar notion of what we would now call descriptive representation, their proponents ultimately were led in different directions. For one, Constant never put forth anything like the Victorians' sophisticated a formula for calibrating the suffrage and the composition of the electorate. He was content to allow popular election to translate into diversity, without diversifying the suffrage across constituencies in order to reflect society's pluralism. Second, as the second half of this chapter argues, Constant sought to fit his representational aims into a capacitarian scheme for the suffrage, and recommended a uniform *cens* that would have narrowed the franchise to the propertied. As Conti has shown, many of the Victorian mirror theorists explicitly differentiated their theories of social representation from the capacitarian model of the French. Conti, *Parliament the Mirror of the Nation*. For a theory of descriptive representation that owes its origins to British thought, see Chapter 5 on Duvergier de Hauranne.
108. *Principles*, 2:394.
109. *Principes*, 2:200.

110. On the distinction between elector and citizen, see Bernard Manin, *The Principles of Representative Government* (Cambridge, UK: Cambridge University Press, 1997), 99.

111. Emmanuel Joseph Sieyès, *Préliminaire de la constitution françoise: Reconnoissance et exposition raisonnée des droits de l'homme et du citoyen* (Paris: Baudoin, 1789), 36.

112. Sewell documents Sieyès' subsequent proposals in Sewell Jr., *A Rhetoric of Bourgeois Revolution*, 177.

113. Crook traces its disappearance in Crook, *Elections in the French Revolution*, 22.

114. "From the beggar, who owns no property, to the king on his throne, there is not a citizen, not an individual, not a human being, who does not have rights. They have different rights; some have political rights; others such and such rights; all have the right to be protected and to be safeguarded from arbitrariness." Quoted in Guy H. Dodge, *Benjamin Constant's Philosophy of Liberalism: A Study in Politics and Religion* (Chapel Hill: University of North Carolina Press, 2012), 113.

115. *Principes*, 2:200–201.

116. Aristotle, *Politics*, 1328b37–1329a2.

117. In 1818, Constant wrote approvingly that the French system "did not entrust its political rights to the poor," giving it one advantage over the English, who gave too much credit to the masses too quickly. Benjamin Constant, "Pensées diverses sur les élections," in *Oeuvres complètes*, ed. Étienne Hofmann, vol. 11 (Berlin: Walter de Gruyter, 2011), 421.

118. *Principes*, 2:208; Compare this statement with Constant's praise of the French electoral system after the passage of the Lainé Law, when neither the "excessive opulence" of the old aristocracy nor the "excessive misery" of the pauper classes held much sway. Constant, "Pensées diverses sur les élections," 421.

119. *Principes*, 2:199.

120. *Principes*, 2:201.

121. *Principes*, 2:220.

122. Though he would later defend the terms of the Lainé Law, he disagreed with other liberals in the debates leading up to its passage. He maintained that the direct tax of 300 francs "supposes too high an income." Holmes, *Benjamin Constant and the Making of Modern Liberalism*, 306, note 18.

123. Constant, "Principles of Politics Applicable to All Representative Governments," 213.

124. Constant, "Pensées diverses sur les élections," 419–421.

125. *Principes*, 2:201.

126. *Principes*, 2: 215. Consider Constant's contrast between the detached scholar, who is "rarely bothered by power" and the proprietor, who seems to display the proper degree of anger against abuses of power.

127. An illuminating study of Cabanis' overlapping medical and political philosophies can be found in Martin S. Staum, *Cabanis: Enlightenment and Medical Philosophy in the French Revolution* (Princeton, NJ: Princeton University Press, 2014). On Cabanis as a political thinker in the school of the Idéologues, see also Welch, *Liberty and Utility*.

128. *Principes*, 2:215–216.

129. *Principes*, 2:215.
130. *Principes*, 2:216.
131. *Principes*, 2:206. See also his statement in Constant, "Pensées diverses sur les élections," 421: "Let the voters [of 300 francs/year] be persuaded that they must consult among themselves, that all having the same interest, they will never be mistaken about [it]."
132. *Principes*, 2:207, 220, 394.
133. *Principes*, 2: 394.
134. *Principes*, 2:221.
135. Benjamin Constant, *Commentary on Filangieri's Work*, trans. Alan Kahan (Indianapolis, IN: Liberty Fund, 2015), 119 and 111.
136. Constant, *Commentary*, 111–112.
137. Benjamin Constant, *Mélanges de littérature et de politique* (Paris: Pichon et Didier, 1829), x.
138. Rosenblatt speculates as to the reasons for Constant's eclipse in the nineteenth and twentieth centuries. Helena Rosenblatt, "Eclipses and Revivals: Constant's Reception in France and America, 1830–2007," in *Cambridge Companion to Constant* (Cambridge, UK: Cambridge University Press, 2009), 351–377.

Chapter 2

1. For glimpses into the rivalry between Guizot and Constant, see J.-P. Aguet, "Benjamin Constant parlementaire sous la monarchie de Juillet (juillet–décembre 1830)," *Annales Benjamin Constant* 2 (1982): 24 and Rosenblatt, *Liberal Values*, chapter 7.
2. Despite its name, Guizot often presented his party's agenda as progressive, claiming that it encouraged "movement in legislation." H.A.C. Collingham, *July Monarchy: A Political History of France, 1830–1848* (London: Addison-Wesley, 1988), 32. On the banquet campaign for suffrage reform that positioned the Left-liberals, members of the dynastic opposition, and the radical republicans against the Guizot government, see John J. Baughman, "The French Banquet Campaign of 1847–8." *The Journal of Modern History* 31, no. 1 (March 1959): 1–15. Guizot's infamous declaration against universal suffrage was printed in *Le Moniteur Universel*, March 27, 1847, 616.
3. On Guizot's roles in the July Monarchy, see Robert L. Koepke, "The Failure of Parliamentary Government in France, 1840–1848," *European Studies Review* 9, no. 4 (October 1979): 433–455; William Fortescue, "Morality and Monarchy: Corruption and the Fall of the Regime of Louis-Philippe in 1848," *French History* 16, no. 1 (March 2002): 83–100.
4. Mark Hulliung articulates one version of this view in *Citizens and Citoyens: Republicans and Liberals in America and France* (Cambridge, MA: Harvard University Press, 2002), x. A similar thesis underlies de Dijn's history of "undemocratic" freedom. De Dijn, *Freedom*.

5. The present chapter is not the first to study Guizot on democracy, though it is the first to disentangle Guizot's various uses of the term across a number of writings and speeches spanning the two regimes. Melvin Richter contrasted Guizot and Tocqueville on the topic in Richter, "Tocqueville and Guizot on Democracy: From a Type of Society to a Political Regime," *History of European Ideas* 30, no. 1 (March 2004): 61–82. Michael Drolet reinterprets Guizot's critiques of democracy through the lens of eighteenth-century debates over human character. Michael Drolet, "Carrying the Banner of the Bourgeoisie: Democracy, Self and the Philosophical Foundations of François Guizot's Historical and Political Thought," *History of Political Thought* 32, no. 4 (2011): 645–690.

6. François Guizot, "De la démocratie dans les sociétés modernes," *Revue française* (October 15, 1837), 208: "All of the ideas of modern democracy and all of its attempts at social organization start from [popular sovereignty] and come back to it."

7. Rosenblatt, *The Lost History of Liberalism*, 88–96. Because Kahan endeavors to glean the history of capacity from parliamentary debates across France, Britain, and Germany, he is attuned to the distinctions between individual and class-based concepts of capacity, but his study overlooks the underlying theoretical divisions between the two views. Kahan, *Liberalism in Nineteenth-Century Europe*.

8. Pierre Rosanvallon, "Guizot et la question du suffrage universel au XIXe siècle"; Aurelian Craiutu, "Guizot's Elitist Theory of Representative Government," *Critical Review* 15, nos. 3–4 (March 2003): 261–284. Craiutu's work has been an invaluable resource for me in writing this chapter.

9. Craiutu's pioneering study of the Doctrinaires includes a chapter on political capacity and representative government, but his aims are quite different from mine. Craiutu intends to tie the concept to the Doctrinaires' systematic political thought rather than to offer a fine-grained analysis of its features. Aurelian Craiutu, *Liberalism under Siege*.

10. The classic argument for Guizot's ideological shift from liberalism to conservatism is Rosanvallon, *Le moment Guizot*. See also Craiutu, *Liberalism under Siege*, 37. Alan Kahan locates Guizot's "definitive break" with liberalism in the 1842 suffrage debates. Kahan, *Liberalism in Nineteenth-Century Europe*, 50. Charles Pouthas argues for the coherence of Guizot's earlier thought in Pouthas, *Guizot pendant la Restauration* (Paris: Plon, 1923). Guizot, for his part, offered little guidance to subsequent scholars who wish to categorize his ideology; he labeled himself a "liberal conservative."

11. Roger Henry Soltau, *French Political Thought in the Nineteenth Century* (New Haven, CT: Yale University Press, 1931); Vincent Starzinger, *The Politics of the Center: The Juste Milieu in Theory and Practice, France and England, 1815–1848* (New York: Transaction Publishers, 1991). In Chapter 3, we will discover that Tocqueville joined the chorus of Guizot's contemporaneous liberal critics.

12. François Guizot, *Des moyens de gouvernement et d'opposition dans l'état actuel de la France* (Paris: Ladvocat, 1821), 185. A thoughtful summary of what was known as "The Great Debate" between liberals and Ultras in this period appears in Larry Siedentop, *Tocqueville* (Oxford: Oxford University Press, 1994), 20–40.

13. For a comprehensive study of the political thought of the Doctrinaires, see Craiutu, *Liberalism under Siege*.

14. Among other proposals, the Ultras sought to revive primogeniture, halt the fragmentation of large estates, curtail the freedom of the press, abolish trial by jury, and as we learned in Chapter 1, engineer electoral laws that favored the richest men out of an already-narrow *le pays légal*. See Jean-Jacques Oechslin, *Le mouvement ultra-royaliste sous la Restauration* (Paris: R. Pichon & R. Durand-Auzais, 1960); David Skuy, *Assassination, Politics, and Miracles: France and the Royalist Reaction of 1820* (Montreal: McGill-Queen's University Press, 2003).

15. Guizot's histories fostered what Siedentop calls "a liberal enthusiasm," and the halls of the Sorbonne became "rallying point[s] for liberal youth." Siedentop, "Introduction," in *The History of Civilization in Europe*, trans. William Hazlitt, ed. Larry Siedentop (Indianapolis: Liberty Fund, 2013), vii. John Stuart Mill hoped that Guizot's historical lectures would be similarly motivating for British liberals. Mill, "London Review (January 1836)," in *Collected Works of John Stuart Mill*, ed. John M. Robson (Toronto: University of Toronto Press, 1963–91), 20:367–393 and "Edinburgh Review (October 1845)," in *Collected Works of John Stuart Mill*, 20:381–421.

16. Guizot, *Histoire des origines du gouvernement représentatif en Europe* (Paris: Didier, 1851), 1:101–102. Hereafter abbreviated *HOGR*. All translations are my own.

17. De Dijn attributes this position to Montesquieu, and situates both Montesquieu and Guizot in a tradition of "aristocratic liberalism" that spanned the eighteenth and nineteenth centuries. Annelien de Dijn, *French Political Thought from Montesquieu to Tocqueville* (Cambridge, UK: Cambridge University Press, 2008). Although Montesquieu is famously regarded as a theorist of "the spirit" of the laws, Guizot did not quite see his predecessor in those terms. He criticized Montesquieu for placing too much emphasis on external forms of government (monarchies, for one) and overlooking the social preconditions of political power. See *HOGR*, 1:85–86.

18. The classic argument about "the social" and "the political" in French liberalism is Siedentop, "Two Liberal Traditions," in *French Liberalism from Montesquieu to the Present Day*, ed. Raf Geenens and Helena Rosenblatt (Cambridge, UK: Cambridge University Press, 2012), 15–35.

19. François Guizot, *Essais sur l'histoire de France: Pour servir de complément aux observations sur l'histoire de France de l'abbé de Mably*, 2nd ed. (Paris, 1824), 87.

20. Guizot argued against the social contract tradition: "The two facts—society and government imply one another; there is no more society without government than there is government without society . . . the necessary coexistence of society and government shows the absurdity of the hypothesis of the social contract." *HOGR*, 1:86–87.

21. *HOGR*, 1:103.

22. Guizot, *Du gouvernement de la France depuis la Restauration, et du ministère actuel* (Paris, 1830), 138–139.

23. Craiutu has convincingly shown how Tocqueville's understanding of the democratic social state originated with the Doctrinaires. Craiutu, *Liberalism under Siege*, 93–100. Another interpretation of "the social state" in *Democracy in America* comes from Michael Zuckert, "On Social State," in *Tocqueville's Defense of Human Liberty*, ed. Joseph Alulis and Peter A. Lawler (New York: Garland, 1993), 3–21.

24. Guizot, *De la peine de mort en matière politique* (Paris: Béchet, 1822), 26.

25. Guizot, *De la peine de mort en matière politique*, 27.

26. Quoted in Rosanvallon, *La démocratie inachévee*, 123, note 1.

27. Guizot, "De la démocratie dans les sociétés modernes," 193-225 at 194.

28. Guizot, *Des moyens de gouvernement et d'opposition dans l'état actuel de la France*, 151.

29. *Archives parlementaires, Deuxième Série* 34 (January 22, 1822), 133.

30. *HOGR*, 1:103.

31. *HOGR*, 1:108.

32. *Le Moniteur Universel*, March 26, 1847, 616.

33. Kahan contends that Guizot "abandoned liberalism" in favor of conservatism in this speech. My argument here emphasizes Guizot's consistency. Kahan, *Liberalism in Nineteenth-Century Europe*, 48.

34. Édouard Alletz, *De la démocratie nouvelle, ou des moeurs et de la puissance des classes moyennes en France* (Paris: F. Lequien, 1837).

35. Auguste Billiard, *Essai sur l'organisation démocratique de la France* (Paris: Hachette, 1837).

36. Although the title of Guizot's pamphlet was an obvious play on *Democracy in America*, Guizot did not include Tocqueville's text among those he chose to review. This was a glaring omission given that its first volume was published two years earlier to great acclaim. For a contemporaneous commentary on Billiard and Alletz and on Guizot's assessments of each of them, see Giuseppe Mazzini, "In Defense of Democracy: A Reply to Mr. Guizot" [1839], in *A Cosmopolitanism of Nations: Giuseppe Mazzini's Writings on Democracy, Nation-Building, and International Relations*, ed. Stefano Recchia and Nadia Urbinati (Princeton, NJ: Princeton University Press, 2009), 66–80.

37. Guizot, "De la démocratie dans les sociétés modernes," 194.

38. Guizot, "De la démocratie dans les sociétés modernes," 197 and 225. Guizot repeats the characterization of democracy as "a cry of war" in his 1849 text, *De la Démocratie en France*. Its use in 1837 (and at least once before in 1816), suggests more consistency across his assessments of political democracy than scholars have argued.

39. Guizot, "De la démocratie dans les sociétés modernes," 197–198.

40. Guizot, "De la démocratie dans les sociétés modernes," 212. There is quite a lot to say about the explicit disagreements between Guizot and Rousseau, and perhaps even more to say about where the two may have agreed. While such comparisons are well beyond the scope of this chapter, later sections do place the two in conversation on the topics of representation and rationality.

41. Guizot, "De la démocratie dans les sociétés modernes," 223.

42. Guizot, *Des moyens de gouvernement et d'opposition dans l'état actuel de la France*, 153.

43. For an overview of nineteenth and twentieth-century arguments that position violence as a vehicle for social and democratic rejuvenation (arguments that were very different from Guizot's), see Kevin Duong, *The Virtues of Violence: Democracy Against Disintegration in Modern France* (Oxford: Oxford University Press, 2020).

44. Guizot, "Philosophie politique: de la souveraineté," in *Histoire de la civilization en Europe*, ed. Rosanvallon (Paris, Gallimard: 1985), 372.

45. Guizot, *The History of Civilization in Europe*, ed. Larry Siedentop and trans. William Hazlitt (Indianapolis, IN: Liberty Fund, 1997), 177. Hereafter abbreviated *HOCE*.

46. Malcolm Crook discusses Napoleonic elections in "The Uses of Democracy," 19–36.
47. *HOGR*, 2:140. Guizot equated Napoleon and Robespierre by coupling the Convention of 1792–5 with the First Empire, and decrying both as despotic.
48. Richard Boyd documents liberals' ambivalent assessments of Bonaparte in "Tocqueville and the Napoleonic Legend," in *Tocqueville and the Frontiers of Democracy*, ed. Ewa Atanassow and Boyd (Cambridge, UK: Cambridge University Press, 2013), 264–290.
49. *HOCE*, 263 and 268.
50. Craiutu identifies affinities between Guizot and Tocqueville on this point. *Liberalism under Siege*, 93–100. We will also remember that the Revolutionary d'Allarde and Le Chapelier laws annihilated corporations and voluntary associations, driving individuals further into a private existence.
51. Guizot, *Memoirs to Illustrate the History of My Time* (London: Richard Bentley, 1858), 1:24 and 26.
52. Pierre-Paul Royer-Collard, *De la liberté de la presse* [1822], in *Discours* (Paris: Librarie de Médicis, 1949), 40.
53. Rosanvallon, *Le moment Guizot*, 87–95; Craiutu, *Liberalism under Siege*, chapter 5. See also Lucien Jaume, "Guizot et la philosophie de la représentation," *Droits* 15 (January 1992): 141–152. The antiliberal Carl Schmitt, who viewed Guizot as *the* exemplar of bourgeois liberalism, wrote that the sovereignty of reason could not actually solve any of the problems produced by political equality. Carl Schmitt, *The Crisis of Parliamentary Democracy*, trans. Ellen Kennedy (Cambridge, MA: MIT Press, 1996).
54. Guizot traced these wrongheaded conceptions of sovereignty to humankind's need to "make their own masters." Guizot, *Philosophie politique: de la souveraineté*, 319–320.
55. Guizot, "De la démocratie dans les sociétés modernes," 208.
56. *HOGR*, 1:98.
57. *HOGR*, 1:26.
58. For a fuller discussion of the Doctrinaires and the press in this period, see André-Jean Tudesq, "Guizot et la Presse sous la Restauration," in *Guizot, les Doctrinaires et la presse, 1820–1830*, edited by D. Roldán (Val-Richer: Fondation Guizot, 1994), 1–10.
59. James Madison, *Federalist 10*, in *The Federalist*, ed. George W. Carey and James McClellan (Indianapolis, IN: Liberty Fund, 2001).
60. *HOGR*, 2:150; 1:94.
61. Mazzini, "In Defense of Democracy," 78.
62. *HOGR*, 2:230; Guizot, "Élections ou de la formation et des opérations des collèges électoraux," in *Discours académiques* (Paris: Didier, 1861), 380–403 at 385.
63. *HOGR*, 1:90.
64. *HOGR*, 2:253.
65. Rosanvallon looks to more recent history and uncovers the origins of sovereign reason in the Revolution and Restoration. *Le moment Guizot*, 87. Craiutu and Jaume both see some version of the sovereignty of reason it in the theories of the Prussian statesman Friedrich Ancillon, whose writings Guizot translated into French. Craiutu, *Liberalism under Siege*, 134–136. Lucien Jaume, *Tocqueville: The Aristocratic Sources of Liberty* (Princeton, NJ: Princeton University Press, 2013), 255–256. H.S. Jones contends that

Guizot "purified" the ideal of sovereign reason from Turgot and Condorcet. Jones, *The French State in Question: Public Law and Political Argument in the Third Republic* (Cambridge, UK: Cambridge University Press, 1993), 23–24.

66. *HOGR*, 1:109. Roberto Romani, for one, interprets Guizotian *raison* as indistinguishable from divine reason. See Romani, "Liberal Theocracy in the Italian Risorgimento," *European History Quarterly* 44, no. 4 (2014): 620–650.

67. *HOGR*, 1:98.

68. *HOGR*, 1:330–331; 2:252.

69. Michael Drolet argues that Guizot's arguments against democracy were grounded in Neoplatonism. Drolet, "Carrying the Banner of the Bourgeoisie."

70. Guizot, "De la démocratie dans les sociétés modernes," 220.

71. *HOGR*, 2:247.

72. *HOGR*, 2:248.

73. *HOGR*, 2:247–248.

74. *HOGR*, 2:245.

75. *HOGR*, 2:245.

76. *HOGR*, 2:242.

77. Frederick B. Artz, "The Electoral System in France During the Bourbon Restoration, 1815–30," *The Journal of Modern History* 1, no. 2 (1929): 210.

78. *HOGR*, 2:231.

79. Most of the references are contained in *HOGR*, 2:Lecture 15.

80. Guizot's attempt to appropriate the idea of the social interest is consistent with Rosanvallon's thesis on the Doctrinaires' motivations more generally. According to Rosanvallon, Guizot and Royer-Collard in particular applied a novel "semantic strategy" to overturn the "mental universe of the Revolution." Pierre Rosanvallon, *La démocratie inachevée: Histoire de la souveraineté du peuple en France* (Paris: Folio, 2003), 115–116.

81. *HOCE*, 61.

82. Guizot was clear to maintain that the incapable remain part of democratic society, though not part of the legal/political nation. "Élections," 386.

83. *HOGR*, 2:246.

84. *HOGR*, 2:253.

85. For a sketch of the ideal of a "new aristocracy" across the thought of French liberals, see Lucien Jaume, "Tocqueville face au thème de 'la nouvelle aristocratie': La difficile naissance des partis en France," *Revue française de science politique* 56 no. 6 (2006): 969–984. Chapter 5 proceeds along the same lines as Jaume's essay, as it compares Guizot's *la nouvelle aristocratie* with that of Tocqueville and Ernest Duvergier de Hauranne, though my analysis departs from Jaume's at key points.

86. Guizot, *Des moyens de gouvernement et d'opposition dans l'état actuel de la France*, 157.

87. *HOGR*, 2:254.

88. *HOGR*, 1:95:

89. Jaume, "Tocqueville face au thème de la 'nouvelle aristocratie.'"

90. Guizot notes that this new aristocracy does not provoke the same fears as other forms of superiority. See *Des moyens de gouvernement et d'opposition dans l'état actuel de la France*, 157–158.

91. Joseph de Maistre, "Study on Sovereignty," in *The Works of Joseph de Maistre*, ed. and trans. Jack Lively (New York: Macmillan, 1965), 116–119.

92. *HOGR*, 1:111.

93. Guizot, *De la peine de mort en matière politique*, 84.

94. *HOGR*, 2:262.

95. *HOGR*, 2:261.

96. Manin, *The Principles of Representative Government*, 30.

97. Crook, *Elections in the French Revolution*, 33–34.

98. Guizot, "Élections," 389.

99. Guizot, "De la démocratie dans les sociétés modernes,"44. See also *Archives parlementaires, Deuxième Série* (February 8, 1831), 66:604.

100. *HOGR*, 2:228.

101. *HOGR*, 2:233.

102. *HOGR*, 2:234–235.

103. *HOGR*, 2:236.

104. Guizot, *Essais sur l'histoire de France*, 88; *HOCE*, 12-13. See also *Memoirs*, 3:3: "time, place, manners, national age, geography, and history" all become determinants of capacity. For Guizot's concessions regarding the "inexact" signs of capacity, see *HOGR*, 2:231.

105. *HOGR*, 1:111.

106. On the 1817 electoral law, see Artz, "The Electoral System in France during the Bourbon Restoration, 1815–1830." Guizot estimated the law enfranchised 140,000 men, but this is probably too generous. Guizot, *Memoirs*, 3:162. Kahan notes that the French were consistently confused about the actual effects of their suffrage laws. Kahan, *Liberalism in Nineteenth-Century Europe*, 37.

107. Alistair Cole and Peter Campbell, *French Electoral Systems and Elections Since 1789* (Aldershot: Gower, 1989), 60.

108. See also Rosanvallon, *Le sacre du citoyen*, 273, who writes that with the law, "the philosophy and practice of the right to vote were suddenly founded on new bases."

109. A sketch of the radical republican position in this period appears in Gianna Englert, "Tocqueville's Politics of Grandeur," *Political Theory* 50, no. 3 (June 2022): 477–503.

110. Liberals in the party of movement such as Odilon Barrot wanted to extend the suffrage as far as possible (though not universally) at the start of the new regime in 1831 to avoid having to reopen the suffrage question every few years. In 1837, Barrot attacked *capacité* head-on in a heated engaged exchange with Guizot. Guizot leaned on the claims from his "De la démocratie dans les sociétés modernes," published that same year. Barrot countered by declaring that a suffrage based on Guizotian *capacité*, which he estimated yielded a franchise of 150,000, could never be representative of the new France—the France that even Guizot recognized. *Archives parlementaires, Deuxième Série* (February 9, 1831), 66:617; Odilon Barrot, *Mémoires posthumes de Odilon Barrot*, 3rd ed. (Paris: Charpentier, 1875), 315–317.

111. On their relationship, see Craiutu, "The Battle for Legitimacy."

112. For an argument that frames Guizotian *capacité* in terms of property, see Johnson, *Guizot*, 74.

113. Guizot, "Élections," 390.

114. Guizot, "Élections," 391.

115. Guizot, "Élections," 390.

116. *Archives parlementaires, Deuxième Série* (May 5, 1837), 110:493–494.

117. Guizot, "Élections," 392.

118. In 1842, Théodore Ducos argued that an "aristocracy of wealth pales before the aristocracy of intelligence and genius." See *Le Moniteur Universel* (February 15, 1842), 307.

119. Rosanvallon, *Le moment Guizot*; Jaume, *L'Individu effacé*; Starzinger, *The Politics of the Center*. A more nuanced version of the argument appears in Drolet, "Carrying the Banner of the Bourgeoisie."

120. Guizot, *Memoirs*, 1:163.

121. In his study of nineteenth-century liberalism, Kahan groups liberals according to whether they adopted an individualist or class-based view of capacity. As I have indicated, even the individualist orientation morphed into a class-based claim before long.

122. Guizot, "Élections," 391.

123. *Des moyens de gouvernement et d'opposition dans l'état actuel de la France*, 266, 264–265.

124. *Des moyens de gouvernement et d'opposition dans l'état actuel de la France*, 267.

125. *HOGR*, 2:262.

126. *HOCE*, 268.

127. Guizot, *Memoirs*, 3:14.

128. Johnson, *Guizot*; Craiutu, *Liberalism under Siege*; Laurent Theis, *François Guizot* (Paris: Fayard, 2008).

129. On the relationship of Guizot's Protestantism to his interest in education, a subject that is beyond the scope of this chapter, see Pierre-Yves Kirschleger, *La religion de Guizot* (Paris: Labor et Fides, 1999).

130. Guizot, *Memoirs*, 3:15

131. Guizot, *Memoirs*, 3:13

132. Guizot, *Memoirs*, 3:2.

133. Guizot, *Memoirs*, 3:4.

134. Guizot advised teachers to "have no fear of interfering in family rights" for the sake of instructing the child. *Memoirs*, 3:330.

135. Guizot, *Essai sur l'histoire et sur l'état actuel de l'instruction publique en France* (Paris, 1816), 2.

136. Jaume, *L'Individu effacé*, 120–169.

137. Guizot, *Essai sur l'histoire et sur l'état actuel de l'instruction publique en France*, 57, 59.

138. Johnson, *Guizot*, 130–133. Guizot's lukewarm Protestantism earned him the title "Pope of the Protestants." For details on particular reforms of the 1833 Law, see Felix Ponteil, *Histoire de l'enseignement en France* (Paris: Sirey, 1966), 197–203. In his 1816 *Essai*, Guizot also called for a corporate body of teachers that would exert superior influence on the administration of national education, akin to that of his new aristocracy in politics.

139. Guizot, *Memoirs*, 3:326. On the role for teachers after the Guizot law, see Sharif Gemie, "'A Danger to Society?' Teachers and Authority in France, 1833–1850," *French History* 2, no. 3 (September 1988): 264–287.

140. Guizot, *Essai sur l'histoire et sur l'état actuel de l'instruction publique en France*, 5.

141. Guizot, *Essai sur l'histoire et sur l'état actuel de l'instruction publique en France*, 24–25.
142. Guizot, *Memoirs*, 3:62.
143. One of the law's early drafts contained a provision to mandate girls' schools in every commune, but these provisions were cut before the final version.
144. Guizot, *Memoirs*, 3:62.
145. Guizot, *Essai sur l'histoire et sur l'état actuel de l'instruction publique en France*, 4.
146. Guizot, *Memoirs*, 3:63.

Chapter 3

1. Portions of this chapter appeared previously in Gianna Englert, "'Not More Democratic, but More Moral': Tocqueville on the Suffrage in America and France," *The Tocqueville Review/La Revue Tocqueville* 42, no. 2 (December 2021): 105–120 and in Englert, "Tocqueville's Politics of Grandeur." I am grateful to the editorial board of *The Tocqueville Review* and to SAGE Publications, the publisher of *Political Theory*, for granting me permission to reprint sections of both articles here.
2. Alexis de Tocqueville, *Democracy in America*, ed. Eduardo Nolla, trans. James T. Schleifer (Indianapolis: Liberty Fund Inc., 2012), 1:14. Hereafter, *DA*. The very recent publication of *The Cambridge Companion to Democracy in America* attests to the text's timeless quality. Richard Boyd, ed., *The Cambridge Companion to Democracy in America* (New York: Cambridge University Press, 2022).
3. James T. Schleifer has identified at least eleven other uses of the word "democracy" in *DA*. James T. Schleifer, *The Making of Tocqueville's "Democracy in America"* (Indianapolis: Liberty Fund, 2000).
4. The following list represents only a select portion of the literature. Michael Zuckert, "On Social State"; Raymond Aron, *Main Currents in Sociological Thought I: Montesquieu, Comte, Marx, Tocqueville—The Sociologists and the Revolution of 1848*, trans. Richard Howard and Helen Weaver (New York: Anchor, 1968); Sanford Lakoff, "Tocqueville, Burke, and the Origins of Liberal Conservatism," *The Review of Politics* 60, no. 3 (1998): 435–464; Jaume, *Tocqueville*, 16–19; Alan S. Kahan, *Tocqueville, Democracy, and Religion: Checks and Balances for Democratic Souls* (Oxford: Oxford University Press, 2015); Jennifer Pitts, *A Turn to Empire: The Rise of Imperial Liberalism in Britain and France* (Princeton, NJ: Princeton University Press, 2009); Ewa Atanassow, "Colonization and Democracy: Tocqueville Reconsidered," *American Political Science Review* 111, no. 1 (2017): 83–96.
5. There are exceptions to this rule. Three stand out: Robert Gannett Jr.'s work that traces Tocqueville on the suffrage, William Selinger's study of Tocqueville and corruption, and Stephen Sawyer's interpretation of Tocqueville as a theorist of the democratic state. Robert T. Gannett, Jr., "Tocqueville and the Politics of Suffrage," *The Tocqueville Review/La Revue Tocqueville* 27, no. 2 (2006): 209–225; William Selinger, "Le grand mal de l'époque: Tocqueville on French Political Corruption," *History of European Ideas* 42, no. 1 (January 2016): 73–94; Stephen W. Sawyer, *Demos Assembled: Democracy and the International Origins of the Modern State, 1840–1880* (Chicago, IL: University of Chicago Press, 2018). In addition, Dana Villa presents Tocqueville as a political actor intent on becoming a "teacher of the

people." Dana Villa, *Teachers of the People: Political Education in Rousseau, Hegel, Tocqueville, and Mill* (Chicago, IL: University of Chicago Press, 2017).

6. Robert D. Putnam, *Bowling Alone: The Collapse and Revival of American Community* (New York: Simon & Schuster, 2000); Jean Bethke Elshtain, "Citizenship and Armed Civic Virtue: Some Critical Questions on the Commitment to Public Life," *Soundings: An Interdisciplinary Journal* 69, no. 1/2 (1986): 99–110.

7. *DA*, 1:6. Emphasis mine.

8. *DA*, 1:28. Ever since Tocqueville's post-war rediscovery by figures such as Raymond Aron and François Furet, scholars have focused their attention on his definition of democracy as a social state. For an alternative history of Tocqueville's reception, see Serge Audier, *Tocqueville retrouvé: Genèse et enjeux du renouveau tocquevillien français* (Paris: J. Vrin, 2004).

9. Tocqueville's name is mentioned at least a dozen times in Kahan's monograph, but almost always it is as a point of reference. Tocqueville's views on the issue are never brought to the forefront. Kahan, *Liberalism in Nineteenth-Century Europe*.

10. Craiutu, *Liberalism under Siege*. See also Craiutu, "Tocqueville and the Political Thought of the French Doctrinaires (Guizot, Royer-Collard, Rémusat)," *History of Political Thought* 20, no. 3 (March 1999): 456–493.

11. This chapter follows in the vein of work by Françoise Mélonio and Jaume, who pit Tocqueville and Guizot as political enemies. While Jaume, for one, writes of the two figures at odds, he only gestures at the heart of their disagreements, and calls Tocqueville a theorist of "subdued popular sovereignty." My goal in this chapter is to dig deeper to uncover the source of their disputes. Françoise Mélonio, *Tocqueville and the French* (Charlottesville: University of Virginia Press, 1998); Jaume, *Tocqueville*. In his intellectual biography of Tocqueville, Brogan has documented Tocqueville's antipathy toward the July Monarchy and his personal dislike of Guizot. Hugh Brogan, *Alexis de Tocqueville: Prophet of Democracy in the Age of Revolution* (London: Profile Books, 2010), 375–406. Jean-Claude Lamberti goes so far as to argue that Tocqueville kept his disagreements with Guizot at the front of his mind as he composed certain chapters of *DA*. According to Lamberti, Tocqueville imagined that he might deliver some of the text of *DA* to confront Guizot in the Chamber. Lamberti, *Tocqueville and the Two Democracies*, trans. Arthur Goldhammer (Cambridge, MA: Harvard University Press, 1989).

12. This chapter contributes to scholarship that portrays Tocqueville as a "strange liberal," or as Welch writes, a thinker who "resisted" the idioms of his time. Cheryl Welch, *De Tocqueville* (New York: Oxford University Press, 2001); Roger Boesche, *The Strange Liberalism of Alexis de Tocqueville* (Ithaca, NY: Cornell University Press, 1987).

13. Alexis de Tocqueville, "Notes pour un Discours," in *Oeuvres Complètes* [hereafter, *OC*], ed. André Jardin, vol. 3, tome 2 (Paris: Gallimard, 1985), 208–212 at 209.

14. For more on this approach beyond what the previous chapter presented, see Stanley Mellon, *Political Uses of History: A Study of Historians in the French Restoration* (Stanford, CA: Stanford University Press, 1958).

15. Eduardo Nolla, "Editor's Introduction," in *DA*, lxvi, note 68.

16. *DA*, 1:14 and 12.

17. *DA*, 1:12, note r.

18. Tocqueville would later contend that the first of these, the Revolution of 1789, was not quite the dramatic rupture with the institutions of the *ancien régime* that its key actors intended. For this argument, see Alexis de Tocqueville, *The Ancien Régime and the French Revolution*, ed. Jon Elster, trans. Arthur Goldhammer (Cambridge, UK: Cambridge University Press, 2011).

19. *DA*, 1:18–19.

20. Nonetheless, Tocqueville's attitude toward Napoleon was much more complicated and ambivalent than those of his fellow liberals Constant and de Staël. On this point, see Boyd, "Tocqueville and the Napoleonic Legend," 264–288 and Sudhir Hazareesingh, *The Legend of Napoleon* (London: Granta, 2005).

21. *DA*, 2:1248. On this theme, see Paul Anthony Rahe, *Soft Despotism, Democracy's Drift: Montesquieu, Rousseau, Tocqueville, and the Modern Prospect* (New Haven, CT: Yale University Press, 2009).

22. Cheryl Welch has argued that Tocqueville's "resistance to the social" put him at odds with Guizot. While this chapter likewise attempts to pinpoint the differences between the two figures, it argues (*contra* Welch) that each of them began from a common vision of the social state, only to reach different conclusions regarding politics. See Cheryl Welch, "Tocqueville's Resistance to the Social," *History of European Ideas* 30, no. 1 (2004): 83–107.

23. For an alternative interpretation that portrays Tocqueville's new political science as an updated form of the ancients' soulcraft, see Harvey C. Mansfield and Delba Winthrop, "Tocqueville's New Political Science," in *The Cambridge Companion to Tocqueville*, ed. Cheryl B. Welch (Cambridge, UK: Cambridge University Press, 2006), 81–107.

24. *DA*, 1:28.

25. *DA*, 1:12.

26. Guizot would target Tocqueville more directly in 1849, when he blamed Tocqueville for inserting equality into the political sphere. François Guizot, *De la démocratie en France* (Paris: Victor Masson, 1849). For other reactions to volume 1 of *DA* in France, see Mélonio, *Tocqueville and the French*.

27. Tocqueville to Royer-Collard, September 27, 1841, *OC*, 11:108. Tocqueville reiterated these sentiments later in Alexis de Tocqueville, *Recollections: The French Revolution of 1848 and Its Aftermath*, ed. Olivier Zunz, trans. Arthur Goldhammer (Charlottesville: University of Virginia Press, 2016), 14–15.

28. Guizot to Tocqueville, April 26, 1842. Quoted in Jaume, *Tocqueville*, 290; Guizot was puzzled by their disagreements at other points as well. After receiving a copy of the 1840 volume of *DA*, Guizot commented, "I take pleasure in your ideas, though I don't agree with them. Why don't we agree?" Quoted in André Jardin, *Tocqueville: A Biography* (New York: Hill and Wang, 1989), 314.

29. *DA*, 1:18.

30. *DA*, 1:18.

31. *DA*, 1:89.

32. *DA*, 1:92.

33. *DA*, 1:313.
34. In addition to press campaigns, republicans in the 1830s held a series of banquets for reform, years before they would form an alliance with the *mouvement* deputies to undertake the well-known public banquet campaign of 1847. At this stage, the republicans generally advocated for a larger electorate rather than a universal suffrage. Within roughly a decade, Alexandre Auguste Ledru-Rollin, Louis Blanc, and Victor Considérant would unite "the social question" with the suffrage question to argue for universal suffrage. See Pamela Pilbeam, *The 1830 Revolution in France* (Houndmills: Palgrave Macmillan, 1991), 167–186. For an excellent article on Blanc's role, see Salih Emre Gerçek, "The 'Social Question' as a Democratic Question: Louis Blanc's Organization of Labor," *Modern Intellectual History* 20, no.2 (2023): 388–416.
35. Malcolm Crook, *How the French Learned to Vote: A History of Electoral Practice in France* (Oxford: Oxford University Press, 2021), 232.
36. *DA*, 1:313–314.
37. *Archives parlementaires*, vol. 66, February 8, 1831, 604.
38. In his chapter on universal suffrage, Tocqueville seemed far less worried about the tyranny of the majority than in other portions of the text. There, he felt that the electoral expression of majority will could act as a pacifying political force.
39. *DA*, 1:311.
40. Alletz led the Doctrinaires' assault on *Democracy in America*, contending that Tocqueville had grossly misinterpreted the progressive forward march of history. Instead of moving toward equality, Alletz argued, the transformations wrought by the new democracy terminated in the rule of the middle class. Alletz, *De la démocratie nouvelle*.
41. After 1848, by contrast, he admitted to feeling personally invigorated as he undertook a campaign under universal male suffrage. Tocqueville, *Recollections*, 76.
42. *DA*, 1:314.
43. *DA*, 1:314 and 317. Constant took note of a similar fact in 1806. "There is *no chance* that these representatives of the people will be intellectually superior . . . Their opinions will be at the level of ideas in the widest circulation." But because Constant was concerned to represent society's interests rather than elevate its superior few, he did not depict this as problem per se. Constant, *Principes*, 2:72. Emphasis added.
44. *DA*, 1:315.
45. Tocqueville to Louis Kergorlay, June 29, 1831, *OC*, 8.1:234.
46. *DA*, 1:316.
47. *DA*, 1:316–317.
48. In the editorial notes to this edition of *DA*, Nolla and Schleifer interpret Tocqueville's ruminations on government in America as variations on the Doctrinaires' central themes. By probing the text further, however, my reading here sheds light on more differences than affinities.
49. *DA*, 1:317.
50. Tocqueville's insights into electoral decision-making resemble those that would inform the field of behavioral economics, including its core assumption about

bounded rationality. For a summary of those assumptions in politics, see Jonathan Bendor et al., *A Behavioral Theory of Elections* (Princeton, NJ: Princeton University Press, 2011).

51. *DA*, 1:95.

52. Tocqueville, *The Ancien Régime and the French Revolution*.

53. *DA*, 1:95.

54. The note can be found in the Nolla/Schleifer edition. According to the editor, it is drawn from Tocqueville's notes on "ideas relative to America." For an explanation of the classification system used in this edition, see the editor's preface in *DA*, 1:xli.

55. *DA*, 1:93, note e.

56. This brief thought experiment brought Tocqueville quite close to an argument that Mill would make in earnest years later in *On Liberty* (1859). Obedience to an "Akbar or a Charlemagne" may be justified for those societies in their "nonage." Mill, *CW*, 18:224.

57. *DA*, 1:93, note e.

58. *DA*, 1:93, note e.

59. One version of the distinction between ordinary and extraordinary politics appears in Richard Tuck, *The Sleeping Sovereign: The Invention of Modern Democracy* (Cambridge, UK: Cambridge University Press, 2016).

60. The literature on Tocqueville's imperialism is vast. For some scholars, there are inherent and irresolvable tensions between Tocqueville's liberalism and his imperialism. Without delving into the details here, his concern that appeals to political capacity might become arguments *against* self-government may introduce one of those tensions into Tocqueville's thought. Melvin Richter, "Tocqueville on Algeria," *The Review of Politics* 25, no. 3 (1963): 362–398; Cheryl B. Welch, "Colonial Violence and the Rhetoric of Evasion: Tocqueville on Algeria," *Political Theory* 31, no. 2 (April 2003): 235–264; Roger Boesche, "The Dark Side of Tocqueville: On War and Empire," *The Review of Politics* 67, no. 4 (2005): 737–752; Jennifer Pitts, "Empire and Democracy: Tocqueville and the Algeria Question," *Journal of Political Philosophy* 8, no. 3 (2000): 295–318.

61. Tocqueville, "La proposition Gauguier," *OC*, 3.2:240.

62. "To know democracy . . . to find lessons there from which we would be able to profit." *DA*, 1:27–28.

63. Tocqueville to Eugène Stöffels, October 5, 1836 in *The Tocqueville Reader*, ed. Olivier Zunz and Alan Kahan (Oxford: Blackwell, 2002), 156–158 at 157.

64. Tocqueville to Eugène Stöffels, October 5, 1836, 157.

65. *DA*, 1:18.

66. Tocqueville to Stöffels, 157.

67. Tocqueville to Gustave de Beaumont, August 9, 1840, in *Alexis de Tocqueville: Selected Letters on Politics and Society*, ed. Roger Boesche (Berkeley: University of California Press, 1985), 142–143.

68. Tocqueville, *Recollections,* 8; Tocqueville, "Lettres sur la situation intérieure de la France," in *OC*, 3.2:95.

69. For a thorough study of Tocqueville on corruption, see Selinger, "Le grand mal de l'époque." While Selinger's study homes in on Tocqueville's remarkable administrative proposals to fight corruption, this chapter looks to his complementary electoral recommendations and later, to his suggestions for reorganizing the suffrage.

70. This was according to one of Tocqueville's calculations, which Beaumont seemed to confirm. Tocqueville, "Réglementation de fonctions publiques et publicité de l'emploi des funds de secours," *OC*, 3.2:219–222 at 220.

71. Tocqueville, "Discussion de l'adresse," January 18, 1842, *OC*, 3.2:206.

72. On the surprising overlap between Tocqueville's opposition and the reformist aims of the political Left, see Englert, "Tocqueville's Politics of Grandeur."

73. Tocqueville, "Discussion de l'adresse," 205.

74. Certain prominent members of the republican Left, from Alexandre Auguste Ledru-Rollin to Louis Blanc to Louis-Antoine Garnier-Pagès, also fought parliamentary corruption in this period. Yet Tocqueville suspected them of colluding with the dynastic Left led by Barrot, and for many reasons—personal as well as political—he was predisposed to distrust their intentions. See Tocqueville, *Recollections*, 52–53.

75. This is the estimate in Gannett, Jr., "Tocqueville and the Politics of Suffrage," 210.

76. Tocqueville, "Discussion de l'adresse," 205.

77. Tocqueville, "Discussion de l'adresse," 205–206.

78. Tocqueville, "Discussion de l'adresse," 205. In addition to Tocqueville's attempts to abolish the system of direct elections, Selinger demonstrates that Tocqueville endeavored to remedy corruption by separating bureaucratic offices from all political or electoral considerations. Selinger, "Le grand mal de l'époque."

79. *DA*, 1:320.

80. *DA*, 1:321.

81. Mélonio presents two-tiered elections as one of the "secrets" of American democracy that Tocqueville wished to tell his countrymen. Mélonio, *Tocqueville and the French*, 24.

82. *DA*, 1:321.

83. As we learned in the previous chapter, Guizot insisted that elections should take place at the local level, where voters have already engaged in the daily habits of public life. For Tocqueville, this proximity between voter and deputy only encouraged patronage.

84. Tocqueville, "Discussion de l'adresse," 206. Once again, Tocqueville seems to anticipate some of the insights about bounded rationality from behavioral economics.

85. Tocqueville, "Notes pour un Discours," *OC*, 3.2:209.

86. Tocqueville, "Discussion de l'adresse," 205.

87. Tocqueville's approach to the suffrage and the electoral law was yet another example of his ambition, as Welch writes, to "take a solitary and original path that disregarded the signs and markers constructed by others." Welch, *De Tocqueville*, 8.

88. Michael Hereth, *Alexis de Tocqueville: Threats to Freedom in Democracy*, trans. George F. Bogardus (Durham, NC: Duke University Press, 1985); Kevin Duong, "The Demands of Glory: Tocqueville and Terror in Algeria," *The Review of Politics* 80, no. 1 (2018): 31–55; Pitts, *A Turn to Empire*.

89. Tocqueville's final extended public discussion of empire was in 1847. See the "Second Report on Algeria," in Alexis de Tocqueville, *Writings on Empire and Slavery*, ed. and

trans. Jennifer Pitts (Baltimore, MD: John Hopkins University Press, 2001), 175–198. He did revisit the subject of European imperialism briefly in 1857 in a series of letters about the Sepoy Rebellion.

90. Tocqueville, "De la classe moyenne et du peuple," OC, 3.2:738–741; Tocqueville, "Question financière," 734–737.

91. Roughly 200,000 men out of a population of 35 million had the right to vote in national elections as a result of the cens in 1831. The numbers for the municipal suffrages would have been higher.

92. Tocqueville, "De la classe moyenne et du peuple," 741.

93. On the administrative side, see Selinger, "Le grand mal de l'époque."

94. Gannett, Jr. takes a different approach than other scholars, and one that comes closest to my own in this chapter. Gannett reads Tocqueville's various responses to the suffrage question as reactions to changing political circumstances. I take that approach further here: Tocqueville's call for suffrage reform was not only a reaction to revolution on the horizon. It was also the next phase of his ongoing plan to combat corruption. Gannett, Jr., "Tocqueville and the Politics of Suffrage."

95. Following pioneering work by Seymour Drescher in the 1960s, scholars over the last few decades have questioned the orthodoxy regarding Tocqueville and social class. For examples, see Drescher's classic Dilemmas of Democracy: Tocqueville and Modernization (Pittsburgh, PA: University of Pittsburgh Press, 1968); Michael Drolet, Tocqueville, Democracy and Social Reform (New York: Palgrave Macmillan, 2003); Eric Keslassy, Le libéralisme de Tocqueville à l'épreuve du paupérisme (Paris: L'Harmattan, 2000); Gianna Englert, "'The Idea of Rights': Tocqueville on The Social Question," The Review of Politics 79, no. 4 (2017): 649–674.

96. Mélonio, Tocqueville and the French; Jon Elster, Alexis de Tocqueville, the First Social Scientist (Cambridge, UK: Cambridge University Press, 2009); Sheldon S. Wolin, Tocqueville between Two Worlds: The Making of a Political and Theoretical Life (Princeton, NJ: Princeton University Press, 2003); Alan S. Kahan, Aristocratic Liberalism: The Social and Political Thought of Jacob Burckhardt, John Stuart Mill, and Alexis de Tocqueville (New York: Oxford University Press, 1992); Brogan, Alexis de Tocqueville.

97. Tocqueville, Recollections, 31.

98. Tocqueville, "Question financière," 735.

99. Tocqueville, "Lettres sur la situation intérieure de la France," OC, 3.2, 95–121 at 114. Perhaps because of his nostalgia, Tocqueville seems to glorify the liberal opposition during the Restoration as a unified force rather than the more fractured coalition that it actually was.

100. Tocqueville, Recollections, 31.

101. Tocqueville, "De la classe moyenne et du peuple," 739.

102. Tocqueville, "Question financière," 735; Tocqueville, Recollections, 8.

103. Tocqueville, Recollections, 8.

104. Tocqueville, Recollections, 12.

105. Tocqueville, "Question financière," 737.

106. Tocqueville, Recollections, 97.

107. Tocqueville, Recollections, 97.

108. As he listened to accounts of the banquets of 1847–8, Tocqueville claimed to have heard notes of "violence" in the radical republicans' speeches. Tocqueville, *Recollections*, 20.

109. Tocqueville, "Speech on the Right to Work," September 12, 1848, in *Compte Rendu des Séances de l'Assemblée Nationale*, 964–967.

110. Tocqueville, "De la classe moyenne et du peuple," 739. For a study that documents not only the disagreements but the more curious affinities between Tocqueville and the radicals in this period, see Englert, "Tocqueville's Politics of Grandeur."

111. The most comprehensive study of Tocqueville's activities during the Second Republic is Sharon B. Watkins, *Alexis de Tocqueville and the Second Republic, 1848–1852: A Study in Political Practice and Principles* (Lanham, MD: University Press of America, 2003).

Chapter 4

1. Throughout this chapter and the one following, I use "universal suffrage" to mean "universal manhood suffrage." This is for the sake of consistency as I move between my own analysis and primary texts from the period, whose authors simply referred to "*le suffrage universel.*" This is also because even most of the more vocal partisans of universal suffrage in this period, including those on the radical Left, assumed that women were best represented politically by their husbands. Very few, if any, French figures shared our twenty-first century sense of "universal." See Anne Verjus, *Le cens de la famille: Les femmes et le vote, 1789–1848* (Paris: Belin, 2002). On the Left and universal suffrage, see Kevin Duong, "What Was Universal Suffrage?" *Theory & Event* 23, no. 1 (2020): 29–65.

2. On the role of the plebiscites in linking emperor to electorate, see Stuart L. Campbell, *The Second Empire Revisited: A Study in French Historiography* (New Brunswick: Rutgers University Press, 1978), 4.

3. Quoted in Louis Girard, *Napoléon III* (Paris: Fayard, 1986), 181.

4. Laboulaye's *Le Parti libéral* was considered a commercial success. It sold over 10,000 copies in five years and was reissued in eight different editions from 1863 to 1872.

5. Writing of the Atlantic revolutions in 1848, Laboulaye admitted that "these were the revolutions that made a political writer of me." Laboulaye, *Questions constitutionnelles* (Paris: Charpentier, 1872), 3.

6. Laboulaye's *Considérations sur la Constitution* (Paris: A. Durand, 1848) included a critique of socialist thought and of elements of the French constitution that he believed had deviated too far from the American model. Similar critiques also appeared in Laboulaye, *La Révision de la constitution* (Paris: A. Durand, 1851).

7. Laboulaye himself reissued Constant's *Cours de politique constitutionnelle* with updated forewords in 1861 and 1872. For the second edition, see Édouard Laboulaye, ed., *Benjamin Constant: Cours de politique constitutionnelle* (Paris: Guillaumin, 1872). Ghins reiterates this point as evidence that Laboulaye constructed a liberal

tradition from whole cloth. Arthur Ghins, "What Is French Liberalism?," *Political Studies*, Online First (October 2022).

8. Édouard Laboulaye, *De La Constitution Américaine et de l'utilité de son étude* (Paris: Hennuyer, 1850), 10. René Rémond named Laboulaye among the triad of French friends of the United States, alongside Tocqueville and the Marquis de Lafayette. René Rémond, *Les États-Unis devant l'opinion française* (Paris: A. Colin, 1962). Jeremy Jennings calls Laboulaye "the most vigorous and articulate member of the 'American school' in France" and the "most impressive" liberal of the post-1848 generation. Jeremy Jennings, *Revolution and the Republic: A History of Political Thought in France Since the Eighteenth Century* (Oxford: Oxford University Press, 2013), 92 and 191. For a biography of Laboulaye, see Jean de Soto, "Édouard Laboulaye," *Revue internationale d'histoire politique et constitutionnelle* 5 (1955): 114–150. On Laboulaye's praise of the American model of executive power, see Stephen W. Sawyer, "An American Model for French Liberalism: The State of Exception in Édouard Laboulaye's Constitutional Thought," *The Journal of Modern History* 85, no. 4 (2013): 739–771.

9. Édouard Laboulaye, *The United States and France* (Boston, MA: The Boston Daily Advertiser, 1862).

10. To read the riveting story of the statue's origins, see Francesca Lidia Viano, *Sentinel: The Unlikely Origins of the Statue of Liberty* (Cambridge, MA: Harvard University Press, 2018).

11. Rosenblatt depicts Laboulaye as an admirer of Constant and defender of religious liberty. Rosenblatt, "On the need for a Protestant Reformation: Constant, Sismondi, Guizot, and Laboulaye," in *French Liberalism from Montesquieu to the Present Day*, 115–133. Edmund Fawcett includes Laboulaye in a list of "four exemplary liberal politicians" who navigated illiberal times, yet his discussion is only paragraphs long. Fawcett, *Liberalism: The Life of An Idea* (Princeton, NJ: Princeton University Press, 2014). André Dauteribes' "Les idées politiques d'Édouard Laboulaye" (PhD diss., Université de Montpellier, 1989) provides a systematic study of Laboulaye's political thought, though the work remains unpublished. The only monograph about Laboulaye in English is Walter Gray's *Interpreting American Democracy in France: The Career of Édouard Laboulaye, 1811–1883* (Newark: University of Delaware Press, 1994). Sawyer's recent work suggests bourgeoning interest in Laboulaye as Tocqueville's torchbearer. Sawyer, *Demos Assembled.*

12. In their respective studies of nineteenth-century liberalism, André Jardin and Louis Girard highlight Laboulaye's leadership role in the liberal party. André Jardin, *Histoire du libéralisme politique de la crise de l'absolutisme à la constitution de 1875* (Paris: Hachette, 1985); Louis Girard, *Les Libéraux français, 1814–1875* (Paris: Aubier, 1985). Jaume briefly discusses Laboulaye as a student of Constant and as a "republican liberal" in Jaume, *L'Individu effacé*, 330 n. 141. Rosanvallon's *Le sacre du citoyen* contains four references to Laboulaye, two of which appear in footnotes. Once again, Sawyer's work offers the most thorough analysis of Laboulaye on the democratic question, though Sawyer focuses on the institutional organization of

the democratic state rather than on Laboulaye's basic definition of "democracy" that informs it.

13. Sudhir Hazareesingh, *From Subject to Citizen: The Second Empire and the Emergence of Modern French Democracy* (Princeton, NJ: Princeton University Press, 1998), 26, 219–227.

14. Hazareesingh, *From Subject to Citizen*, 26.

15. Laboulaye, *Le Parti libéral, son programme et son avenir* (Paris: Charpentier, 1863), 5. Hereafter abbreviated *LPP*.

16. *LPP*, 134.

17. My argument here challenges the interpretation of the "anti-democratic" Laboulaye put forward by de Dijn in *French Political Thought from Montesquieu to Tocqueville*, 158–70.

18. Shortly after the Revolution of 1848, Guizot fled to England. When he returned to France, he wisely kept his distance from politics. From 1849 until his death in 1874, he completed a multi-volume history of the Glorious Revolution and a study of Christianity along with his *Memoirs*.

19. Pierre Jules Baroche, *Compte rendu des séances de l'Assemblée nationale législative*, 8, May 23, 1850, 130–131. Tocqueville, who sat on the constitutional committee, held that universal suffrage was a way to *counter* the socialist threat. See Watkins, *Alexis de Tocqueville and the Second Republic*, 445–447.

20. Adolphe Thiers, Session of May 24, 1850 in *Discours parlementaires de M. Thiers* (Paris: Calmann Levy, 1879), 9:44.

21. Thiers, *Discours parlementaires de M. Thiers*, 9:39.

22. "La Constitution Républicaine du 4 Novembre 1848," in *Les Constitutions de la France depuis 1789*, ed. Godechot, 266–267.

23. Barrot briefly entertained the idea of an indirect electoral scheme, despite knowing that it could never be implemented. Charles Alméras, *Odilon Barrot, avocat et homme politique (1791–1873)* (Paris: Presses Universitaires de France, 1951), 190–191.

24. Thiers, *Discours parlementaires de M. Thiers*, 39–41.

25. In the industrial cities of Lille and Nimes, the outcomes were similar to those in Paris. In Roubaix, a major center of textile production in the north, the number was as high as eighty percent. Rosanvallon, *Le sacre du citoyen*, 402.

26. Léon Faucher, *Compte rendu des séances de l'Assemblée nationale législative*, 8, May 18, 1850, 48–50.

27. Ferdinand Béchard, *Compte rendu des séances de l'Assemblée nationale législative*, 8, May 22, 1850, 88.

28. Rosanvallon characterizes this strategy as an attempt to "outwit" universal suffrage with a "*compromis bâtard.*" Rosanvallon, *Le sacre du citoyen*, 402.

29. Thiers, *Discours parlementaires de M. Thiers*, 9:40.

30. I am indebted to the monographs by Rosanvallon and Kahan, from which the framework for the previous section is drawn.

31. Rosanvallon, *Le sacre du citoyen*, 402. Tocqueville predicted as much. He predicted that "the only sure result is [the law] it will eliminate three million voters, most

of which, if we must maintain the principle of universal suffrage, deserve to be maintained." Nassau Senior, "Conversations with Alexis de Tocqueville," *OC*, 6.2:261.

32. Girard, *Les Libéraux français*, 170–171. Girard presents liberals as the "great losers" of the Empire, since they lost both parliamentary power and the fight over the franchise.

33. Louis-Napoleon Bonaparte, "Proclamation du 18 janvier 1852."

34. A fascinating retelling of Laboulaye's fate in the early years of the Empire can be found in Viano, *Sentinel*, chapter 11.

35. Roger Price, *The French Second Empire: An Anatomy of Political Power* (Cambridge, UK: Cambridge University Press, 2001), part II.

36. Jardin, *Histoire du libéralisme politique*. In the 1857 elections, only five liberals were elected to the *Corps législatif*. In the 1863 elections, members of the liberal party won three times as many seats.

37. Price, *The French Second Empire*, 301–304.

38. Gray, *Interpreting American Democracy in France*, 64.

39. Girard, *Les Libéraux français*, 188.

40. The eminent historian Guido de Ruggiero described liberalism as a "chaotic mixture" in his effort to capture the state of the liberal party. Guido de Ruggiero, *The History of European Liberalism*, trans. R.G. Collingwood (London: Humphrey Milford, 1927), 203.

41. On debates over centralization versus decentralization, see Hazareesingh, *From Subject to Citizen*, chapter 3. De Dijn presents a more straightforward story and frames decentralization as the opposition's "rallying cry" in this period. De Dijn, *French Political Thought from Montesquieu to Tocqueville*, 173.

42. This chapter focuses on one of the fault lines that divided liberals in this period. As Hazareesingh has argued, there were certainly others: provincial versus Parisian liberalisms, economic versus political, secular and religious. See Hazareesingh, *From Subject to Citizen*, 184–189.

43. This camp included Émile Ollivier and Lucien-Anatole Prévost-Paradol.

44. For a similar interpretation, see George Armstrong Kelly, who argues that liberalism traveled from the world of politics into the world of critique across the century. Kelly, *The Humane Comedy: Constant, Tocqueville, and French Liberalism*, rev. ed. (Cambridge, UK: Cambridge University Press, 2007), 225.

45. *LPP*, v.

46. *LPP*, 14, 299.

47. *LPP*, v.

48. *LPP*, 5, 7.

49. *LPP*, 122.

50. *LPP*, 15–19.

51. Many of Laboulaye's reflections on religion appear in his discussion of Benjamin Constant in *Revue nationale et étrangère, politique, scientifique et littéraire*, 3 (Paris: 1861) and in *La liberté religieuse* (Paris: Charpentier, 1858). See also Rosenblatt, "On the need for a Protestant Reformation."

52. Laboulaye would go on to decry the "despotism of the single Chamber" in his extended argument in favor of parliamentarism. *LPP*, 125–130.

53. *LPP*, 130.

54. Laboulaye knew full well, however, that universal suffrage in theory was not universal in practice. He served as president of the French Anti-Slavery Society and frequently corresponded with abolitionists in the North. In 1842, he published his *Recherches sur la condition civile et politique des femmes* (Paris: A. Durand, 1842), a history of women from ancient Rome to the present. Laboulaye stopped short of advocating for women's suffrage in that text. However, in tracing the history of marriage, he encouraged women of the nineteenth century to agitate for higher wages and to take control over their dowries.

55. As we will discuss briefly at the start of Chapter 5, not all of his contemporaries agreed with Laboulaye regarding the virtues of the American republic.

56. *LPP*, 134. Notice that Laboulaye sided with the likes of Constant and even Guizot against Tocqueville in denouncing indirect elections as illiberal.

57. *LPP*, 12. Emphasis added.

58. *LPP*, viii.

59. Constant, "The Liberty of the Ancients Compared with that of the Moderns," in *Political Writings*, 323.

60. Laboulaye was never a categorial opponent of the plebiscite. He approved of the plebiscite in 1870, which he described as the expression of constituent power in the people. The U.S. Minister to France John Bigelow refers to conversations with Laboulaye about this issue. See Bigelow, "Laboulaye," in *Bluntschli, Lieber, and Laboulaye*, ed. Daniel Coit Gilman (Baltimore, MD: Johns Hopkins University, 1884), 28–42.

61. *LPP*, viii.

62. *LPP*, 12.

63. *LPP*, 126–127.

64. *LPP*, 125.

65. In an otherwise complimentary review of *Democracy in America*, Laboulaye accused Tocqueville of employing a capacious and elastic concept of "democracy" in his work, so much so that he used the term to encompass every vice and weakness of the Americans. Édouard Laboulaye, *L'état et ses Limites* (Paris: Charpentier, 1865). Stephen Sawyer explores Laboulaye's other departures from Tocqueville in *Demos Assembled*, 76–98.

66. Laboulaye to Francis Lieber, September 25, 1865. Quoted and translated in Gray, *Interpreting American Democracy in France*, 152. Laboulaye and Lieber, along with the Swiss Jurist Johann Bluntschli, corresponded so often on matters of public and international law that they referred to themselves as "a scientific clover-leaf."

67. *LPP*, vi–vii.

68. *LPP*, vii.

69. *LPP*, x.

70. *LPP*, 7–8.

71. Laboulaye engaged in a similar discussion of self-government in his essay on centralization. "Centralization . . . has to be replaced by the free government of the individual by himself, self-government, for which we lack the word because we do not possess its substance." Laboulaye, *L'État et ses limites*, 72.

72. Napoleon's decree of March 1852 encouraged the creation of mutual aid societies. The Law of May 1864 abolished the crime of coalition, thus decriminalizing unions. See Alan R.H. Baker, *Fraternity Among the French Peasantry: Sociability and Voluntary Associations in the Loire Valley, 1815–1914* (Cambridge, UK: Cambridge University Press, 2004), 170–176. For more on the Empire's shift toward decentralization after 1860, see Hazareesingh, *From Subject to Citizen*.

73. See Gray, *Interpreting American Democracy in France*, 69–70.

74. David I. Kulstein, "Economics Instruction for Workers during the Second Empire," *French Historical Studies* 1, no. 2 (1959): 225–234. On musical societies for the workers, which were state-sponsored, see Jane Fulcher, "The Orphéon Societies: Music for the Workers in Second-Empire France," *International Review of the Aesthetics and Sociology of Music*, 10, no. 1 (1979) 47–56; William H. Sewell, *Work and Revolution in France: The Language of Labor from the Old Regime to 1848* (Cambridge: Cambridge University Press, 1980). For Laboulaye's positive assessment of these organizations, see Laboulaye, "De l'éducation," *Discours populaires* (Paris: Charpentier, 1869).

75. *LPP*, 309.

76. *LPP*, 310.

77. *LPP*, 310.

78. Guizot wrote of world-altering events that "take possession of all that exists in society, transform it, and place everything in an entirely new position . . . that which [man] sees, he has never seen before; what he saw once, no longer exists as he saw it." *HOGR*, 1:59. The Revolution of 1848 did for Laboulaye what 1789 did for Guizot. "The February Revolution of 1848 destroyed all my plans and overturned all of my ideas." Laboulaye, "Avertissement," *Questions constitutionnelles* (Paris: Charpentier, 1872), 3.

79. *LPP*, x–xi.

80. *LPP*, 134.

81. In the final paragraph of *LPP*, Laboulaye presented the "program of French democracy" as inseparable from that of French liberalism, both of which could be summarized in "three words: individual, social, and political freedoms." *LPP*, 313. Liberalism and democracy were thus joined under the banner of three freedoms.

82. *DA*, 1:12, note r.

83. *LPP*, 150.

84. *LPP*, 7.

85. *LPP*, 151.

86. *LPP*, 151.

87. *LPP*, 151.

88. *LPP*, 151.

89. Édouard Laboulaye, "Avertissement de la présente édition," in *Cours de Politique Constitutionnelle* (Paris: Guillaumin, 1872), i.

90. Laboulaye, "Introduction," in *Cours de Politique Constitutionnelle*, viii. Rosenblatt has documented how the influence of Sainte-Beuve's reviews redirected the public's attention from Constant's politics onto his rather scandalous personal life and tarnished his reputation as a result. See Rosenblatt, *Liberal Values*, chapter 7.

91. Laboulaye, "Introduction," xii.

92. This is not to deny Laboulaye's *political* liberalism, which is evident from his personal forays into French constitution-making and his poetic praise of the American Constitution, as well as in his writings on ministerial responsibility and a two-chambered parliament.

93. Constant, *De la religion*.

94. Édouard Laboulaye, "Benjamin Constant," in *Revue Nationale et Étrangère, Politique, Scientifique et Littéraire* (Paris, 1861), 7:513. Rosenblatt was among the first to unearth the spiritual roots out of which Constant's liberalism grew.

95. See especially Édouard Laboulaye, *La liberté religieuse* (Paris: Charpentier, 1858).

96. *LPP*, 8.

97. *LPP*, 175.

98. Unlike Tocqueville, Laboulaye never visited the country he so admired, often blaming ill health. He portrayed a stylized version of America in his 1863 novel, in which the entire city of Paris is transported to Massachusetts. Initially dismissive of the new World, the novel's protagonist comes to appreciate America's singular virtues. Édouard Laboulaye, *Paris en Amérique* (Paris: Charpentier, 1863).

99. *LPP*, 176.

100. Édouard Laboulaye, "Les Bibliothèques Populaires," in *Discours Populaires* (Paris: Charpentier, 1869) 11.

101. Laboulaye, "Introduction," xii. Laboulaye seemed to agree with Constant that most individuals would naturally discover that the truth lie in liberal Protestantism.

102. Laboulaye, "Introduction," xiii.

103. On the influence of Mann and Channing on Laboulaye, see Gray, *Interpreting American Democracy*.

104. *LPP*, 169.

105. *LPP*, 171.

106. Laboulaye, "Introduction," xxiv.

107. Laboulaye, "Introduction," 139.

108. *LPP*, 68.

109. Laboulaye, "De l'éducation," in *Discours Populaires* (Paris: Charpentier, 1869), 82.

110. Laboulaye placed his work in the tradition of the Guizot Law. Laboulaye, "L'instruction publique et le suffrage universel," in *L'État et ses limites* (Paris: Charpentier, 1863), 210.

111. Laboulaye, "L'instruction publique et le suffrage universel," 210–211.

112. Laboulaye, "L'instruction publique et le suffrage universel," 152–153.

113. He translated Benjamin Franklin's correspondence into French. Édouard Laboulaye ed., *Correspondance de Benjamin Franklin* (Paris: L. Hachette, 1866).

114. Mill qualified this proposal to exclude three groups from the franchise: those who could neither read nor write nor follow the basic rules of arithmetic, those who do not pay taxes, and those on parish relief. J.S. Mill, "Thoughts on Parliamentary Reform," in *The Collected Works of John Stuart Mill*, ed. John M. Robson (Toronto: University of Toronto Press, 1963–91), 19:311–340. On Millean and liberal political exclusions more generally, see Gianna Englert, "Liberty and Industry: John Locke, John Stuart Mill, and the Economic Foundations of Political Membership," *Polity* 48, no.4 (2016): 551–579.

115. Mill did not place his complete faith in the vote either, which he called "*one of* the chief instruments both of moral and intellectual training for the popular mind." Mill, "Thoughts on Parliamentary Reform," 322–323.

116. Mill, "Thoughts on Parliamentary Reform," 322.

117. *LPP*, 153. Laboulaye cited an 1817 pamphlet by Joseph Fiévée, who sided with the Ultras before 1820, for evidence of precisely how far France had drifted from the principles of free government that motivated the revolutionaries. Fiévée decried practices of electoral interference as nefarious efforts to "annihilate" constitutional freedoms by means of "trickery and seduction." Writing in 1863, Laboulaye concluded that Fiévée's reflections, "so correct at the time of a limited suffrage, have lost none of their truth or their force today." *LPP*, 154.

118. Price, *The French Second Empire*, 106. For a history of electoral corruption in the long nineteenth century, see Marcus Kreuzer, "Democratisation and Changing Methods of Electoral Corruption in France from 1815 to 1914," in *Political Corruption in Europe and Latin America*, ed. Walter Little and Eduardo Posada-Carbón (London: Palgrave Macmillan, 1996), 97–112.

119. Price, *The French Second Empire*, 107–108.

120. Some of Laboulaye's contemporaries chose to believe that universal suffrage would become "self-regulating" with time, and therefore regarded universal suffrage as a palatable, if from far from ideal, option. In an 1870 manifesto, the *Ligue de la Decentralisation* proclaimed that "it is by giving universal suffrage the opportunity to exercise itself freely and often that it will come to regulate itself." (Paris: 1870), 4.

121. *LPP*, 156.

122. Laboulaye, "Introduction," xx.

123. See Hazareesingh, *From Subject to Citizen*, 223.

Chapter 5

1. Antoine Isaac Silvestre de Sacy, *Journal des débats politiques et littéraires* (Paris, 1863).

2. Other assessments of eighteenth- and nineteenth-century American life "through European eyes" can be found in Aurelian Craiutu and Jeffrey C. Isaac, eds. *America Through European Eyes* (State College, PA: Penn State University Press, 2009).

3. Ernest Duvergier de Hauranne, *Huit mois en Amérique, lettres et notes de voyage*, 2 vols. (Paris: Lacroix, 1866).

4. Ernest Duvergier de Hauranne, "La démocratie et le droit de suffrage: II. Le suffrage universel," *Revue des Deux Mondes (1829–1971)* 74, no. 4 (1868): 785–821.

5. Raymond Huard, *La naissance du parti politique en France* (Paris: Presses de la Fondation nationale des sciences politiques, 1996), 13; Spitzer, "Restoration Political Theory," 68. J.A.W. Gunn challenges the view that the term *parti* was synonymous with faction, but concedes that a "party spirit" was seen as factious and divisive. J.A.W. Gunn, *When the French Tried to Be British: Party, Opposition, and the Quest for Civil Disagreement, 1814–1848* (Montréal: McGill-Queen's University Press, 2009).

6. On Prosper's opposition to the July Monarchy, see Fortescue, "Morality and Monarchy," 88; on his clashes with Guizot, see Jaume, *L'Individu effacé*, 158–164; Rosanvallon, *Le sacre du citoyen*, 282. Prosper also wrote on electoral reform to counter corruption under the July Monarchy. Prosper Duvergier de Hauranne, *De la réforme parlementaire et de la réforme électorale* (Paris: Paulin, 1847).

7. Ralph H. Bowen and Albert Kress, "Historical Introduction," in *A Frenchman in Lincoln's America: Huit Mois En Amérique, Lettres et Notes de Voyages, 1864–1865* (Chicago: R.R. Donnelley & Sons, 1974), xxi–xxii.

8. The confusion stems from the fact that the two also had similar first names. The younger Duvergier de Hauranne is Louis-Prosper-Ernest. See Adolphe Robert and Gaston Cougny, *Dictionnaire des parlementaires français: depuis le 1er mai 1789 jusqu'au 1er mai 1889* (Paris: Bourloton, 1889), 2:544–546.

9. Girard, *Les libéraux français*, 270. See also Price, *The French Second Empire*, 301–302.

10. Jaume, *L'Individu effacé*, 546, note 35.

11. Gunn's work on party and opposition ends in 1848. Gunn, *When the French Tried to Be British*.

12. On the French reaction to the text, see Bowen and Kress, "Historical Introduction."

13. Vincent Guillin and Djamel Souafa, "La réception de Stuart Mill en France," *La Vie des idées*, May 18, 2010, http://www.laviedesidees.fr/La-reception-de-Stuart-Mill-en.html; Gregory Conti, "Charles Dupont-White: An Idiosyncratic Nineteenth-Century Theorist on Speech, State, and John Stuart Mill," *Global Intellectual History*, July 22, 2021, 1–46; Sudhir Hazareesingh, *Intellectual Founders of the Republic: Five Studies in Nineteenth-Century French Republican Political Thought* (Oxford: Oxford University Press, 2005), chapter 2.

14. Georgios Varouxakis, "French Radicalism through the Eyes of John Stuart Mill," *History of European Ideas* 30, no. 4 (December 2004): 433–461; Guillin and Souafa, "La réception de Stuart Mill en France."

15. I acknowledge the different currents and strands of nineteenth-century British radicalism but use the term in a specific way in this chapter to refer to an ideology of democratic reform associated with the political incorporation of the working classes. See Eugenio F. Biagini and Alastair J. Reid, *Currents of Radicalism: Popular Radicalism, Organised Labour and Party Politics in Britain, 1850–1914* (Cambridge, UK: Cambridge University Press, 1991).

16. On the contrary—it was envisioned as a stopgap to stall further democratization. Robert Saunders, *Democracy and the Vote in British Politics, 1848–1867: The Making of the Second Reform Act* (Surrey: Ashgate, 2011).

17. Jonathan Parry, *The Rise and Fall of Liberal Government in Victorian Britain* (New Haven, CT: Yale University Press, 2009), 216.

18. The Anglophile Lucien-Anatole Prévost-Paradol, for one, thought that an *incremental* extension of suffrage would protect those views in the minority from being crowded out by an ignorant, enfranchised mob. Lucien Anatole Prévost-Paradol, *La France nouvelle* (Michel Lévy frères, 1868), 63–64.

19. Ernest Duvergier de Hauranne, "La démocratie et le droit de suffrage: I. Les théoriciens du droit de suffrage," *Revue des Deux Mondes (1829–1971)* 74, no. 3 (1868): 611.

20. And by default, also Constant's warnings. Benjamin Constant, "The Liberty of the Ancients Compared with That of the Moderns," in *Constant: Political Writings*, 309–328.

21. "La démocratie et le droit de suffrage I," 611.

22. He did not, however, mention Laboulaye by name, nor did he target the arguments of *LPP*.

23. "La démocratie et le droit de suffrage II," 786.

24. "La démocratie et le droit de suffrage I," 613.

25. "La démocratie et le droit de suffrage I," 612.

26. "La démocratie et le droit de suffrage I," 618.

27. "La démocratie et le droit de suffrage I," 612–613.

28. "La démocratie et le droit de suffrage I," 608.

29. "La démocratie et le droit de suffrage I," 613.

30. "La démocratie et le droit de suffrage I," 609.

31. This chapter does not take up the issue of whether Duvergier de Hauranne got English reform right—that is, whether he understood and accurately represented the Reform Bill and its defenders. This issue is secondary to our purposes here.

32. "La démocratie et le droit de suffrage I," 613.

33. On the many moving pieces and maneuvers behind the reform, see Saunders, *Democracy and the Vote in British Politics, 1848–1867*.

34. Additionally, Duvergier de Hauranne embraced the concept of utility, which had a complicated association with the Revolution. For the most part, the French spurned the concept. As Cheryl Welch argues, even the most modest Anglo consequentialism signaled "self-deception, social and political instability, the justification of terror, craven collaboration, and cynical raison d'état" for the French. Cheryl Welch, "'Anti-Benthamism': Utilitarianism and the French Liberal Tradition," in *French Liberalism from Montesquieu to the Present Day*, ed. Raf Geenens and Helena Rosenblatt (Cambridge, UK: Cambridge University Press, 2012), 134–152.

35. "La démocratie et le droit de suffrage I," 613. Emphasis mine.

36. "La démocratie et le droit de suffrage I," 613.

37. In his work on this period, Greg Conti differentiates the Victorian "mirror theorists" such as Mill, Hare, and Lorimer from "democrats" of the period such as A.V. Dicey, who subscribed to a uniform scheme for the suffrage, with or without the aim to mirror society. Duvergier de Hauranne, however, does not draw any such distinctions in the essay. While bearing Conti's typology in mind, this chapter follows Duvergier de Hauranne's lead on terminology. Conti, *Parliament the Mirror of the Nation*.
38. "La démocratie et le droit de suffrage I," 613.
39. John Stuart Mill wrote of "the exceedingly strange and lamentable incapacity of Britain and France to understand or believe the real character or springs of action of each other." Duvergier de Hauranne tried to overcome their "incapacity." "Mill to Gustave d'Eichtal," in *CW*, 13:465.
40. "La démocratie et le droit de suffrage I," 618.
41. "La démocratie et le droit de suffrage I," 615.
42. "La démocratie et le droit de suffrage I," 614.
43. "La démocratie et le droit de suffrage I," 614–615.
44. "La démocratie et le droit de suffrage I," 615.
45. Conti, *Parliament the Mirror of the Nation*.
46. Guizot, *Histoire parlementaire de France: Recueil complet des discours prononcés dans les chambres de 1819 à 1848* (Paris: Michel Lévy, 1863), 3:554–556.
47. "La démocratie et le droit de suffrage I," 619.
48. See also Jeremy Jennings, "Doctrinaires and Syndicalists: Representation, Parties, and Democracies in France," *Journal of Political Ideologies* 11, no. 3 (October 2006): 269–288.
49. Kahan, *Liberalism in Nineteenth-Century Europe*, 111.
50. Duvergier de Hauranne, "La démocratie et le droit de suffrage I," 698.
51. "La démocratie et le droit de suffrage II," 643; "La démocratie et le droit de suffrage I," 615.
52. Kahan, *Liberalism in Nineteenth-Century Europe*, 197–198.
53. "La démocratie et le droit de suffrage II," 785.
54. "La démocratie et le droit de suffrage I," 618–619.
55. "La démocratie et le droit de suffrage I," 616–617.
56. "La démocratie et le droit de suffrage I," 619.
57. "La démocratie et le droit de suffrage I," 626.
58. Conti, *Parliament the Mirror of the Nation*.
59. James Lorimer, *Constitutionalism of the Future, Or Parliament the Mirror of the Nation* (London: Longmans, Green, Reader and Dyer, 1867); Conti compares Mill and Lorimer in *Parliament the Mirror of the Nation*, 64–67.
60. On the place of plural voting proposals in the conversation over representation, see Conti, *Parliament the Mirror of the Nation*, 54–67. Conti persuasively recognizes the nuances of the debate about plural voting, which was conceived of either as a good in itself (Mill) or a tool to serve the goal of descriptive representation (Lorimer). He captures the divisions on this question in a more nuanced way than Duvergier de Hauranne did in his review of British writings on the vote.

61. James Lorimer, "Mr. Mill on Representative Government," *The North British Review* 35 (1861): 557.

62. As Guillin and Souafa have shown, other French figures weighed in on the matter of social representation around this same time. Guillin and Souafa, "La réception de Stuart Mill en France."

63. On this influence, see Paul B. Kern, "Universal Suffrage without Democracy: Thomas Hare and John Stuart Mill," *The Review of Politics* 34, no. 3 (1972): 306–322; On this influence in Mill's own words, see John Stuart Mill, "Armand Carrel," in *Collected Works of John Stuart Mill*, ed. J.M. Robson, vol. 20 (Toronto, 1985); Both Hare and Mill were proponents of proportional representation, which combined elements of Victorian mirror theory with a Guizot-inspired capacitarian threshold for the franchise.

64. "La démocratie et le droit de suffrage I," 630.

65. "La démocratie et le droit de suffrage I," 635.

66. "La démocratie et le droit de suffrage I," 636.

67. "La démocratie et le droit de suffrage I," 638.

68. "La démocratie et le droit de suffrage I," 638–639.

69. Duvergier de Hauranne was willing to raise the issue of women's suffrage, which Mill "in his boldness" had resolved and Lorimer appears "not to have thought of." "La démocratie et le droit de suffrage I," 619, 638.

70. "La démocratie et le droit de suffrage I," 638.

71. "La démocratie et le droit de suffrage I," 643.

72. "La démocratie et le droit de suffrage I," 643.

73. "La démocratie et le droit de suffrage I," 643.

74. Rosanvallon, *Le peuple introuvable*, 39.

75. Pierre Rosanvallon, *The Demands of Liberty: Civil Society in France since the Revolution*, trans. Arthur Goldhammer (Cambridge, MA: Harvard University Press, 2007), 14.

76. Huard, *La naissance du parti politique en France*, 13; Spitzer, "Restoration Political Theory," 68; J.A.W. Gunn challenges the view that party was synonymous with faction. Gunn, *When the French Tried to Be British*.

77. The mode of secret voting in the Chamber, adopted after 1820, also aimed to limit party affiliation since it allowed deputies to conceal their decisions. A discussion of the secret vote can be found in Gunn, *When the French Tried to Be British*, 117–118.

78. Prosper de Barante, *La vie politique de M. Royer-Collard* (Paris, 1861), 2:215–216.

79. Girard, *Napoléon III*, 182.

80. Speech of May 28, 1872, quoted in Price, *The French Second Empire*, 106.

81. Price insightfully describes party organizations as political "tendencies" in *The French Second Empire*, 259.

82. These defining features of the party are outlined in Huard, *La naissance du parti politique en France*.

83. On the continued opposition to parties in the early twentieth century, see Nicolas Roussellier, "Brilliant Failure: Political Parties Under the Republic Era in France (1870–1914)," in *Organizing Democracy: Reflections on the Rise of Political*

Organizations in the Nineteenth Century, ed. Henk te Velde and Maartje Janse (New York: Springer, 2017), 145–164.

84. Guizot, *HOGR*, 2:343.
85. Guizot, *HOGR*, 2:249–250.
86. "La démocratie et le droit de suffrage I," 621.
87. Tocqueville, *Recollections*, 4; Tocqueville, *DA*, 1:280–281.
88. Duvergier de Hauranne praised Thomas Hare in particular for his insights into the representation of minorities. "La démocratie et le droit de suffrage I," 610–611.
89. "La démocratie et le droit de suffrage II," 797.
90. "La démocratie et le droit de suffrage II," 798.
91. *Huit mois*, 1:79.
92. *Huit mois*, 2:215.
93. *Huit mois*, 1:91.
94. *Huit mois*, 1:215.
95. *Huit mois*, 1:216.
96. *Huit mois*, 2:23.
97. *Huit mois*, 2:31.
98. *Huit mois*, 2:24.
99. *Huit mois*, 2:27.
100. *Huit mois*, 2:23.
101. Although Jaume acknowledges that Duvergier de Hauranne's work on parties fell on deaf ears when it was published, he doesn't follow the thinker's influence into the Third Republic. Jaume, "Tocqueville face au thème de la 'nouvelle aristocratie,'" 969.
102. "La démocratie et le droit de suffrage II," 798.
103. Alexis de Tocqueville, "Speech to the Chamber of Deputies 27 January 1848," in *Democracy in America*, trans. J.P. Mayer (New York: Harper & Row, 2006).
104. Tocqueville elsewhere criticized the "petty ideas" of the July Monarchy as unworthy of the label "party." Alexis de Tocqueville, "Lettres sur la situation intérieure de la France," in *OC*, 3.2:95.
105. In this way, Tocqueville's reawakening of great parties mirrored his call for imperialism. Both projects aimed at the rejuvenation of domestic politics. See Pitts, *A Turn to Empire* and Englert, "Tocqueville's Politics of Grandeur."
106. Tocqueville, *DA*, 1:4.
107. Duvergier de Hauranne seemed to share Tocqueville's critical assessment of the July Monarchy. "La démocratie et le droit de suffrage II," 806–807.
108. Quagliariello importantly writes of the changing nature of American parties in the intervening years between Tocqueville's 1831 journey and Duvergier de Hauranne's in 1864. Gaetano Quagliariello, *Politics Without Parties: Moisei Ostrogorski and the Debate on Political Parties on the Eve of the Twentieth Century* (Aldershot, UK: Avebury, 1996), 69–70.
109. "La démocratie et le droit de suffrage II," 789.
110. "La démocratie et le droit de suffrage II," 790.
111. On this interpretation, see Jaume, "Tocqueville face au thème de la 'nouvelle aristocratie.'"

112. He was also critical of the bourgeoisie in recent history and skeptical of their true ability to lead the nation. "La démocratie et le droit de suffrage II," 819.

113. "La démocratie et le droit de suffrage II," 790.

114. He also tried consciously to avoid having anyone confuse his argument with a defense of aristocratic privilege. See Duvergier de Hauranne, "La démocratie et le droit de suffrage II," 792.

115. Daniel Ziblatt identifies organized political parties led by conservative elites as independent variables in the emergence and persistence of democratization. Ziblatt's cases are Britain and Germany. Daniel Ziblatt, *Conservative Parties and the Birth of Democracy* (Cambridge, UK: Cambridge University Press, 2017).

116. We discussed some of the state's tactics to manage the electorate in Chapter 4.

117. "La démocratie et le droit de suffrage II," 800.

118. "La démocratie et le droit de suffrage II," 800.

119. "La démocratie et le droit de suffrage II," 797.

120. "La démocratie et le droit de suffrage II," 800.

121. Nancy Rosenblum, *On the Side of the Angels: An Appreciation of Parties and Partisanship* (Princeton, NJ: Princeton University Press, 2008), 119–126.

122. "La démocratie et le droit de suffrage II," 799.

123. "La démocratie et le droit de suffrage I," 624.

124. Rosenblum, *On the Side of the Angels: An Appreciation of Parties and Partisanship*, 456–57.

125. "La démocratie et le droit de suffrage I," 624.

126. *Huit mois*, 1:23–24.

127. Huard, *La naissance du parti politique en France*.

128. While both Guizot and Tocqueville are cited in Duvergier de Hauranne's 1868 essays on democracy, Constant is not.

129. Mill, *Considerations on Representative Government*, ed. J.M. Robson, *The Collected Works of John Stuart Mill*, 19 (Toronto: University of Toronto Press, 1963).

130. Dana Villa puts forward a similar critique of Rousseau, Tocqueville, Hegel, and Mill, all of whom, Villa argues, set out to educate a newly politicized "people" in the art of politics. Villa, *Teachers of the People*.

131. Jaume interprets Duvergier de Hauranne in light of this theme of the new aristocracy, in line with Guizot. But as my interpretation suggests, there is more to Duvergier de Hauranne's praise of parties than their "aristocratic" character. Jaume, "Tocqueville face au thème de la 'nouvelle aristocratie."

132. Rosenblum, *On the Side of the Angels*, 457.

Conclusion

1. The long road to women's suffrage would wind throughout the next century. French women did not receive the vote until 1944. This history is elaborated most recently in Crook, *How the French Learned to Vote*, chapter 2.

2. Fouillée's essay was written in response to Edmond Schérer's widely read essay against democracy from the previous year. Schérer cited the failure of the Paris Commune of 1871 to insist that the lower classes were so incapable of serving their own interests that they could never be entrusted to choose the government. Fouillée took the publication of Schérer's work as an opportunity to reopen the more general discussion about capacity in a democracy. Alfred Fouillée, "La Philosophie Du Suffrage Universel," *Revue Des Deux Mondes (1829–1971)* 65, no. 1 (1884): 103–129. I am grateful to Alan Kahan for suggesting that I integrate Fouillée's thought into this conclusion.

3. Melissa Schwartzberg, "Epistemic Democracy and Its Challenges," *Annual Review of Political Science* 18 (2015): 187–203.

4. Brennan, *Against Democracy*. The reemergence of the epistemic challenge to democracy suggests that political capacity (or one of its many variants) is not exactly the "dead language" that Kahan and others, writing in the 1990s and early 2000s, once declared it to be. Claims for political capacity or political reason or other forms of expertise have returned in full force to meet the latest crisis of democracy's dissolution. For another take on the possibility of epistocracy, see Somin, *Democracy and Political Ignorance*. For Kahan's declaration of the death of political capacity, see Kahan, *Aristocratic Liberalism: The Social and Political Thought of Jacob Burckhardt, John Stuart Mill, and Alexis de Tocqueville*) as well as the conclusion to *Liberalism in Nineteenth-Century Europe*.

5. Fouillée, "La Philosophie Du Suffrage Universel," 112.

Works Cited

Primary Sources

Alletz, Édouard. *De la démocratie nouvelle, ou des moeurs et de la puissance des classes moyennes en France*. Paris: F. Lequien, 1837.

Archives parlementaires de 1787 à 1860: Recueil complet des débats législatifs et politiques des chambres françaises, Deuxième Série (1800 à 1860). Edited by M.J. Madival and M.E. Laurent. Paris, 1879–1913.

Aristotle. *Politics*. Edited and translated by Carnes Lord. Chicago: University of Chicago Press, 2013.

Barante, Prosper de. *La Vie Politique de M. Royer-Collard*. 2 vols. Paris, 1861.

Barrot, Odilon. *Mémoires posthumes de Odilon Barrot*. Paris: Charpentier, 1875.

Bigelow, John. "Laboulaye." In *Bluntschli, Lieber, and Laboulaye*. Edited by Daniel Coit Gilman, 27–42. Baltimore: Johns Hopkins University, 1884.

Billiard, Auguste. *Essai sur l'organisation démocratique de la France*. Paris: Hachette, 1837.

Burke, Edmund. *Reflections on the Revolution in France*. In *Select Works of Edmund Burke*. Indianapolis: Liberty Fund, 1999.

Cabanis, Pierre-Jean-Georges. *Quelques considérations sur l'organisation sociale en général, et particulièrement sur la nouvelle constitution*. Paris, 1800.

Compte rendu des séances de l'Assemblée nationale législative, vol. 8. May 16–June 26, 1850. Paris, 1850.

Condorcet, Nicolas de. *Plan de constitution présenté à la Convention nationale, les 15 et 16 février 1793*. Paris, 1793.

Condorcet, Nicolas de. "Sur l'admission des femmes au droit de cité." *Journal de la société de 1789*, July 3, 1790.

Constant, Benjamin. *De la force du gouvernement actuel de la France et de la nécessité de s'y rallier*. Paris, 1796.

Constant, Benjamin. *Des effets de la Terreur*. Paris, 1797.

Constant, Benjamin. *Réflexions sur les constitutions, la distribution des pouvoirs, et les garanties, dans une monarchie constitutionnelle*. Paris: H. Nicolle, 1814.

Constant, Benjamin. *De la Liberté des brochures, des pamphlets et des journaux, considérée sous le rapport de l'intérêt du gouvernement*. Paris, 1814.

Constant, Benjamin. Speech on Bonaparte. *Journal des débats politiques et littéraires*. March 19, 1815.

Constant, Benjamin. *Considérations sur le projet de loi relatif aux élections, adopté par la Chambre des Députés*. Paris: Delaunay, 1817.

Constant, Benjamin. *Des élections de 1818*. Paris: Béchet, 1818.

Constant, Benjamin. *De la proposition de changer la loi des élections*. Paris: Poulet, 1819.

Constant, Benjamin. *Des Motifs qui ont dicté le nouveau projet de loi sur les élections*. Paris: Béchet aîné, 1820.

Constant, Benjamin. *Second Discours prononcé par Benjamin Constant sur la loi des élections.* Grenoble: Barnel, 1820.

Constant, Benjamin. *Mélanges de littérature et de politique.* Paris: Pichon et Didier, 1829.

Constant, Benjamin. "Pensées diverses sur les élections." In *Oeuvres complètes*, vol. 11. Edited by Étienne Hofmann, 418–423. Berlin: Walter de Gruyter, 2011.

Constant, Benjamin. *Principes de politique applicables à tous les gouvernements.* Edited by Etienne Hofmann, 2 vols. Genève: Librairie Droz, 1980.

Constant, Benjamin. *Principles of Politics Applicable to All Representative Governments.* In *Constant: Political Writings.* Edited and translated by Biancamaria Fontana, 170–307. Cambridge, UK: Cambridge University Press, 1988.

Constant, Benjamin. "The Liberty of the Ancients Compared with that of the Moderns." In *Constant: Political Writings.* Edited and translated by Biancamaria Fontana, 308–328. Cambridge, UK: Cambridge University Press, 1988.

Constant, Benjamin. *The Spirit of Conquest and Usurpation and Their Relation to European Civilization.* In *Constant's Political Writings.* Edited and translated by Biancamaria Fontana, 44–165. Cambridge, UK: Cambridge University Press, 1988.

Constant, Benjamin. *Fragments d'un ouvrage abandonné sur la possibilité d'une constitution républicainedans un grand pays.* Paris: Aubier, 1991.

Constant, Benjamin. *Commentary on Filangieri's Work.* Translated by Alan Kahan. Indianapolis, IN: Liberty Fund, 2015.

Duvergier de Hauranne, Ernest Prosper. *Huit mois en Amérique, lettres et notes de voyage.* 2 vols. Paris: Lacroix, 1866.

Duvergier de Hauranne, Ernest Prosper. "La démocratie et le droit de suffrage: I. Les théoriciens du droit de suffrage." *Revue des Deux Mondes (1829–1971)* 74, no. 3 (1868): 608–643.

Duvergier de Hauranne, Ernest Prosper. "La démocratie et le droit de suffrage: II. Le suffrage universel." *Revue des Deux Mondes (1829–1971)* 74, no. 4 (1868): 785–821.

Duvergier de Hauranne, Ernest Prosper. *La République conservatrice.* Paris: G. Baillière, 1873.

Duvergier de Hauranne, Prosper. *De la réforme parlementaire et de la réforme électorale.* Paris: Paulin, 1847.

Fouillée, Alfred. "La Philosophie du suffrage universel." *Revue des Deux Mondes (1829–1971)* 65, no. 1 (1884): 103–129.

Gouges, Olympe de. *Déclaration des droits de la femme et de la citoyenne.* Paris, 1791.

Guizot, François. *Quelques idées sur la liberté de la presse.* Paris, 1814.

Guizot, François. *Essai sur l'histoire et sur l'état actuel de l'instruction publique en France.* Paris, 1816.

Guizot, François. *Des moyens de gouvernement et d'opposition dans l'état actuel de la France.* Paris: Ladvocat, 1821.

Guizot, François. *De la peine de mort en matière politique.* Paris: Béchet, 1822.

Guizot, François. *Essais sur l'histoire de France: Pour servir de complément aux observations sur l'histoire de France de l'abbé de Mably.* Paris, 1824.

Guizot, François. *Du gouvernement de la France depuis la Restauration, et du ministère actuel.* Paris, 1830.

Guizot, François. "De la démocratie dans les sociétés modernes." *Revue française*, October 15, 1837.

Guizot, François. *De la démocratie en France.* Paris: Victor Masson, 1849.

Guizot, François. *Histoire des origines du gouvernement représentatif en Europe.* 2 vols. Paris: Didier, 1851.

Guizot, François. *Memoirs to Illustrate the History of My Time.* London: Richard Bentley, 1858.

Guizot, François. "Élections ou de la formation et des opérations des collèges électoraux." In *Discours académiques*, 379–420. Paris: Didier, 1861.

Guizot, François. "Philosophie politique: de la souveraineté." In *Histoire de la civilization en Europe.* Edited by Pierre Rosanvallon, 305–389. Paris: Gallimard, 1985.

Guizot, François. *The History of Civilization in Europe.* Edited by Larry Siedentop. Translated by William Hazlitt. Indianapolis, IN: Liberty Fund, 2013.

Laboulaye, Édouard. *Recherches sur la condition civile et politique des femmes.* Paris: A. Durand, 1842.

Laboulaye, Édouard. *Considérations sur la Constitution.* Paris: A. Durand, 1848.

Laboulaye, Édouard. *De la Constitution Américaine et de l'utilité de son étude.* Paris: Hennuyer, 1850.

Laboulaye, Édouard. *La liberté religieuse.* Paris: Charpentier, 1858.

Laboulaye, Édouard. "Benjamin Constant." In *Revue Nationale et Étrangère, Politique, Scientifique et Littéraire*, vol. 7. Paris: Charpentier, 1861.

Laboulaye, Édouard. *The United States and France.* Boston: The Boston Daily Advertiser, 1862.

Laboulaye, Édouard. *Le Parti libéral: son programme et son avenir.* Paris: Charpentier, 1863.

Laboulaye, Édouard. "L'instruction Publique et Le Suffrage Universel." In *L'État et ses Limites.* Paris: Charpentier, 1863.

Laboulaye, Édouard. *Paris en Amérique.* Paris: Charpentier, 1863.

Laboulaye, Édouard, ed. *Correspondance de Benjamin Franklin.* Paris: L. Hachette, 1866.

Laboulaye, Édouard. "De l'éducation," In *Discours Populaires.* Paris: Charpentier, 1869.

Laboulaye, Édouard. "Les bibliothèques populaires." In *Discours Populaires.* Paris: Charpentier, 1869.

Laboulaye, Édouard. "Introduction." In *Cours de politique constitutionnelle, ou collection des ouvrages publiés sur le gouvernement représentatif par Benjamin Constant.* Paris: Guillaumin, 1872.

Laboulaye, Édouard. "Avertissement de la présente edition." In *Cours de politique constitutionnelle.* Paris: Guillamin, 1872.

Laboulaye, Édouard. *Questions constitutionnelles.* Paris: Charpentier, 1872.

Leboyer, Olivia. *Élite et libéralisme.* Paris: CNRS Editions, 2012.

Lorimer, James. "Mr. Mill on Representative Government." *The North British Review* 35 (1861): 534–563.

Lorimer, James. *Constitutionalism of the Future, Or Parliament the Mirror of the Nation.* London: Longmans, Green, Reader and Dyer, 1867.

Madison, James. "Federalist 10." In *The Federalist*, edited by George W. Carey and James McClellan, 42–48. Indianapolis, IN: Liberty Fund, 2001.

Maistre, Joseph de. "Study on Sovereignty." In *The Works of Joseph de Maistre*, edited and translated by Jack Lively, 116–119. New York: Macmillan, 1965.

Mazzini, Giuseppe. "In Defense of Democracy: A Reply to Mr. Guizot." In *A Cosmopolitanism of Nations: Giuseppe Mazzini's Writings on Democracy, Nation-Building, and International Relations*, edited and translated by Stefano Recchia and Nadia Urbinati, 66–80. Princeton, NJ: Princeton University Press, 2009.

Mill, John Stuart. *The Collected Works of John Stuart Mill*. 33 vols. Edited by J.M. Robson. Toronto: University of Toronto Press, 1963–1991.

M.J.V. *Le cri d'un Ultra, ou le "vade-mecum" de l'électeur honnête homme*. Paris: Delaunay, 1818.

Necker, Jacques. "Sur l'élection des membres des assemblées provinciales," in *De l'administration des finances de la France*, vol. 2. Paris: Jean-Pierre Heubach, 1784.

Necker, Jacques. *Dernières vues de politique et de finance*. Paris, 1802.

Plato. *Republic*. Translated by Allan Bloom. New York: Basic Books, 1968.

Plato. *Statesman*. Translated by Julia Annas and Robin Waterfield. Cambridge, UK: Cambridge University Press, 1995.

Prévost-Paradol, Lucien Anatole. *La France nouvelle*. Paris: Michel Lévy Frères, 1868.

Proudhon, Pierre-Joseph. *De la capacité politique des classes ouvrières*. Paris: Librairie internationale, 1868.

Rousseau, Jean-Jacques. *The Social Contract and Other Later Political Writings*. Translated by Victor Gourevitch. Cambridge, UK: Cambridge University Press, 1997.

Royer-Collard, Pierre-Paul. *De la liberté de la presse*. In *Discours*. Paris: Librarie de Médicis, 1949.

Sacy, Antoine Isaac Silvestre de. *Journal des débats politiques et littéraires*. Paris, 1863.

Sieyès, Emmanuel Joseph. *Préliminaire de la constitution françoise: Reconnoissance et exposition raisonnée des droits de l'homme et du citoyen*. Paris: Baudoin, 1789.

Sieyès, Emmanuel Joseph. "Constitutional Observations." In *Emmanuel Joseph Sieyès: The Essential Political Writings*. Edited and translated by Oliver W. Lembcke and Florian Weber, 186–194. Leiden: Brill Academic, 2014.

Smith, Adam. *The Theory of Moral Sentiments*. Indianapolis, IN: Liberty Fund, 1982.

Thiers, Adolphe. *Discours parlementaires de M. Thiers*, vol. 9. Paris: Calmann Levy, 1879.

Tocqueville, Alexis de. *Oeuvres complètes*, vol. 3, tome 2. Edited by André Jardin. Paris: Gallimard, 1985.

Tocqueville, Alexis de. *The Tocqueville Reader*. Edited and translated by Olivier Zunz and Alan Kahan. Oxford: Blackwell, 2002.

Tocqueville, Alexis de. *Alexis de Tocqueville: Selected Letters on Politics and Society*. Edited and translated by Roger Boesche. Berkeley: University of California Press, 1985.

Tocqueville, Alexis de. *Writings on Empire and Slavery*. Edited and translated by Jennifer Pitts. Baltimore MD: Johns Hopkins University Press, 2001.

Tocqueville, Alexis de. *The Ancien Régime and the French Revolution*. Edited by Jon Elster. Translated by Arthur Goldhammer. Cambridge: Cambridge University Press, 2011.

Tocqueville, Alexis de. *Democracy in America*. 2 vols. Edited by Eduardo Nolla. Translated by James T. Schleifer. Indianapolis, IN: Liberty Fund, 2012.

Tocqueville, Alexis de. *Recollections: The French Revolution of 1848 and Its Aftermath*. Edited by Olivier Zunz. Translated by Arthur Goldhammer. Charlottesville: University of Virginia Press, 2016.

Wollstonecraft, Mary. *A Vindication of the Rights of Woman with Strictures on Political and Moral Subjects*. London: J. Johnson, 1792.

Secondary Sources

Aberdam, Serge. *Démographes et démocrates: L'oeuvre du comité de division de La Convention Nationale*. Paris: Société des études robespierristes, 2004.

Aguet, J.-P. "Benjamin Constant parlementaire sous la monarchie de Juillet (juillet–décembre 1830)." *Annales Benjamin Constant* 2 (1982): 3–45.

Alexander, Robert. *Re-Writing the French Revolutionary Tradition: Liberal Opposition and the Fall of the Bourbon Monarchy.* Cambridge, UK: Cambridge University Press, 2004.

Alexander, Robert. "Benjamin Constant as a Second Restoration Politician." In *The Cambridge Companion to Constant,* edited by Helena Rosenblatt, 146–170. Cambridge, UK: Cambridge University Press, 2009.

Alméras, Charles. *Odilon Barrot, avocat et homme politique (1791–1873).* Paris: Presses Universitaires de France, 1958.

Applebaum, Anne. *Twilight of Democracy: The Seductive Lure of Authoritarianism.* New York: Doubleday, 2020.

Aron, Raymond. *Main Currents in Sociological Thought I: Montesquieu, Comte, Marx, Tocqueville—The Sociologists and the Revolution of 1848.* Translated by Richard Howard and Helen Weaver. New York: Anchor, 1968.

Artz, Frederick B. "The Electoral System in France During the Bourbon Restoration, 1815–30," *The Journal of Modern History* 1, no. 2 (1929): 205–218.

Atanassow, Ewa. "Colonization and Democracy: Tocqueville Reconsidered." *American Political Science Review* 111, no. 1 (2017): 83–96.

Atanassow, Ewa. *Tocqueville's Dilemmas, and Ours: Sovereignty, Nationalism, Globalization.* Princeton, NJ: Princeton University Press, 2022.

Audier, Serge. *Tocqueville retrouvé: Genèse et enjeux du renouveau tocquevillien français.* Paris: J. Vrin, 2004.

Baker, Alan R.H. *Fraternity Among the French Peasantry: Sociability and Voluntary Associations in the Loire Valley, 1815–1914.* Cambridge: Cambridge University Press, 2004.

Balland, Robert. "De l'organisation à la restriction du Suffrage Universel en France." In *Reaction et Suffrage Universel En France et En Allemagne, 1848–50,* edited by Jacques Droz, 67–173. Paris: M. Rivière et Cie, 1963.

Bastid, Paul. *Benjamin Constant et sa doctrine.* Paris: Armand Colin, 1966.

Baughman, John J. "The French Banquet Campaign of 1847–8." *The Journal of Modern History* 31, no. 1 (March 1959): 1–15.

Bell, Duncan. *Reordering the World: Essays on Liberalism and Empire.* Princeton, NJ: Princeton University Press, 2016.

Bell, Duncan. "What Is Liberalism?" *Political Theory* 42, no. 6 (2014): 682–715.

Bendor, Jonathan, Daniel Diermeier, David A. Siegel, and Michael M. Ting. *A Behavioral Theory of Elections.* Princeton, NJ: Princeton University Press, 2011.

Biagini, Eugenio F., and Alastair J. Reid. *Currents of Radicalism: Popular Radicalism, Organised Labour and Party Politics in Britain, 1850–1914.* Cambridge, UK: Cambridge University Press, 1991.

Bobbio, Norberto. *Liberalism and Democracy.* London: Verso, 2005.

Boesche, Roger. "The Dark Side of Tocqueville: On War and Empire." *The Review of Politics* 67, no. 4 (2005): 737–752.

Boesche, Roger, ed. *Alexis de Tocqueville: Selected Letters on Politics and Society.* Berkeley: University of California Press, 1985.

Boesche, Roger. *The Strange Liberalism of Alexis de Tocqueville.* Ithaca, NY: Cornell University Press, 1987.

Bowen, Ralph H., and Albert Kress. "Historical Introduction." In *A Frenchman in Lincoln's America: Huit mois en Amérique, lettres et notes de voyages, 1864–1865.* Chicago: R.R. Donnelley & Sons, 1974.

Boyd, Richard. *Uncivil Society: The Perils of Pluralism and the Making of Modern Liberalism*. Lanham, MD: Lexington Books, 2004.

Boyd, Richard. "Tocqueville and the Napoleonic Legend." In *Tocqueville and the Frontiers of Democracy*, edited by Ewa Atanassow and Richard Boyd, 264–288. Cambridge, UK: Cambridge University Press, 2013.

Boyd, Richard, ed. *The Cambridge Companion to Democracy in America*. Cambridge, UK: Cambridge University Press, 2022.

Brennan, Jason. *Against Democracy*. Princeton, NJ: Princeton University Press, 2016.

Brogan, Hugh. *Alexis de Tocqueville: Prophet of Democracy in the Age of Revolution*. London: Profile Books, 2010.

Campbell, Stuart L. *The Second Empire Revisited: A Study in French Historiography*. New Brunswick, NJ: Rutgers University Press, 1978.

Caplan, Bryan. *The Myth of the Rational Voter: Why Democracies Choose Bad Policies*. Princeton, NJ: Princeton University Press, 2011.

Cole, Alistair and Peter Campbell. *French Electoral Systems and Elections Since 1789*. Aldershot: Gower, 1989.

Collingham, H.A.C. *July Monarchy: A Political History of France, 1830–1848*. London: Addison-Wesley, 1988.

Conti, Gregory. "Charles Dupont-White: An Idiosyncratic Nineteenth-Century Theorist on Speech, State, and John Stuart Mill." *Global Intellectual History* 8, no. 1 (July 2021): 1–46.

Conti, Gregory. *Parliament the Mirror of the Nation: Representation, Deliberation, and Democracy in Victorian Britain*. Cambridge, UK: Cambridge University Press, 2019.

Coppolani, Jean Yves. *Les élections en France à l'époque napoléonienne*. Paris: Albatros, 1980.

Craiutu, Aurelian. "Tocqueville and the Political Thought of the French Doctrinaires (Guizot, Royer-Collard, Rémusat)." *History of Political Thought* 20, no. 3 (March 1999): 456–493.

Craiutu, Aurelian. "The Battle for Legitimacy: Guizot and Constant on Sovereignty." *Historical Reflections/Réflexions Historiques* 28, no. 3 (2002): 471–491.

Craiutu, Aurelian. "Guizot's Elitist Theory of Representative Government." *Critical Review* 15, nos. 3–4 (January 2003): 261–284.

Craiutu, Aurelian. *Liberalism under Siege: The Political Thought of the French Doctrinaires* Lanham, MD: Lexington Books, 2003.

Craiutu, Aurelian. *A Virtue for Courageous Minds: Moderation in French Political Thought, 1748–1830*. Princeton, NJ: University Press, 2012.

Craiutu, Aurelian and Jeffrey C. Isaac, eds. *America Through European Eyes: British and French Reflections on the New World from the Eighteenth Century to the Present*. State College, PA: Penn State University Press, 2009.

Crook, Malcolm. *How the French Learned to Vote: A History of Electoral Practice in France*. Oxford: Oxford University Press, 2021.

Crook, Malcolm. *Elections in the French Revolution: An Apprenticeship in Democracy, 1789–1799*. Cambridge, UK: Cambridge University Press, 2002.

Crook, Malcolm. "The Uses of Democracy: Elections and Plebiscites in Napoleonic France," in *The French Experience from Republic to Monarchy, 1792–1824: New Dawns in Politics, Knowledge and Culture*, edited by Máire F. Cross and David Williams, 58–71. London: Palgrave Macmillan UK, 2000.

Dauteribes, André. "Les idées politiques d'Édouard Laboulaye." PhD diss., Université de Montpellier, 1989.

de Dijn, Annelien. *French Political Thought from Montesquieu to Tocqueville*. Cambridge, UK: Cambridge University Press, 2008.

de Dijn, Annelien. *Freedom: An Unruly History*. Cambridge, MA: Harvard University Press, 2020.

de Luca, Stefano. "Benjamin Constant and the Terror." In *The Cambridge Companion to Constant*, edited by Helena Rosenblatt, 92–114. Cambridge, UK: Cambridge University Press, 2009.

de Ruggiero, Guido. *The History of European Liberalism*. Translated by R.G. Collingwood. London: Humphrey Milford, 1927.

de Soto, Jean. "Édouard Laboulaye." *Revue internationale d'histoire politique et constitutionelle* 5 (1955): 114–150.

Delbouille, Paul. "Aux sources de la démocratie libérale: Benjamin Constant." *Revue d'Histoire littéraire de la France* 106, no. 2 (2006): 259–270.

Dodge, Guy H. *Benjamin Constant's Philosophy of Liberalism: A Study in Politics and Religion*. Chapel Hill: University of North Carolina Press, 2012.

Drescher, Seymour. *Dilemmas of Democracy: Tocqueville and Modernization*. Pittsburgh, PA: University of Pittsburgh Press, 1968.

Drolet, Michael. *Tocqueville, Democracy and Social Reform*. New York: Palgrave Macmillan, 2003.

Drolet, Michael. "Carrying the Banner of the Bourgeoisie: Democracy, Self and the Philosophical Foundations of François Guizot's Historical and Political Thought." *History of Political Thought* 32, no. 4 (2011): 645–690.

Duong, Kevin. "The Demands of Glory: Tocqueville and Terror in Algeria." *The Review of Politics* 80, no. 1 (2018): 31–55.

Duong, Kevin. *The Virtues of Violence: Democracy Against Disintegration in Modern France*. Oxford: Oxford University Press, 2020.

Duong, Kevin. "What Was Universal Suffrage?" *Theory & Event* 23, no. 1 (2020): 29–65.

Edelstein, Daniel. *On the Spirit of Rights*. Chicago: University of Chicago Press, 2018.

Elshtain, Jean Bethke. "Citizenship and Armed Civic Virtue: Some Critical Questions on the Commitment to Public Life." *Soundings: An Interdisciplinary Journal* 69, nos. 1–2 (1986): 99–110.

Elster, Jon. *Alexis de Tocqueville, the First Social Scientist*. Cambridge, UK: Cambridge University Press, 2009.

Englert, Gianna. "'The Idea of Rights': Tocqueville on The Social Question." *The Review of Politics* 79, no. 4 (2017): 649–674.

Englert, Gianna. "Usurpation and 'The Social' in Benjamin Constant's *Commentaire*." *Modern Intellectual History* 17, no. 1 (June 2018): 1–30.

Englert, Gianna. "'Not More Democratic, but More Moral': Tocqueville on the Suffrage in America and France." *The Tocqueville Review/La Revue Tocqueville* 42, no. 2 (December 2021): 105–120.

Englert, Gianna. "Tocqueville's Politics of Grandeur." *Political Theory* 50, no. 3 (June 2022): 477–503.

Fawcett, Edmund. *Liberalism: The Life of An Idea*. Princeton, NJ: Princeton University Press, 2014.

Fortescue, William. "Morality and Monarchy: Corruption and the Fall of the Regime of Louis-Philippe in 1848." *French History* 16, no. 1 (March 2002): 83–100.

Fukuyama, Francis. *The End of History and the Last Man*. New York: Simon and Schuster, 2006.

Fulcher, Jane. "The Orphéon Societies: Music for the Workers in Second-Empire France." *International Review of the Aesthetics and Sociology of Music* 10, no. 1 (1979): 47–56.

Gannett, Jr., Robert T. "Tocqueville and the Politics of Suffrage." *The Tocqueville Review/ La Revue Tocqueville* 27, no. 2 (2006): 209–225.

Garsten, Bryan. "From Popular Sovereignty to Civil Society in Post-Revolutionary France." In *Popular Sovereignty in Historical Perspective*, edited by Richard Bourke and Quentin Skinner, 236–269. Cambridge, UK: Cambridge University Press, 2016.

Garsten, Bryan. "Representative Government and Popular Sovereignty." In *Political Representation*, edited by Alexander S. Kirshner, 90–110. Cambridge, UK: Cambridge University Press, 2010.

Gauchet, Marcel. "Constant." In *Dictionnaire Critique de la Révolution Française*, edited by François Furet and Mona Ozouf, 924–933. Paris: Flammarion, 1988.

Gemie, Sherif. "'A Danger to Society?' Teachers and Authority in France, 1833–1850." *French History* 2, no. 3 (September 1988): 264–287.

Gerçek, Salih Emre. "Alexis de Tocqueville's Reluctant 'Democratic Language.'" *The Review of Politics* 83, no. 1 (2020), 1–24.

Gerçek, Salih Emre. "The 'Social Question' as a Democratic Question: Louis Blanc's Organization of Labor." *Modern Intellectual History* 20, no. 2 (July 2022): 388–416.

Ghins, Arthur. "Benjamin Constant and the Politics of Reason." *History of European Ideas* 44, no. 2 (2018): 224–243.

Ghins, Arthur. "Benjamin Constant and Public Opinion in Post-Revolutionary France." *History of Political Thought* 40, no. 3 (2019): 484–514.

Ghins, Arthur. "'Popular Sovereignty· That I Deny': Benjamin Constant on Public Opinion, Political Legitimacy and Constitution Making." *Modern Intellectual History* 19, no. 1 (2022): 128–158.

Ghins, Arthur. "What Is French Liberalism?" *Political Studies*, Online First (October 2022), https://journals.sagepub.com/doi/abs/10.1177/00323217221126727.

Girard, Louis. *Les Libéraux français: 1814–1875*. Paris: Aubier, 1985.

Girard, Louis. *Napoléon III*. Paris: Fayard, 1986.

Godechot, Jacques, ed. *Les constitutions de la France depuis 1789*. Paris: Flammarion, 1995.

Grange, Henri. "De l'influence de Necker sur les idées politiques de Benjamin Constant." *Annales Benjamin Constant* 2 (1982): 73–80.

Gray, Walter. *Interpreting American Democracy in France: The Career of Édouard Laboulaye, 1811–1883*. Newark: University of Delaware Press, 1994.

Guillin, Vincent, and Djamel Souafa. "La réception de Stuart Mill en France." *La Vie des idées*, May 18, 2010. http://www.laviedesidees.fr/La-reception-de-Stu art-Mill-en.html.

Gunn, J.A.W. *When the French Tried to Be British: Party, Opposition, and the Quest for Civil Disagreement, 1814–1848*. Montréal: McGill-Queen's University Press, 2009.

Hazareesingh, Sudhir. *From Subject to Citizen: The Second Empire and the Emergence of Modern French Democracy*. Princeton, NJ: Princeton University Press, 1998.

Hazareesingh, Sudhir. *Intellectual Founders of the Republic: Five Studies in Nineteenth-Century French Republican Political Thought*. Oxford: Oxford University Press, 2005.

Hazareesingh, Sudhir. *The Legend of Napoleon*. London: Granta, 2005.

Hereth, Michael. *Alexis de Tocqueville: Threats to Freedom in Democracy*. Translated by George F. Bogardus. Durham, NC: Duke University Press, 1985.

Herzog, Don. *Poisoning the Minds of the Lower Orders*. Princeton, NJ: Princeton University Press, 2021.

Hofmann, Etienne. Les "Principes de politique" de Benjamin Constant: La genèse d'une oeuvre et l'évolution de la pensée de leur auteur, 1789–1806. Geneva: Droz, 1980.

Holmes, Stephen. Benjamin Constant and the Making of Modern Liberalism. New Haven, CT: Yale University Press, 1984.

Huard, Raymond. La naissance du parti politique en France. Paris: Presses de la Fondation nationale des sciences politiques, 1996.

Hulliung, Mark. Citizens and Citoyens: Republicans and Liberals in America and France. Cambridge, MA: Harvard University Press, 2002.

Innes, Joanna and Mark Philp. "'Democracy' from Book to Life: The Emergence of the Term in Active Political Debate to 1848." In Democracy in Modern Europe: A Conceptual History, edited by Jussi Kurunmäki, Jeppe Nevers, and Henk te Velde, 16–34. New York: Berghahn, 2018.

Jainchill, Andrew. Reimagining Politics after the Terror: The Republican Origins of French Liberalism. Ithaca, NY: Cornell University Press, 2008.

Jardin, André. Histoire du libéralisme politique de la crise de l'absolutisme à la constitution de 1875. Paris: Hachette, 1985.

Jardin, André. Tocqueville: A Biography. New York: Hill and Wang, 1989.

Jaume, Lucien. "Guizot et la philosophie de la representation." Droits 15 (January 1992): 141–152.

Jaume, Lucien. L'Individu effacé, ou la paradoxe du libéralisme français. Paris: Fayard, 1997.

Jaume, Lucien. "Tocqueville face au thème de 'la nouvelle aristocratie': La difficile naissance des partis en France." Revue française de science politique 56, no. 6 (2006): 969–984.

Jaume, Lucien. Tocqueville: The Aristocratic Sources of Liberty. Princeton, NJ: Princeton University Press, 2013.

Jennings, Jeremy. "Doctrinaires and Syndicalists: Representation, Parties, and Democracies in France." Journal of Political Ideologies 11, no. 3 (October 2006): 269–288.

Jennings, Jeremy. "A Note on Freedom of the Press in Restoration France." Journal of Modern Italian Studies 17, no. 5 (December 2012): 568–573.

Jennings, Jeremy. Revolution and the Republic: A History of Political Thought in France Since the Eighteenth Century. Oxford: Oxford University Press, 2013.

Johnson, Douglas. Guizot: Aspects of French History, 1787–1874. Westport, CT: Praeger, 1976.

Jones, H.S. The French State in Question: Public Law and Political Argument in the Third Republic. Cambridge, UK: Cambridge University Press, 1993.

Kahan, Alan S. Aristocratic Liberalism: The Social and Political Thought of Jacob Burckhardt, John Stuart Mill, and Alexis de Tocqueville. New York: Oxford University Press, 1992.

Kahan, Alan S. Liberalism in Nineteenth-Century Europe: The Political Culture of Limited Suffrage. New York: Palgrave Macmillan, 2003.

Kahan, Alan S. Tocqueville, Democracy, and Religion: Checks and Balances for Democratic Souls. New York: Oxford University Press, 2015.

Kelly, George Armstrong. The Humane Comedy: Constant, Tocqueville, and French Liberalism, rev. ed. (Cambridge, UK: Cambridge University Press, 2007)

Kern, Paul B. "Universal Suffrage without Democracy: Thomas Hare and John Stuart Mill." The Review of Politics 34, no. 3 (1972): 306–22.

Keslassy, Eric. Le libéralisme de Tocqueville à l'épreuve du paupérisme. Paris: L'Harmattan, 2000.

Kirschleger, Pierre-Yves. La religion de Guizot. Paris: Labor et Fides, 1999.

Kloppenberg, James T. *Toward Democracy: The Struggle for Self-Rule in European and American Thought*. Oxford: Oxford University Press, 2016.

Koepke, Robert L. "The Failure of Parliamentary Government in France, 1840–1848." *European Studies Review* 9, no. 4 (October 1979): 433–455.

Kreuzer, Marcus. "Democratisation and Changing Methods of Electoral Corruption in France from 1815 to 1914." In *Political Corruption in Europe and Latin America*, edited by Walter Little and Eduardo Posada-Carbó, 97–112. London: Palgrave Macmillan, 1996.

Kulstein, David I. "Economics Instruction for Workers during the Second Empire." *French Historical Studies* 1, no. 2 (1959): 225–234.

Lakoff, Sanford. "Tocqueville, Burke, and the Origins of Liberal Conservatism." *The Review of Politics* 60, no. 3 (1998): 435–464.

Lamberti, Jean-Claude. *Tocqueville and the Two Democracies*. Translated by Arthur Goldhammer. Cambridge, MA: Harvard University Press, 1989.

Le Breton, Michel and Dominique Lepelley. "Une analyse de la loi électorale du 29 juin 1820." *Revue économique* 65, no. 3 (2014): 469–518.

Levitsky, Steven and Daniel Ziblatt. *How Democracies Die*. New York: Crown, 2018.

Levy, Jacob T. *Rationalism, Pluralism, and Freedom*. Oxford: Oxford University Press, 2015.

Levy, Jacob T. "Pluralism without Privilege? *Corps Intermédiaires*, Civil Society, and the Art of Association." In *Organizations, Civil Society, and the Roots of Development*, edited by Naomi Lamoreaux and John J. Wallis, 83–108. Chicago: University of Chicago Press, 2017.

Manent, Pierre. *An Intellectual History of Liberalism*. Translated by Rebecca Balinski. Princeton, NJ: Princeton University Press, 1996.

Manin, Bernard. *The Principles of Representative Government*. Cambridge, UK: Cambridge University Press, 1997.

Mansfield, Harvey C., and Delba Winthrop. "Tocqueville's New Political Science." In *The Cambridge Companion to Tocqueville*, edited by Cheryl B. Welch, 81–107. Cambridge, UK: Cambridge University Press, 2006.

Mellon, Stanley. *The Political Uses of History: A Study of Historians in the French Restoration*. Stanford, CA: Stanford University Press, 1958.

Mélonio, Françoise. *Tocqueville and the French*. Translated by Beth G. Raps. Charlottesville: University of Virginia Press, 1998.

Nolla, Eduardo. "Editor's Introduction." In *Democracy in America* by Alexis de Tocqueville, xlvii–cxlix. Indianapolis, IN: Liberty Fund, 2012.

Oechslin, Jean-Jacques. *Le mouvement ultra-royaliste sous la Restauration*. Paris: R. Pichon, 1960.

Palmer, R.R. "Notes on the Use of the Word 'Democracy,' 1789–1799." *Political Science Quarterly* 68 no. 2 (1953): 203–226.

Parry, Jonathan. *The Rise and Fall of Liberal Government in Victorian Britain*. New Haven, CT: Yale University Press, 2009.

Pilbeam, Pamela. *The 1830 Revolution in France*. Basingstoke: Palgrave Macmillan, 1991.

Pitts, Jennifer. *A Turn to Empire: The Rise of Imperial Liberalism in Britain and France*. Princeton, NJ: Princeton University Press, 2009.

Pitts, Jennifer. "Empire and Democracy: Tocqueville and the Algeria Question." *Journal of Political Philosophy* 8, no. 3 (2000): 295–318.

Plattner, Marc F. "Liberalism and Democracy: Can't Have One Without the Other," *Foreign Affairs*, March 1, 1998. https://www.foreignaffairs.com/articles/1998-03-01/liberalism-and-democracy-cant-have-one-without-other.

Plattner, Marc F. "From Liberalism to Liberal Democracy." *Journal of Democracy* 10, no. 3 (1999): 121–134.

Plessis, Alain. *The Rise and Fall of the Second Empire, 1852–1871.* Cambridge, UK: Cambridge University Press, 1985.

Price, Roger. *The French Second Empire: An Anatomy of Political Power.* Cambridge, UK: Cambridge University Press, 2001.

Ponteil, Felix. *Histoire de l'enseignement en France.* Paris: Sirey, 1966.

Pouthas, Charles. *Guizot pendant la Restauration.* Paris: Plon, 1923.

Putnam, Robert D. *Bowling Alone: The Collapse and Revival of American Community.* New York: Simon & Schuster, 2000.

Quagliariello, Gaetano. *Politics Without Parties: Moisei Ostrogorski and the Debate on Political Parties on the Eve of the Twentieth Century.* Aldershot: Avebury, 1996.

Rahe, Paul Anthony. *Soft Despotism, Democracy's Drift: Montesquieu, Rousseau, Tocqueville, and the Modern Prospect.* New Haven, CT: Yale University Press, 2009.

Rausch, Fabian. "The Impossible *Gouvernement Représentatif*: Constitutional Culture in Restoration France, 1814–30." *French History* 27, no. 2 (June 2013): 223–248.

Rémond, René. *Les États-Unis devant l'opinion française.* 2 vols. Paris: A. Colin, 1962.

Richter, Melvin. "Tocqueville on Algeria." *The Review of Politics* 25, no. 3 (1963): 362–398.

Richter, Melvin. "Tocqueville and Guizot on Democracy: From a Type of Society to a Political Regime." *History of European Ideas* 30, no. 1 (March 2004): 61–82.

Robert, Adolphe, and Gaston Cougny. *Dictionnaire des parlementaires français: Depuis le 1er mai 1789 jusqu'au 1er mai 1889,* vol. 2. Paris: Bourloton, 1889.

Romani, Roberto. "Liberal Theocracy in the Italian Risorgimento." *European History Quarterly* 44, no. 4 (2014): 620–650.

Rosanvallon, Pierre. *Le moment Guizot.* Paris: Gallimard, 1985.

Rosanvallon, Pierre. "Guizot et la question du suffrage universel au XIXe siècle." In *François Guizot et la culture politique de son temps,* edited by Marina Valensie, 129–145. Paris: Gallimard, 1991.

Rosanvallon, Pierre. *Le sacre du citoyen: Histoire du suffrage universel en France.* Paris: Folio, 2001.

Rosanvallon, Pierre. *Le Peuple introuvable: Histoire de la représentation démocratique en France.* Paris: Gallimard, 2002.

Rosanvallon, Pierre. *La Démocratie inachevée: Histoire de la souveraineté du peuple en France.* Paris: Folio, 2003.

Rosanvallon, Pierre. "Political Rationalism and Democracy in France in the 18th and 19th Centuries." *Philosophy & Social Criticism* 28, no. 6 (November 2002): 689–700.

Rosanvallon, Pierre. *Le Modèle politique français: La société civile contre le jacobinisme de 1789 à nos jours.* Paris: Seuil, 2004.

Rosanvallon, Pierre. *The Demands of Liberty: Civil Society in France since the Revolution.* Translated by Arthur Goldhammer. Cambridge, MA: Harvard University Press, 2007.

Rosenblatt, Helena. "Why Constant? A Critical Overview of the Constant Revival." *Modern Intellectual History* 1, no. 3 (October 2004): 439–453.

Rosenblatt, Helena. "Re-Evaluating Benjamin Constant's Liberalism: Industrialism, Saint-Simonianism and the Restoration Years." *History of European Ideas* 30, no. 1 (2004): 23–37.

Rosenblatt, Helena. *Liberal Values: Benjamin Constant and the Politics of Religion.* Cambridge, UK: Cambridge University Press, 2008.

Rosenblatt, Helena. "Eclipses and Revivals: Constant's Reception in France and America, 1830–2007." In *The Cambridge Companion to Constant*, 351–377. Cambridge, UK: Cambridge University Press, 2009.

Rosenblatt, Helena. "On the Need for a Protestant Reformation: Constant, Sismondi, Guizot, and Laboulaye." In *French Liberalism from Montesquieu to the Present Day*, edited by Raf Geenens and Helena Rosenblatt, 115–133. Cambridge, UK: Cambridge University Press, 2012.

Rosenblatt, Helena. *The Lost History of Liberalism: From Ancient Rome to the Twenty-First Century.* Princeton, NJ: Princeton University Press, 2018.

Rosenblum, Nancy. *On the Side of the Angels: An Appreciation of Parties and Partisanship.* Princeton, NJ: Princeton University Press, 2008.

Roussellier, Nicolas. "Brilliant Failure: Political Parties Under the Republic Era in France (1870–1914)." In *Organizing Democracy: Reflections on the Rise of Political Organizations in the Nineteenth Century*, edited by Henk te Velde and Maartje Janse, 145–164. New York: Springer, 2017.

Rubinelli, Lucia. *Constituent Power: A History.* Cambridge, UK: Cambridge University Press, 2020.

Saunders, Robert. *Democracy and the Vote in British Politics, 1848–1867: The Making of the Second Reform Act.* Surrey: Ashgate, 2011.

Sawyer, Stephen W. "An American Model for French Liberalism: The State of Exception in Édouard Laboulaye's Constitutional Thought." *The Journal of Modern History* 85, no. 4 (2013): 739–771.

Sawyer, Stephen W. *Demos Assembled: Democracy and the International Origins of the Modern State, 1840–1880.* Chicago, IL: University of Chicago Press, 2018.

Schleifer, James T. *The Making of Tocqueville's Democracy in America.* Indianapolis, IN: Liberty Fund, 2000.

Schmitt, Carl. *The Crisis of Parliamentary Democracy.* Translated by Ellen Kennedy. Cambridge, MA: MIT Press, 1996.

Schwartzberg, Melissa. "Epistemic Democracy and Its Challenges." *Annual Review of Political Science* 18 (2015): 187–203.

Selinger, William. "Le grand mal de l'époque: Tocqueville on French Political Corruption." *History of European Ideas* 42, no. 1 (January 2016): 73–94.

Selinger, William. *Parliamentarism, From Burke to Weber.* Cambridge, UK: Cambridge University Press, 2019.

Selinger, William and Gregory Conti. "The Lost History of Political Liberalism." *History of European Ideas* 46, no. 3 (April 2020): 341–354.

Sewell, William H. *Work and Revolution in France: The Language of Labor from the Old Regime to 1848.* Cambridge, UK: Cambridge University Press, 1980.

Sewell, William H. *A Rhetoric of Bourgeois Revolution: The Abbé Sieyes and What Is the Third Estate?* Durham, NC: Duke University Press, 1994.

Siedentop, Larry. *Tocqueville.* Oxford: Oxford University Press, 1994.

Siedentop, Larry. "Two Liberal Traditions." In *French Liberalism from Montesquieu to the Present Day*, edited by Raf Geenens and Helena Rosenblatt, 1–12. Cambridge, UK: Cambridge University Press, 2012.

Siedentop, Larry. "Introduction." In *The History of Civilization in Europe*, edited by Larry Siedentop. Translated by William Hazlitt, vii–xli. Indianapolis, IN: Liberty Fund, 2013.

Skuy, David. *Assassination, Politics, and Miracles: France and the Royalist Reaction of 1820*. Montreal: McGill-Queen's University Press, 2003.

Sonenscher, Michael. "Introduction," in *Sieyès: Political Writings: Including the Debate Between Sieyes and Tom Paine in 1791*, edited and translated by Michael Sonenscher, xxxi–xxxiii. Cambridge, MA: Hackett, 2003.

Soltau, Roger. *French Political Thought in the Nineteenth Century*. New Haven, CT: Yale University Press, 1931.

Somin, Ilya. *Democracy and Political Ignorance: Why Smaller Government Is Smarter*. Stanford, CA: Stanford University Press, 2013.

Spitzer, Alan B. "Restoration Political Theory and the Debate over the Law of the Double Vote." *The Journal of Modern History* 55, no. 1 (March 1983): 54–70.

Starzinger, Vincent. *The Politics of the Center: The Juste Milieu in Theory and Practice, France and England, 1815–1848*. New York: Transaction Publishers, 1991.

Staum, Martin S. *Cabanis: Enlightenment and Medical Philosophy in the French Revolution*. Princeton, NJ: Princeton University Press, 2014.

Theis, Laurent. *François Guizot*. Paris: Fayard, 2008.

Timmermans, Nora. "Benjamin Constant, Political Power, and Democracy." *History of European Ideas* 48, no. 3 (March 2022): 246–262.

Todorov, Tzvetan. *A Passion for Democracy: Benjamin Constant*. New York: Algora Publishing, 2007.

Tuck, Richard. *The Sleeping Sovereign: The Invention of Modern Democracy*. Cambridge, UK: Cambridge University Press, 2016.

Tudesq, Jean. "Guizot et la Presse sous la Restauration." In *Guizot, les Doctrinaires et la presse, 1820–1830*, edited by D. Roldán, 1–10. Val-Richer: Fondation Guizot, 1994.

Urbinati, Nadia. *Representative Democracy: Principles and Genealogy*. Chicago IL: University of Chicago Press, 2006.

Varouxakis, Georgios. "French Radicalism through the Eyes of John Stuart Mill." *History of European Ideas* 30, no. 4 (December 2004): 433–61.

Verjus, Anne. *Le cens de la famille: Les femmes et le vote, 1789–1848*. Paris: Belin, 2002.

Viano, Francesca Lidia. *Sentinel: The Unlikely Origins of the Statue of Liberty*. Cambridge, MA: Harvard University Press, 2018.

Villa, Dana. *Teachers of the People: Political Education in Rousseau, Hegel, Tocqueville, and Mill*. Chicago, IL: University of Chicago Press, 2017.

Vincent, Steven K. "Benjamin Constant, the French Revolution, and the Origins of French Romantic Liberalism." *French Historical Studies* 23, no. 4 (October 2000): 607–637.

Vincent, Steven K. *Benjamin Constant and the Birth of French Liberalism*. New York: Palgrave Macmillan, 2011.

Watkins, Sharon B. *Alexis de Tocqueville and the Second Republic, 1848–1852: A Study in Political Practice and Principles*. Lanham, MD: University Press of America, 2003.

Welch, Cheryl B. *Liberty and Utility: The French Idéologues and the Transformation of Liberalism*. New York: Columbia University Press, 1984.

Welch, Cheryl B. *De Tocqueville*. Oxford: Oxford University Press, 2001.

Welch, Cheryl B. "Tocqueville's Resistance to the Social." *History of European Ideas* 30, no. 1 (2004): 83–107.

Welch, Cheryl B. "Utilitarianism and the French Liberal Tradition." In *French Liberalism from Montesquieu to the Present*, edited by Raf Geenens and Helena Rosenblatt, 134–152. Cambridge, UK: Cambridge University Press, 2012.

Wolin, Sheldon S. *Tocqueville between Two Worlds: The Making of a Political and Theoretical Life*. Princeton, NJ: Princeton University Press, 2003.

Wood, Dennis. *Benjamin Constant: A Biography*. New York: Routledge, 2002.

Zakaria, Fareed. "The Rise of Illiberal Democracy." *Foreign Affairs* 76, no. 6 (1997): 22–43.

Zeldin, Theodore. *The Political System of Napoleon III*. London: Macmillan, 1958.

Ziblatt, Daniel. *Conservative Parties and the Birth of Democracy*. Cambridge, UK: Cambridge University Press, 2017.

Zuckert, Michael. "On Social State." In *Tocqueville's Defense of Human Liberty*, edited by Joseph Alulis and Peter A. Lawler, 3–21. New York: Garland, 1993.

Index

For the benefit of digital users, indexed terms that span two pages (e.g., 52–53) may, on occasion, appear on only one of those pages.